I0115338

BRAINWASHED!

AMERICA'S CULTURAL REVOLUTION

BARRY HOWARD MINKIN

Insight Press * USA

OTHER BOOKS BY BARRY MINKIN:

PLAYING WITH DUST

(Insight Press * USA)

AMERICA'S DEEPENING DIVIDE

(Insight Press * USA)

THE GREAT UNRAVELING

(Insight Press * USA)

TEN GREAT LIES THAT THREATEN WESTERN CIVILIZATION

(Insight Press * USA)

ECONOQUAKE

(Prentice Hall)

FUTURE IN SIGHT

(Simon & Schuster)

THE STATUS OF BIOTECHNOLOGY

(Frost & Sullivan)

INSIGHT PRESS * USA

INSIGHT PRESS * USA – A MINKIN AFFILIATES IMPRINT
1660 MOUNT VERNON DRIVE
SAN JOSE, CA 95125
COPYRIGHT 2020 BY BARRY MINKIN

All rights reserved. No part of this book may be reproduced in any form or means, electronic or mechanical, including photocopying, recording, or any information storage or retrieval system without permission in writing from Insight Press*USA the publisher, phone 650-780-9800, or e-mail barryminkin@earthlink.net.

This publication is designed to present only the author's recollection and opinion about the many people, places and events presented in this book. The author and publisher specially disclaim any liability, loss or risk, personal or otherwise, which may be incurred as a consequence, directly or indirectly, from use of any contents of this work.

Minkin, Barry Howard

ISBN- 13   978-0-9792904-8-0

Catalog suggestions:

1. Internal threat to America 2. Reverse discrimination 3. Left–wing threats 4. Diversity as a threat 5. Israel–Palestinian myths 6. Left–wing funding 7. Economic fallacies 8. Media bias 9. Illegal immigration myths 10. University brainwashing 11. Subtle trends 12. Race relations 13. Government agencies' special interest 14. Judicial loopholes help illegal aliens 15. Black and left-wing hate 16. Civil Rights Act subversion 17. What the Left believes 18. Failed Black leaders 19. Islamic propaganda in primary education 20. Failed Black education 21. Black vs. police myths
I. Title

ACKNOWLEDGEMENTS

My thanks go first to Lois, whose goodness, love, and support have never wavered.

I'm grateful to Alex, whose views shared by most of her peers drastically differ from mine. She motivated me because of her being open to changing those views when the facts warrant it.

Hat's off to those willing to tell the truth and those willing to listen to the truth.

Thanks also to Kathryn and Jim, John and Teresa, and Hilda and Dr. Zin, for encouraging me to get my unpopular but important views into print. I also give my heartfelt love to my great family and friends who do not share my strongly felt truths expressed in this book.

I'm so grateful to Kristin Waller for doing a great book editing.

I give my sincere respect to those who fought the external threats to our democracy and to those who will fight the growing internal threats.

Finally, I dedicate this book in loving memory of Isadore (Joe) and Reba Minkin and for those we remember with such deep love in my extended family.

TABLE OF CONTENTS

INTRODUCTION

"Those who do not look upon themselves as a link connecting the Past with the Future do not perform their duty to the world."

Daniel Webster (1820)

Today is Labor Day 2020. My recent autobiography, *Playing with Dust,* was to be the capstone on top of my previous works. I did not plan or want to ever be writing another book at this late chapter of my life. But like no other time in my life, I've become completely obsessed and frustrated that I have not as yet been able to explain to others some critical, highly controversial, unique insights that will soon dramatically impact their lives and their children's future for generations.

I do feel I've done my very best to have warned the public of the disaster right ahead, that so many of you still do not see. Indeed, my similar written warnings and insights go back 15 years and can be found in *Ten Great Lies that Threaten Western Civilization* and more recently in *America's Deepening Divide.* This book of over 100,000 words is my last attempt to get through to you. For all our sakes, I ask that you please read it with an open mind. As Joseph Conrad noted and I am feeling more every day: *"the messenger can't rest until the message is delivered."*

As I write this second paragraph, currently stirring in my mind is the image of a car speeding out of control around the sharp curves on Highway 1 and almost certain to fall over the cliff and roll into the sea. I feel helpless, an observer on the sandy shoulder of the road, wildly waving my arms trying to prevent an inevitable disaster. The closer they get toward the cliff, the more I'm feeling sickened and depressed. Everyday I'm coming closer to the very painful realization that my role will be explaining how this historic tragedy happened having not being able to prevent it.

Sadly, I'm a great witness to how and why this catastrophe happened. It turns out due to random time and chance events in my life, I understand how subtle events

I've observed link together like the chain of evidence a prosecutor might be presenting to the jury in an "open and shut case." Moreover, I'm uniquely able to follow the pending catastrophe from the moment of its inception at an event I was at in the 1970s, until it happened on November 3, 2020. In my terrible dream, I watch those trapped in the car, including people and values I love so much, slowly sink into the abyss. I know I tried to prevent that inevitable outcome.

The car of course is our great country. The driver is the radical Left and the diversity and victimization mob, and the passengers the America people and values. The cliff they've fallen over was the recent election.

Why didn't the passengers make the driver stop or at least scream about the consequences of their dangerous out of control behavior? Perhaps they were unaware of the danger since warnings had been mysteriously blocked on the media. Some just along for the ride did not understand that their driver was playing a dangerous game of chicken with their lives as well as their children's and country's future. Others just didn't like the previous driver's brash personality even though he had a historic record of wins. Indeed, they disliked the previous driver so much that they chose a driver with a decade's long record of being asleep at the wheel. Doesn't trading an accomplished driver over personality issues, to one that is sleepy and corrupt, seem like eating dog crap because you don't like broccoli?

Being 80, the impact of America's Cultural Revolution won't impact my remaining life significantly, but I fear greatly for our children and grandkids. Being a professional futurist for five decades, I have made hundreds of predictions in writing that have been spot on. I would love to say my last predictions bode for a bright future for America; as you see below, sadly, I can't. *Since emotion and subjectivity were required for the years of brainwashing, I will present "Demon Questions" in bold italics throughout the book that may help you reevaluate your own ingrained views. I encourage your skepticism but please promise to keep an open mind. The saying goes: "If you meet Buddha on the road, kill him." In other words, think for yourself.*

My Predictions

1. The U.S. economy will never again perform as well as it did during the Trump administration before the China virus.

2. There will continue to be migration from blue states to red states.

3. The only "systemic racism" will continue to be against non-handicapped, straight, white males.

4. The Dems will try to pack the Supreme Court, making it a political ally for their agenda rather than an independent branch of the government.

5. Color and race over merit will be legitimized for admissions and jobs.

6. The country will be more divided than any time since the Civil War.

7. Union membership will be required and grow as productivity will fall.

8. Alliances and cooperation with the EU will expand.

9. Government corruption will expand as more "pork projects" are handed out to party hacks and minority members for supporting the Biden win.

10. John Kerry's failed Iran policy will be resurrected. Iran will be given U.S. aid as Kerry again advises Biden.

11. Hunter Biden's corruption charges from his "work" in China, Ukraine, and Russia will be dropped. Joe will also be implicated by the "Biden corruption tapes" but not charged.

12. The DOJ Durham probe will bring charges against Comey, Brennan, Clinton, Rice, Holder, Biden, and Obama for "Obamagate," (the Russian collusion hoax to spy on and frame Trump) but will not be pursued by a Biden Justice Department.

13. Crime will rise in blue states as police budgets are cut and more pro-criminal prosecutors supported by Soros organizations are elected.

14. Taxes and fees will increase steadily.

15. The "Green New Deal" banning fossil fuels will be a disaster.

16. Gun rights will be shredded.

17. White privilege and revisionist history will be required from grade school to college.

18. Divisive hyphenated feminist "I hate men" and Black studies "I hate Whites" will be required university core courses.

19. The victimization and diversity business will grow as companies continue to be sued with fallacious racism claims because minorities are not represented according to the proportion of their population. However, sports teams will be exempt and unlike government, business and universities will not need to have Whites, women, Hispanics, and LGBT representation according to representation in the population.

20. Illegal aliens will receive healthcare.

21. Obamacare will be resuscitated and paid for by expensive, unsustainable, poorly run government options.

22. Budget-busting deficit spending will continue with no talk of a balanced budget.

23. Failed states like New York and California with enormous pension liability will be bailed out by the Feds.

24. Chain migration will flood our country and will bankrupt our welfare programs.

25. Marijuana will be legalized throughout the U.S.

26. Mexican and Black gangs will control neighborhoods throughout the country as ICE budgets are cut.

27. The media except for FOX and OAN will continue to be a propaganda arm for the government.

28. The government will continue to harass Trump, his organization, and supporters including a reconciliation commission like in South Africa.

29. Less qualified minorities will be given more executive positions.

30. Quality and productivity will decline throughout American business as requirements for unions and minority representation increase.

31. China will continue its trade surplus with the U.S. with Biden's support.

32. Business travel will decline.

33. Vacancy rates will skyrocket for apartments and office space in blue states.

34. Relations with Cuba, China, and Venezuela will improve while relations with Israel deteriorate.

35. Red states will be opposed to most federal policies that will be favoring blue states.

36. Reparations for Blacks will be given but only if Dems win Senate.

37. Statehood for D.C. will be voted for if Dems win Senate.

38. Having destroyed Trump, their only natural predator, the government swamp monsters will quickly repopulate and then multiply in the D.C. cesspool. Many federal government employees will rarely show up to work since nobody will care enough to challenge them. D.C. will be the perfect environment for "feather bedding" and patronage for party loyalists and minorities, who will feel free to make their own work rules rather than follow "White protocols." Government unions will grow larger and of course vote for propositions giving them pay raises and amazing benefits that private sector workers could only wish for.

39. Anti-Semitic hate crimes will increase.

40. Hard working Americans will once again be overregulated and squeezed by high taxes as class warfare excels between them and a growing rich government class that will rule like royals. Old government dynasties like the eight-decade Pelosi, Newsome, Getty, and Brown mafia will also further enrich fortunes made exploiting California. *Did you know, for example, about the corrupt deal where Governor Pat Brown gave the concession to operate to Squaw Valley? The resort developed by the taxpayers for the 1960 Olympics was awarded to William Newsom and his partner John Pelosi. John of course is married to the Baltimore mafia boss's daughter Nancy.*

41. Biden will not be prosecuted for blatant corruption; Hunter Biden and Joe's brother will be identified as the "bag men" for Joe in this massive corruption scandal as significant as "Watergate."

42. Hunter will not be held accountable though pedophilia involving him was found on his "smoking gun" computer and turned over to the FBI.

43. The media, including social media, blocked reporting the validity of the Biden tapes proving massive corruption. These blockbuster charges confirmed under oath by his business partner will remain censored. Keeping this bumbling candidate from the public scrutiny will work successfully in this election because of the cover provided by accomplices in the fake news, the biased debate commission, Big Tech, and social media. *Did you ever hear Biden being asked questions about this vast corruption scandal? Did you know the FBI had this damning information about Biden during the Trump impeachment hoax but didn't disclose it?*

44. Biden's cabinet will select based on color and sex over merit, including a woman or Black heading DOD.

45. Biden will open the doors again for immigration from majority Muslim countries that hate America. They will migrate to Minnesota and Michigan radicalizing cities like has happened in England.

46. Biden will rejoin the redistribution of American wealth exercise called the Paris Climate Accord.

47. Biden will rejoin the WHO that according to the WSJ, "had disclosed information intended to minimize the risk of the China virus becoming an epidemic, with the explicit purpose of covering China's failure to handle the crisis."

48. Joe will lift tariffs against China because he is severely compromised due to his involvement in his family corruption scandal involving that country.

49. Biden will get the U.S. more involved with international organizations like the UN, World Court, WTO, EU, and NATO.

50. The amazing gains ICE and Trump have made securing our borders will revert back to chaos under Biden.

These are my predictions. What do you see about the future for America and democracy that has Biden supporters dancing in the street?

Mega and Micro Trends

Over my five decades as a futurist I've often been asked how do I even know what *is* happening, much less what will happen? The "news" describes today's accelerating changes by round-the-clock firing of a barrage of random facts (and too often fiction), people and events, catapulted into social media, the internet, radio, and television daily. Lacking a structure into which to fit this data, we experience it as random sound bites. *However, the changes we are experiencing are neither random nor independent of one another.* This important observation is the underlying theme of my success predicting the future. Let's look at some of the patterns I see underlying some of today's events and I will share how subtle changes in our belief systems that I've followed for years helped bring us to this tragic point.

We are all very aware that throughout history powerful forces have changed the direction of civilizations and impacted the quality of life for generations to come. Some forces behind these changes, such as wars, pandemics, and major science and technology breakthroughs, were quite apparent to those who lived through them.

At other times, however, humanity failed to see the changes a force was making on society, even as those changes were occurring. The automobile, for example, made remote commerce and commuting from the suburbs possible. But as it did so, it eroded core city shopping districts and contributed to the urban blight of empty and decrepit buildings.

Even subtler, less apparent forces had significant, though often unrecognized, impacts. Their effects were recognized only by later generations, even when those effects were often greater—either more beneficial or more devastating— than those occasioned by traumatic events. For example, the development of the internet and the early history of Christianity had undeniable impacts on the future of the world and everyone in it, but in the early stages, those who would be most impacted by these events were completely unaware of the dramatically altered futures with which they and their children would be presented.

I've observed how subtle forces have influenced generations of Americans since the 1970s; those forces are about to change America for the worst.

This book is about the devastating impacts on American/Western values and thought brought about by subtle changes in belief systems and ideas that few have followed or understand. **Over the past five decades there has been a** complete reversal of America's and much of the world's moral compass. The reversal of values and beliefs is a trend that is having an increasing negative impact on today's world, and will prove an even stronger negative force for future generations. The changes were so subtle, and introduced and reinforced by previously trustworthy segments of society, that most accept them as truth and reality.

Being a professional futurist for over 50 years, I'm usually way ahead of society in identifying and tracking trends. Not many things surprise me. But for a decade I've been shocked almost daily with the conclusions and perceptions I hear in the media about issues, people, events, and other subject matter. Often these opposite views are worlds apart from my view of reality. At times I feel I've woken up in a world where black is white and white is black. For the first time in my life, I can even envision the remote but real possibility of a scenario where America evolves into an Orwellian society with a brutal policy of draconian control by propaganda, disinformation denial of the truth (doublethink), and manipulation of the past. *Would an American Cultural Revolution turn our great democracy into a Hell hole like Mao's China, Hitler's Germany, Stalin's Russia, or Kim's Korea, or something completely different?*

Already there is profound confusion as to basic dichotomies such as, what is right and what is wrong? What is true and what is false? Who is good and who is evil? Daily media couches the confusion in such questions as: Is Black Lives Matter (BLM) a positive or negative force? Are groups like the ACLU, Southern Poverty Law Center, and the UN impartial organizations or are they pushing a biased agenda? Is systemic racism a real problem in America? And so on.

As someone who has been paid for over 50 years to be an objective observer of our world, it became a mission for me to understand why my usually accurate view of reality was differing so much from today's younger generation, trusted friends and family, as well as the 'mainstream' media. My conclusions about how our moral compass began to swing wildly and why it will devastate our country without a major corrective calibration are presented in this book.

I've concluded that today, we live in a period where many of our most important beliefs are simply wrong! Yet, a cabal of headline-grabbing politicians, cable news contributors, pseudo intellectual professors, special interest groups, professional organizations, social media, Big Tech organizations, and clergy continually inculcate our society with false creeds. These beliefs are today's idols, worshipped with the same dangerous, unquestioning, irrational religious fervor as ancient man-made images of golden calves. They have indeed become our 'idol threats.'

The hated Nazi propaganda minister, racist Joseph Goebbels, helped develop and promote the beliefs that the Aryan race was superior to other races, that Hitler was Germany's savior, and that the Jews caused all of Germany's economic problems. Millions of people lost their lives before Goebbels and Hitler were toppled and the threat to world stability ended. Goebbels said, "A lie told often enough becomes the truth."

On the other hand, my late uncle Tony, a decorated WWII veteran would cock his head and look up with an unforgettable twinkle in the eye when confronted with lies and beliefs that did not compute with his real worldview. The next words out of his mouth would always be, "You don't believe that shit, do you?" If Uncle Tony were living today, he would be as flabbergasted as I am at the lies that so much of humanity accepts as truth.

Who am I and why write this Controversial Book?

My motivations are simple. For over 60 years, I and other organizations have learned they could trust my predictions. **I've never been surer that there will be trouble ahead.** As I wrote in *America's Deepening Divide*, an on-going American cultural revolution is deeply dividing America. The Biden platform, like accelerating pressure on deep mid-ocean fault lines, will push opposing forces against each other so hard that there will be a dramatic shattering of a landscape that was stable for years and increased likelihood of a devastating tsunami in the not-too-distant future. Of course, in our case I'm referring to a cultural revolution that will destroy our culture, economy, education, political, and social systems that have served us well for hundreds of years.

Those who are behind and want to increase pressure for this revolution are using dangerous fibs to brainwash future generations of Americans. Americans, being some of the nicest, most generous and fairest people in the world, are also the most gullible and vulnerable to flimflammers selling myths about systemic racism and the like still being rampant in the country. Learning in school and other trusted sources about the scourge of slavery, the "Jim Crow" era, and watching cops shoot Blacks on TV makes us social warriors the target demographic for brainwashing.

I would not be writing this book if we still had real journalistic integrity and the media and search engines presented (as Dragnet's Joe Friday would say) "just the facts" rather than "propaganda"; the application and methodology of which I studied in my graduate Social Psychology course. Indeed, the number of outlets for facts are becoming less and less, as a cloud of censorship and propaganda usually seen only in totalitarian countries descends on America.

That means there are very few people like me left who, like those in a stereotypical domestic argument, would choose to be right rather than happy. Sure it's easier to be seen standing along the side of those claiming to be social justice warriors even if they are being manipulated like puppets. Truth tellers cannot be worried about being popular and liked, called a racist, being alienated by family and friends, losing a job or a sponsor, having a show canceled, failing to use the politically correct language, challenging a radical professor, listening to opposing viewpoints, or being targeted and defamed by left-wing radicals or our own government.

I'm proud to be one among the group willing to tell the truth; whether it is declaring for all to hear that the Emperor is naked or that systemic racism against Blacks is a pernicious lie—even though that lie is the foundation stone of the Biden administration—or that Google and the monolithic fake news media are the propaganda arm for the far Left and victimization advocates.

Among the heroes in the shrinking band of truth tellers are: Dennis Prager, Jason Riley, David Horowitz, Sebastian Gorka, Candice Owens, Tucker Carlson, Mark Levin, John Solomon, Larry Elder, Patrick Husain, Ben Shapiro, Conrad Black, Karl Rove, Matt Gaetz, Jim Jordan, Laura Ingram, Nikki Haley, Sarah Sanders, Thomas Fitton, Kimberly Strassel, Charlie Kirk, Oxford Chancellor Patten, Jason Chaffetz, Michelle Malkin, Joe Concha and Victor Davis Hanson. These are people whose commentary I trust and you can too.

My insights into the pending catastrophe have been sharpening into focus for over half of my eighty years. I understand today's events more clearly than at any other time in my life, and with decades of successful predictions in writing, that's saying something. Indeed, Mark Twain warned, "Watch what you say to people who buy ink by the barrel." Perhaps I should have heeded his warning, but when my predictions published in seven books, numerous blogs, and in scores of consulting assignments proved correct over time, I learned that I can trust my insights, as many others have. Indeed, 'real world' Minkin was even invited to make predictions on *Larry King Live* TV show to a worldwide audience, and the publication *Critical Factors,* called me "a candidate for guru of the decade."

For more than 40 years, including ten with Stanford Research Institute (SRI International), I've been paid by scores of companies, governments, and other organizations all over the world to identify trends that present opportunities and threats that might impact them. I'm always hired to be an objective outside observer and to always "tell it like it is." My five decades working in the "real world" has honed my ability to quickly find the pony in a room full of horse crap, whether in a corporate setting or more often in the media.

Moreover, my education as an organizational psychologist prepared me to know what is valid or fact, versus what appears to be true on the surface but is not. What we call "face validity." When I was Employment Supervisor for Coca-Cola Bottling Company of New York, I used my years of training and sophisticated human resource tools, such as depth interviewing and testing, to hire the most qualified people for the NYSE Company. I took great pride in my hiring success at that time when there was real racial inequality, and I'm very proud of my role in achieving significant breakthroughs for the civil rights movement. Therefore, I feel immune to the overused slur of being called a "racist," particularly by those who support today's reality; the terrible racism against Whites and Asians.

More specifics about my time fighting discrimination are found later in the book. It is also very important to state up front that I view most Blacks, immigrants, Muslims, students, and other struggling groups as victims, not targets, of scorn. Indeed, my goal is to help these groups by spotlighting and attacking those forces that, in pursuing their own agendas, use these people as pawns on a political chessboard. *We can all agree that there was real discrimination against Blacks in employment, housing, and in many sectors including entertainment, restaurants, hotels, transportation, and other accommodations in the past. Moreover, slavery which I speak about on Caribbean and South America cruises was an abomination. My point however is that you would be hard pressed to find an example of such discrimination now. Do you agree?*

Chapter 1
BRAINWASHED

"A great civilization is not conquered from without, until it has destroyed itself from within."

Will Durant

"Truth will ultimately prevail where there is pains to bring it to light."

George Washington

"I concluded that we live in a world where a large percentage of the population has been brainwashed as thoroughly as the Chinese 'Red Guard' generation that was lost to Maoist propaganda. The brainwashing has been very effective because many of the people and institutions we have been taught to trust have slowly instilled their distorted views over decades."

Barry Howard Minkin

When I presented the above premise in a blog to my futurist colleagues in the World Future Society, they were not happy. Members, who are used to sharing trends in technology, engineering, economics, and science, reacted to me as if I was some heretic; like a Martin Luther who insulted the accepted religious dogma of his time. To suggest a large percentage of the America is brainwashed they thought was just hogwash, a true offensive, a leap too far. After some insulting responses and having my follow-up blog censored, I dropped out of the group. With so many lifelong friends and family also responding negatively, perhaps I'm on the wrong track. I'm not! I've never been more than willing to present my open and shut case and let you the jury decide the truth of my case after reading this book.

I will identify (no CNN, MSNBC, *Washington Post*, or *New York Times* "anonymous source" nonsense) those individuals and organizations that are manipulating, controlling, and have indeed brainwashed generations to pursue their own agenda—some for profit and some not. They will continue to destroy our bedrock American and Western civilization values, dimming all hope for a bright future for the next couple of generations.

Propaganda is the detergent used for brainwashing.

"Revolution is not a crime! Rebellion is justified!" "Dare to think, dare to act." Such were the slogans that stirred China's youth to rebellion during their Cultural Revolution—the words repeatedly blared over loudspeakers across the country, on the radio, and printed in Party newspapers. An example of this also came in August 1966, when Mao issued his first Cultural Revolution "big character poster," or a political tract written in big Chinese characters, urging the Red Guards to rebel and "bombard the headquarters."

"Bombard the Headquarters" became the slogan that justified wrestling authority from government officials who were so-called "capitalist roaders." The slogan led to countless officials and party cadres being persecuted for their "bad class background" as land owners, bourgeois intellectuals, or friends of Westerners. Prominent "capitalist roaders" at the time included President Liu Shaoqi, who died in prison in 1969 following severe persecution, and late paramount leader Deng Xiaoping, who survived the Cultural Revolution and lived to engineer China's opening and reform period.

Accompanied by the personality cult of Chairman Mao Zedong, the chief instigator of the movement, millions were inspired by the propaganda to turn on their fellow citizens—even their own parents—during the decade of collective madness that seized the country from May 1966. Their unquestioning obedience allowed the Maoist Communist party to use the Red Guards and the Chinese people to destroy his political enemies, including those who opposed his policies and those who refused to accept his revolution.

In this early phase of "America's Cultural Revolution," we as yet have no personality cult like a Mao; but like the Chinese Cultural Revolution, we do have slogans and groups ready to destroy political enemies and those opposed to left-wing and diversity dogma. **The most overused slogan for the American Cultural Revolution is also its biggest lie, so-called "systemic racism."**

Our "red guard" BLM Marxist and Antifa anarchist are also sent to the streets to destroy political enemies and our values by their leaders. These domestic terrorist leaders openly brag about their willingness to destroy the country if, like BLM leaders say, they "don't get what we want." BLM also professed on their website "a need to destroy the nuclear family"; sadly something too many of these bastards from single-parent families never had. Such provocative statements were taken down after this anti-American, anti-Semitic group received millions from brainwashed foundations, corporations, and individuals willing to pay for the destruction of their own country and even their children's future.

Like Mao, we also have a corrupt media that serves as a propaganda arm. Our media works for the Democrat party. Indeed, less than a week before our most important election we hit the lowest points in history of the press in America. In an unprecedented attempt at election interference, the mainstream media and the oligarchs in Big Tech decided to put a "protective wall" around Joe Biden's candidacy. This is according to Gerry Baker, *Wall Street Journal's* editor at large, who called out the "lapdog press" for blacking out explosive Tony Bobulinski claims during a Tucker Carlson interview. Bobulinski, a former decorated Navy officer and former business associate of Hunter Biden, met with Joe Biden twice; he said Biden's brother shrugged off concerns that Joe Biden's ties to his son's business deals could put a future presidential campaign at risk. He said they would use "plausible deniability" if they were caught (which they have been). This is raising serious questions about whether the "lapdog press" is still worthy of public trust. *Do you think this historical censorship of probable massive corruption by the Biden family cost Trump the election?*

Moreover, the fact that the FBI is also looking into pedophilia charges against Hunter after viewing his laptop, like Joe's groping of intern Tara Reade, hasn't even elicited a whisper from the "me too" and women's movement screams of their hypocrisy. Though Joe did nothing note worthy in 47 years living off the government teat, it seems he was very successful heading up lucrative money laundering and corruption schemes for his crime family. Perhaps he got advice from Nancy Pelosi, whose father was a mafia chieftain in neighboring Baltimore. *Sorry for the cheap shot Nancy; let's get back to my major premise.*

Try to clear your mind and open it to facts that will challenge your closely held belief system. Play along with me and please read this book accepting my silly assumption that through years of subtle manipulation, your views of the world do not jive with reality.

You have indeed been brainwashed! How could you not be? I would also have likely been brainwashed if the vast percentage of teachers I was told to respect, and paid dearly to learn from, instead taught a revisionist version of history that fit their virulent bias against Whites, Jews, males, and American/ Western history and values.

Moreover, if most of the news and social media, businesses, civil rights leaders, professional organizations, professional teams, leagues, universities, churches, charities, foreign countries, clubs, communication providers, utilities, star athletes, search engines, unions, major consumer brands, entertainment industry, family, friends, and government also uniformly repeated these slogans and aggressively defended and supported the groups using these slogans, my brainwashing would not only be plausible but very probable.

Is it possible all these sectors have been brainwashed and have been brainwashing you? Sounds crazy but let's deconstruct my broad wild claim into workable pieces to examine.

"THE GREAT CON"

The power of one!

The father of what became the multibillion-dollar victimization and divisity business was Jessie Jackson. Jackson had strong credentials including being in the vicinity when MLK was killed. Blanketing his greed and ambition under preacher garb, this physically imposing charismatic leader rushed in to fill the vacuum left by the death of MLK. He became Clinton's go-to guy to bring and keep Black voters in the Democrat camp. He was rewarded for his effort with the government seal of approval for various get rich schemes including some usurping U.S. foreign policy. For example, he was paid handsomely for his support and access to Clinton contacts by dictators and terrorists like Omar Khadafy. *Are you ready to hear the incredible true story of how Jackson's greed led to unquestioning acceptance of the myth of systemic racism by most sectors of our society?*

Deep pockets and spineless executives made business an early target for a lucrative extortion scheme I call "The Great Con"; a form of blackmail by Black males. It begins with lawyers working with Black mafia Godfathers like Jessie Jackson and Al Sharpton identifying an organization with deep pockets a "mark" to extort.

Color the facts strategy

The con goes like this: First they hire an expert booster, perhaps from an Ivy League school, who they know will support their position. The expert then prepares a slick statistical presentation of the obvious. There are fewer Blacks than White or Asian-American employees in all levels of high tech or some other company or industry that requires a high degree of skills and/or education. The expert then predicts what the numbers would be if Blacks were represented according to their proportion of the U.S. population. Besides their own cadre of private lawyers, they bring in friendly lawyers from the EEOC to threaten legal action by the government to remedy the situation.

The fallacy is to see this disparity of minorities in an organization as proof of systemic racism.

Those of us with at least half a brain know there are other factors involved; most importantly and obvious is the scarcity of candidates having the experience, academic requirements, or skills needed to be hired based on the job requirements. But predictably the obvious reasons are quickly devalued or completely ignored. Instead, pressure is exerted by lawyers and from their friends in the EEOC (Equal Employment Opportunity Commission). This self-immolation is enthusiastically supported by the brainwashed "woke" corporate employees since it is consistent with their academic teaching and the party line that our country is systemically racist; a theme that is unquestionably parroted by other sectors of society. *Do you agree that the easily proved obvious reasons such as a lack of required academic credentials, previous experience, or skills are the likely reason for the discrepancies by race and gender in business?*

Multibillion-dollar victimization and divisity business.

To avoid any controversy and having EEOC vultures looking through their books, subjecting them to being harassed and to negative media attacks, most eunuch executives and boards choose to roll over like lap dogs and allow the extortionists to make millions. By always settling out of court, they inadvertently expanded this extortion to other business. In fact, "The Great Con" would expand and develop into what has become a multibillion-dollar victimization and divisity business. These self-serving minority squeaky wheels will provide the stage, script, and collect and distribute the bacon from the Biden big government pig trough. *Did you know that almost every charge of discrimination is settled out of court and Jessie Jackson, Al Sharpton, and others made millions from these settlements? This is why business would rather parrot the false systemic racism slogans. Indeed, they already paid heavily for protection from further attacks from the victimization and divisity extortionists.*

At all cost never stop shouting the myths and slogans since they are the life blood of The Great Con.

At the final presidential debate, Joe Biden didn't give any hint about whether if elected he would pack the Supreme Court, which would of course destroy our government's brilliant system of checks and balances. But he was very clear that his administration was going to deal with the buzz word called "systemic racism." Like the "Police target Blacks"; "Hands up don't shoot"; "no justice, no peace"; "Trump is a racist" etc.; these slogans are vaporous and, as I will show, not at all supported by facts. Nevertheless, such slogans provide cover for dangerous groups like Antifa, New Black Panther Party, and Black Lives Matter to destroy our cities and pervert American history and values in our version of the Mao Cultural Revolution. *You will hear these myths and lies because they are required for the victimization and diversity private and public extortion schemes to work. If there is no systemic racism, how will you justify giving billions in government grants to minority cons to study and fix the problem?*

Warriors or pawns?

Sure, it feels good believing you are helping an oppressed minority break the chains holding them back from equal justice. I sure felt that way doing my thing at Coca-Cola to advance civil rights in the '60s and '70s. But unlike you, I watched the pendulum swing away from racism toward Blacks, women, gays, and those with a handicap, to overt racism against White, straight, non-handicapped males. I observed how the media swallowed the con, that Blacks not getting jobs or admission to schools was due to some bogus hoax; currently branded "systemic racism" rather than obvious inability to compete based on merit. For sure, the power behind the Biden throne is the multibillion-dollar victimization and "divisity" (my word to mean causing divisiveness) industry. This industry created the hyphenated study courses; out of which angry, obnoxious graduates inject their "I hate Whites, men, and America," cancer into organization of all types. *Do you think indoctrinating students with the personal views by professors is better than hearing diverse views and letting the students decide?*

The brainwashed, many very good liberal but naive people, are made to think they are "social justice" warriors out doing good for society. But, in reality they are pawns being moved by politically astute conmen for their personal gains. These robot warriors are programmed to march to support and excuse Black criminal behavior from groups like BLM Marxists and Antifa anarchists— committed to destroy our country. Completely ignoring facts, they instead swallow propaganda, such as the total hoax that police target Blacks for racist reasons. They compound the problems by voting for politicians and prosecutors that came out of the same robot factory who support criminals and anarchists over law-abiding Americans.

Junk journalism

To reinforce all the brainwashing from school and work, you have a media that parrots left-wing, divisity, and Democratic Party dogma. They learned the lesson from the mugging of business and dutifully hire a mix of people based on their color, sex, and sexual preferences over merit. They work with leaders of the victimization/divisity con game like Van Jones and Al Sharpton, who chirp the same negative left-wing tunes 24 hours a day. *Do you ever get your news from FOX or OAN or watch a Prager University video for some balance?*

Think for example, that you are someone who has been watching CNN or MSNBC to get all your news about President Trump, who in spite of media and political hot air head wind has made historical accomplishments; such as having the greatest economy in the history of the country for Blacks, women, Hispanics, and Asians, and being nominated for at least five Nobel peace prizes. *With over 95% of coverage about him being negative on these and most other news outlets, you probably knew little or anything about his long impressive list of accomplishments.* But, I'm sure you are very familiar with the years of lies about Russian collusion or his not calling out White Supremist groups and other libel that perfectly fit the only narrative you have been taught since your school days. *Did you know these or any of the long lists of historic Trump accomplishments? Sadly, you don't have a clue if you only depend on the monolithic propaganda sources comprised of MSDNC, CNN, NBC, ABC, CBS, PBS, or the once great New York Times or Washington Post for your news.*

Google helps the victimization/diversity cancer metastasize across America.

If I wanted to hear diverse views to make up my own mind about what was being taught or learned from the media or other source, I might search Google. But what would happen if I searched for voices supportive of: American values and our Founders? People who are incensed by Black Lives Matter (BLM) looting and destruction might be using the search engine to find sites with facts about the disproportionally high percentage of crime committed by Blacks and illegal immigrants or about Black/police interaction. Others might search for information about Biden corruption, liberal bias, or almost any other view not considered politically correct by left-wing professors, or their propaganda media sources listed above.

What you would find is almost all those sites critical of regressive progressive views have been censored or found after miles of searching, barely surviving in the lonely outback of searches. Seems like the "woke" little students all had the same biased schooling. Those who did best goose-stepping to the party line, including China's, were hired into the Google monoculture to protect and reinforce the Left and diversity propaganda—while censoring opposing pro-American facts and beliefs. **Big Tech monopolies destroying free speech hurt our democracy; do you agree?**

You can reverse the brainwashing, if you read this book with an open mind and are *willing to accept facts* and ignore myths. *Do you have the courage to check your automatic emotional responses at the door and recalibrate your assumptions and beliefs?*

I wrote this book to help move the world toward a better future, and to help right our moral compass, by providing a voice to the suppressed silent majority of fair-minded independent thinkers. Moreover, I have provided a manifesto that will hopefully fortify students like my grandkids with facts, as they are subjected to years of university and societal brainwashing. This brainwashing is more pervasive and dangerous in America than the Chinese virus. Hopefully, this book will help cure or lessen the impacts of the brainwashing pandemic that will sadly flourish under a Biden administration.

First let's check how brainwashed you are:

It truly amazes me how so many nice liberals, radical left-wingers, as well as those in the diversity mob gang, are blind to simple facts and reality. The Left hollers for facts and science with issues like the China virus and climate change; yet hold onto lies and myths like systemic racism, a religious dogma that must be believed on faith even if it is false. To free people from left-wing mind control and help calibrate how far their current belief system diverges from facts, I developed a simple reality check tool: the Left Wing/Diversity Brainwashed Continuum (LDBC).

Using a point scale and this tool you can begin to calibrate how far your views are from reality.

LDBC

Make a column numbered 1-60. If you think the statement is mostly true mark T; if mostly false mark F.

1. Teaching children in elementary school that they should apologize to their black classmates because they are the beneficiaries of so-called "White privilege" is a good thing.
2. The Biden family is not corrupt.
3. Black Lives Matter is a positive force.
4. I support Antifa.
5. I like that athletes kneel for our national anthem.

6. There is systemic racism in America.
7. The only plausible explanation for George Floyd's death was the cop's knee on his neck.
8. Jacob Blake was shot because he was a black man.
9. After the riots, the cops were finally found guilty in a court of law in the Freddie Gray, Trayvon Martin, and Michael Brown cases.
10. It is OK with me that colleges and universities accept Blacks with lower scores than Whites and Asians for admission.
11. Trump was found guilty of Russian collusion.
12. 9/11 was justified by U.S. actions.
13. Illegal aliens should be given full coverage for healthcare.
14. Israel intentionally kills innocent Palestinians.
15. There should be a Black, Hispanic, & woman on all admissions committees.
16. The Black Panthers, Louis Farrakhan, and Malcolm X are American heroes.
17. Most Blacks are in jail because they are victims of the system.
18. Goggle is an objective search engine.
19. Blacks are underrepresented in high tech due to systematic racism.
20. The far right commits most of the hate crimes in America.
21. Racism against Blacks in the U.S. is getting worse.
22. America's history should be taught only after the arrival of slaves.
23. Western history and literature should be scrapped and replaced by African, Native American, and Hispanic history.
24. The freedom of speech of left-wing professors is under attack.
25. The liberal press is being muzzled.
26. Fox News is biased, but BBC, CBS, MSNBC, and CNN are fair.
27. Iran having an atomic bomb is all right with me.
28. Biden did not use his influence to get the Ukraine prosecutor building a case against his son fired.
29. I'm OK with a socialist agenda in America.
30. I'm for reparations for Blacks.
31. We should have an open border policy.
32. Black's commit proportionately less crime than Whites.
33. We should make union membership mandatory in all states.
34. Government unions are a good idea.
35. Trump's claim that the economy before the China virus was the best in history for Blacks, Asians, Hispanics, and women is a lie.
36. Voter fraud is a myth.
37. It is wrong to ask for a voter's ID.

38. I'm for chain migration that brings extended immigrant families into the country.
39. Obama united the country and Trump divided it.
40. Eliminating all fossil fuels is a workable idea.
41. The Paris Climate Accord was a good deal for the U.S.
42. I'm willing to give up my current health care for a program run by the Federal government.
43. Trump should have shut down the whole U.S. economy to help stop the pandemic.
44. The protests in Portland and Seattle should not be called riots.
45. Defunding the police is a good idea.
46. Cops disproportionately shoot blacks.
47. Federal laws requiring changes in local zoning law to require more multifamily low-income housing in the suburbs is a good idea.
48. I'm willing to pay higher taxes to fund the "Green New Deal"
49. Trump was for the Iraq war and Biden was against it.
50. Dr. Ford's FBI girlfriend did **not** try to get a witness to change her testimony in the Kavanaugh confirmation.
51. Dropping test scores and instead picking students randomly is a good idea.
52. The pandemic **did not** originate in a lab in Wuhan China.
53. Hyphenated courses like Black history should be a requirement at all universities.
54. I support CA law requiring boardrooms to diversify according to race and sexual preference.
55. Being White gives one a much better chance of getting into Harvard.
56. Norway, Denmark, and Sweden have a higher minimum wage than the U.S.
57. In the U.S. the rich pay less than half of all taxes.
58. The media was right not reporting on the Biden family corruption and child porn found on Hunter Biden's computer.
59. Voting on ACB to the Supreme Court was illegal and unprecedented by the Senate.
60. Packing the Supreme Court and making D.C. and Puerto Rico states will not impact the checks and balances between the three branches of government.

ALL 60 STATEMENTS ARE MOSTLY FALSE.

I will present facts refuting each of the above statements throughout this book. If you answered true to 20 or more of the above statements, your brainwashing is complete and sadly there is little chance of your recovery.

Moreover, it seems the majority of voters in swing states are also brainwashed having given Biden a win. With the Left winning the Senate, I predict the America we know and I love will no longer exist.

Tragically, we are now ripe for a Dangerous American Cultural Revolution!

In an interview with G. Edward Griffin in 1984, former KGB informant Yuri Bezmenov exposed the insidious operations of the Soviet Union and how the Communist apparatus viciously overtakes the conscience of a country. *It seems we could add Russia and China to the many sectors within our own country that are reinforcing destructive anti-American left-wing/diversity brainwashing and myths—naively supported by the majority of Biden voters. With or without intent, supporting these myths is leading to the destruction of our democracy.*

Yuri Bezmenov reiterated that the U.S. was in a state of undeclared war, against the principles on which it was founded, under the Communist conspiracy. "You don't have to be paranoid... Unless the United States wakes up, the time bomb is ticking every second and the disaster is coming closer and closer. Unlike myself, you will have nowhere to defect," he emphasized.

He began his interview by revealing that people who toed the Soviet foreign policy, in their home country, were elevated to positions of power through media and manipulation of public opinion.

The concept of 'Ideological Subversion'

Yuri Bezmenov explained that KGB was more concerned about the psychological warfare against the American government through ideological subversion rather than espionage activities, which constituted only 15% of their work. He highlighted how **brainwashing** techniques were used on the American population to infuse an ideology, distinct from Americanism. He further emphasized how manipulation of public opinion can make people **reject obvious facts to cater to the existing perceptions and interests.**

Demoralization of a population

The former KGB informant stated that the Soviet Intelligence Agency used four methods to alter the mindset and behavior of people in foreign countries. The first step is that of demoralization, which according to him took 15 to 20 years. *During the phase, young people are influenced to question the integrity of a country and raise suspicions through media propaganda and academia. Perception takes the center stage and facts become meaningless. He attributes it to the lack of moral standards in society.*

For a population self-absorbed in a world of propaganda, and theories of Marxism and Leninism, truth loses its grip on the society. The older generation also loses control over the population due to consistent attacks on their moral fabric. Yuri Bezmenov revealed that the 'demoralization' phase was completed before the interview and the Soviet Union was surprised at the ease of its execution. He also explained how those from the 60s were occupying high positions in the government, mass media, and civil services at the time of the interview. Yuri Bezmenov further claimed that another 20 years would be needed to create a new generation of patriotic American citizens.

Destabilization, Crisis, and Normalization

As per the former KGB informant, destabilization of a country—also referred to as the second step—meant altering the nation's foreign relations, economy, and defense systems. He said that the process takes 2 to 5 years to execute. He stated that the Marxist-Leninist hold over the American defense and economic sector was 'fantastic.' Bezmenov said that he never thought that the process would be so easy to execute in the U.S. when he landed there in 1971. He highlighted that a country could be brought to a state of crisis, the third step, in as short of time as six weeks and cited the example of Central America to make his point.

Coupled with a violent change in power structure and economy, the fourth phase of normalization is kicked in which can last indefinitely. The word normalization is derived from Soviet propaganda that seeks to downplay a drastic change in a country as a normal phenomenon. *"This will happen in America if you allow the schmucks to bring the country to crisis, promise people all kinds of goodies and paradise on Earth, destabilize your economy, eliminate the principle of free-market competition, put a Big Brother government in Washington, D.C. with benevolent things,"* he remarked. *Bingo! Do you think the KGB will be dancing in the street along with the Biden supporters?*

The Left /Right Continuum

As I study the history of countries in South America and Europe for my next cruise talk, my mind keeps coming back to the events happening now in our own country and how similar unrest unfolded throughout history. In Brazil and most of South America for example, in the 1930s political groups copying the deep political divisions in Europe, polarized many countries into the right/left extremes of fascism and communism. Representatives of these extremes continue to cause unrest in the politics of these countries to this very day.

Often when in power, the Left tries to implement some economic and social policies that are revolutionary. The promise of free everything and don't worry, you can do your own thing since big government will take care of you is enticing to most people. Unfortunately, these utopian pipe-dreams have <u>always</u> failed in other settings. They are instead replaced by the real-world nightmare—poverty and stagflation. At some point, the Right with the support of the military in its role as a "moderating power," takes control through a coup. This dynamic repeats itself over and over in Latin America and Europe; it destroys economies and the social cohesion that binds a country together.

The U.S is currently dividing into such an unmanageable country and is about to destroy itself from within. More concerning is that I don't see any moderating power in the future to prevent a complete split. Indeed, the puppet masters behind curtains are also sabotaging the institutions set up to stop their revolution. They instead are using their nefarious efforts to defund the police, eliminate the Department of Homeland Security (DHS), and help elect prosecutors who support criminals over victims. ***Are you beginning to understand my concerns?***

Our Brainwashed Generation

Like the generation of children who grew up brainwashed under Mao, or children who are still studying terrorism in the Madras' of Pakistan or the Jew-hating classrooms in Gaza and Iran, we in the U.S. have lost a generation of our children to the prophets and profits of the victimization and "divisity" shell-game.

Any self-respecting country teaches each successive generation about its history, ideals, failures, and achievements. Patriotism is how a country survives, because love for one's own is the strongest and most reliable motivator for self-defense against anarchy, crime, and foreign predation; all of those protections are necessary for a country to exist at all. Patriotism, love of our values, historic accomplishments, brilliant constitution, and our history with its blemishes was the powerful force behind the USA chants at Trump rallies.

On the other hand, today's American Left shows us daily in words and deeds that they have no respect for our country, its flag, founders, constitution, or history. Since they despise it so much, they should never lead it! *Does that make sense to you? It does to me!* That is why the usual suspects in the fake news immediately denounced President Trump's new initiative for teaching American children to respect and understand the country providing them the best security in the world, the biggest social welfare state, and the most expensive education system in the world.

Over the years I watched the pendulum of racism swing all the way from Blacks to Whites and Asians. I discuss how this happened in the next couple of chapters. I stood up and my accomplishments helped break through many barriers when there was real racism against Blacks, as you will learn in the next chapter. Now I stand up as strongly against the cancer of "reverse racism" against straight White, non-handicapped males, and Asians. *Will you speak up against "reverse racism"? It is already widespread in the Biden Administration.*

Racism Against White Men and Their Children

California was quietly trying to sneak through Proposition 16. It was just a month before the election when I learned about it and jumped out of my chair. Prop 16 would actually allow an applicant's color, race, and sex (rather than merit) to be determinants in hiring and admissions. This is just the latest example of how the brainwashed, overwhelmed by the media obsession with the impacts of the China virus, might have allowed the cancer of reverse discrimination to spread to our country's vital organs; as it is already doing in completely Democrat controlled California. We have hit the bottom with this insult to our most basic American values that would allow public agencies to consider an applicant's race, color, sex, ethnicity, or country they came from, in making decisions about public education or hiring for employment. Sounds like "big brother" government joined the divisity mob to force race and sex over merit. *Would you have supported this proposition?*

Early in my career, I was an Employment Supervisor for the Coca-Cola Bottling Company, Director of Human Resources for Slant/Fin Corporation, as well as Department Manager for the Stanford Research Institute's (SRI) Human Resource Consulting Group; I took pride in my excellent long term success of hiring the most qualified people for every position posted. I had trained on the graduate level in all types of interviewing, testing, job analysis, labor relations, reference checking, training, and compensation. An applicant's past success, experience, education, skills, and pay range were important, as were previous employment references, criminal check, and proof of citizenship. What was not important was an applicant's race, color, religion, sexual orientation, or national origin. *Why would I care about an applicant's race or other such factors that have nothing to do with who is the best candidate for the posted job?*

Moreover, I would be damaging the cornerstone of the Civil Rights Act which clearly states that: "Any deliberate attempt to maintain a racial balance, whatever such balance might be, would involve a violation of Title VII because maintaining such a balance would require an employer to hire or refuse to hire on the basis of race." This example of reverse racism, California Proposition 16, also went against Section 703j of the Civil Rights Act of 1964.

Congress debated the issues of racial preferences and proportional representation. The result of the debate was the adoption of **Section 703(j) of the Act, which states that nothing in the Act "shall be interpreted to require any employer ... to grant preferential treatment to any individual or group because of race ... of such individual or group" in order to maintain a racial balance.** *Did you know granting preferential treatment to any race including Blacks is a direct violation of the Civil Rights Act?*

Senators Clark and Case, who steered that section of Title VII through the legislative process, left no doubt about Congress's intent at the time. **Read this:**

"Any deliberate attempt to maintain a racial balance, whatever such balance might be, would involve a violation of Title VII because maintaining such a balance would require an employer to hire or refuse to hire on the basis of race. It must be emphasized that discrimination is prohibited to any individual."

Ask yourself my friends; do you support hiring or refusal to hire based on race? Do you support the most basic and enduring American value that all men are created equal? The cancer of reverse racism spreading through the current political body does not!

Corporate Boardroom Diversity Law

It seems that the victimization and "divisity" mafia, made up of greedy self-serving Black "leaders" and their codependent brainwashed left-wing supporters, has found an easy mark in the eunuch Governor of California. How about another blatant example of reverse racism and "Big Brother" government over-reach?

California did have another proposition to mandate diversity in private business. **This bill would ban all-White corporate boards.** More than 600 publicly held companies with California headquarters would be required to be extorted by the 2020 additions to "The Great Con," requiring a person of color on the board. This is as dumb and wrong as corporations and their shareholders being required to summit quietly to a lobotomy—cutting out healthy, functional brain tissue and replacing it with tissue selected for its color. Such transplants may grow rich and gain unearned prestige but are programmed to force the spread of color down throughout the corporation. Like the transplant board member, this spread is usually regardless of ability, education, skills, seniority, or experience.

Indeed, American basic values and the core of the Civil Rights Act that have been so vital to our democracy are quickly being eaten away by the noxious, deleterious cancer spread by those who could never get ahead by merit, so therefore they must cheat. They do this by changing the rules as well as playing odious race and sex cards against those who compete on their ability. Society should show our distain but never respect those who used their color or sex in admission or getting a job. They are cheating society, lowering standards with their racism to those who play by fair color-blind rules.

Who is better than the business shareholders to know the best person to be put on their Board of Directors? Imagine then this latest chutzpah of the mismanaged failing California state government telling private companies the color and sex of people they must select to sit on their board of directors. Their disgusting motive is to enrich themselves and their "good fellows." They use this unearned, top-down power to spread the late-stage racist cancer that has already destroyed much of the public sector and our universities. These meritless appointments and admission into government, universities, and the private sector have and will continue to substantially dilute the power and respect of these organizations. *Did you see any laws mandating quotas based on race or sex? Would you want the state to tell you or your company what sex and race your board of directors must be? Do you approve Biden administration support for these reverse discrimination policies?*

Racist White Privilege Brainwashing Begins in First Grade

To me the above policies are disgusting and go against every American value I cherish. But I have never been more upset by the many dangerous pervasions of "social justice"; then to watch hopelessly as reverse racist cancer is currently maliciously and sneakily being injected into an innocent generation of elementary students. Indeed, the radical Left is using your tax dollars to indoctrinate your children and grandchildren to hate America and for years they've gotten away with it. *Did you know that?*

- In California, a teacher assigned students to write letters to the Oakland police department demanding an end to "racial profiling"—*for a math class*.
- Teachers are reading a book called "A is for Activist" to first grade students—teaching them "F is for feminist, T is for trans, X is for Malcolm X."
- An Illinois principal invited a BLM activist—who celebrated the execution-style killings of Chicago police—to speak at career day.

There's even a national program called Black Lives Matter at School pushing for this indoctrination—*and they've already succeeded in Seattle, Philadelphia, Los Angeles, Chicago, Detroit, Boston, New York City, Baltimore, and Washington, D.C.*

But they won't stop there. The Black Lives Matter racists won't be happy until they've conquered every school district in America—and programmed every boy and girl to believe that all white people are racist, the United States is evil, and capitalism must be overthrown. Alexandria Cortez (AOC) and other victimization and divisty extortionists are already using the Capitol mostly peaceful protest by thousands of Trump supporters and the inexcusable actions of a few dozen misfits (including a professional BLM protest organizer) who rampaged and entered the Capitol as a weapon of destruction of the masses. These extortionists are mislabeling and totally exaggerating the unfortunate actions of a few into an insurrection, and branding the millions of Trump supporters, including those in our military as white supremacists (while hypocritically totally ignoring the ongoing attacks on government facilities by Antifa and BLM), as an excuse to get funding and make millions programming all children to accept the dangerous onerous systemic racism myth. This is a disgusting, divisive form of child abuse and racial discrimination that is immoral and should be a criminal offense. You have to have had your grey matter completely brainwashed to think it is OK for your child or grandchild to be taught to feel ashamed or guilty about the whiteness of their skin.

Why should we allow these left-wing racist radicals to teach our children to despise themselves for something they had nothing to do with?! Leave our kids alone! *Can we at least agree about this?*

Not much time left to wake the "woke."

Iceberg ahead!

Social media and Google has become the propaganda arm for radical progressives and the victimization/divisity mob.

Writing this book, *what most dismayed, shocked, and enlightened me was how far left biased the Google search engine has become.* It used to be that a student could turn to the search engine to counter the misguided pap spewed by their radical professors. Today it is the largest purveyor of left-wing myths and whitewash to cover over objective reality. It was envisioned as a place designed for independent thinkers to escape the obvious political censorship and partisan bias of the fake news.

In the past I would have looked to Google for fair and balanced coverage of Trump; rather than watch daily the over 90% negative "Bizarro World" coverage by CNN, MSNBC, CBS, NPR, and ABC; or from once proud, but now sullied media outlets like *The New York Times*, *The Atlantic*, and *The Washington Post*. But it seems Google inexplicably instead is colluding with other big-tech firms (some of whom are also media owners with an allegiance to the Democrat Party) to push a naive extreme left-wing agenda that at some point will surely come back and bite them.

As I did research for this book, I've become painfully aware of how much more blatantly biased and so out of touch with reality the Google search engine has become even since my previous books. Indeed, I found even the most obnoxious, dangerous radical opinions from openly biased left-wing groups are given the front pages of Google searches to spew their venom; while moderate views or those that criticize China, if not censored, are relegated to the remote lonely acres at the end of searches.

For example, my reality based on five decades of personal experience and objective observation and research is that systemic racism, bias against Blacks, police targeting Blacks, is a hoax perpetuated by self-serving victimization and diversity hustlers and extortionists. These flimflam losers survive only because they are supported by years of brainwashing in the once trusted academia and media. They are also given the government "Good Housekeeping" seal of approval as well as gangster muscle from accomplishes in the corrupt EEOC and the "swamp." As I mentioned before, support for my views and other objective independent sources are consistently found in the far back of the search engine; well after pages of left-wing propaganda supporting these myths and the organizations promoting them.

Some examples: I've recently became aware of how the devious plot discussed above of injecting race into early education is surprisingly, like most radical left-wing ideology, being reinforced and protected by Google, social media, and fake news media. For example, try to research the topic of teaching about so-called "White privilege" in grade school or BLM burning, looting, and assaulting police in our cities on Google. Any comments that reflect what a dangerous, divisive, terrible idea White privilege is or BLM's criminal racist behavior is delegated far back in the search pages.

As an exercise, try searching Google for sites about: Left-wing bias in the media, BLM rioting, left-wing support of terrorism, Black police interaction, Joe Biden's major corruption being uncovered, Hunter Biden pedophilia, riots in the street caused by radical left-wing protestors from Antifa, affirmative action, illegal immigration, Black crime rates, "Three Strike" benefits found in FBI studies, asbestos fraud, China virus or Black Caucus corruption.

What you will find in all these searches is a very obvious left-wing bias. Excuses for bad behavior, in almost every site, will be found in the important front pages. For example, there isn't a scintilla of evidence that conservative groups instigated any of those nightly riots; yet Google, social media, and the fake news portray these Trump supporters as White Supremacist instigators and BLM as innocent protestors and victims. *Is it the right-wing that is looting, burning, and confronting cops in the Left run cities?*

How about searching the issue of court packing that would radically destroy America's constitutional balance of power? What you would find is pages of defense for this dastardly act that even the Democratic congress under FDR called "dangerous abandonment of constitutional principle" and an "invasion of judicial power" before he backed down. But for the Google monoculture, brainwashed radical social justice pawns such anti-American radical revolutionary nonsense deserves top billing.

I believe that Google has decided its good business to collude with the radical far-left, China, and fake news media's attempt at an American Cultural Revolution. This is in spite of their CEOs' ludicrous lying to Congress that Google is not biased. It seems the weak leadership at the top of Google has decided to employ an inefficient participatory approach to the company's management.

That decision was reinforced after the November 2018 walkout by a massive number of employees who decided that they didn't like the way the company management handled a sexual harassment claim. This unprecedented mutiny against management helped give exceptional power to the naive university brainwashed, young employees in Google to push a broader left-wing social justice agenda at work. This collective activism produced a monoculture at Google and other high-tech companies that is reinforced through employee town halls and cancerous, divisive, employee "social justice" cells. These company sponsored cells called Employee Resource Groups (ERG's) meet regularly and represent most groups in the victimization and divisity coalition; including of course Blacks, women, and gays. There are also Community Resource Groups to deal with issues like mental health.

These groups push the Tech Oligarchs' tentacles into areas far beyond their business products and services and reinforce their brainwashed workforce monoculture's unquestioning support of the divisive Great Con. The only divisity not represented, and instead black-balled and censored in Silicon Valley, are independent and conservative voices. The problem for America in the case of the Google monopoly is that their brainwashed social warriors seriously infected the objectivity of the world's most used search engine. In fact, they changed an important tool into an online propaganda arm of the "fake news." Moreover, anti-American far-left sites will almost always be found on the coveted first few pages of a search.

The far-left sites are populated by dangerous groups that either support or are themselves aggressively on our streets pushing for an American Cultural Revolution. The sad reality is Google, by giving prime front page positioning and consolidation of left-coast views in its search engine, has in fact become a publisher of material; that is dangerously too radical and out of step with the country. Defending the fatedly flawed "immigration lottery" or denying left-wing media bias in the first search pages are some of the many examples of the out of touch Google left-wing monoculture that I will present throughout this book.

Google left-wing views are thankfully still out of touch regarding the immigration lottery, though you would never know it by doing a Google search. Opposite from what is found in a Google search; Americans have clearly expressed a strong majority view that immigration is too high and should be lowered. That view was expressed by 83% of respondents in a large national Roper poll. Clearly, the 55,000 immigrant lottery visas would be a prime candidate for elimination in any reductions. The Commission on Immigration Reform tacitly adopted that position by eliminating the lottery from its recommended immigration framework.

As for left-wing media bias, I present mucho proof of it in the last chapter. But a Google search would present pages denying such bias exists. They conveniently hide the fact that even pluralities of Democrats, including Governor Cuomo of New York, now say the press is too liberal and anti-Trump.

As for Google, Facebook, and Twitter using "independent sources" to evaluate material presented, that has been dead on arrival (DOA) for fair-minded people. These "referees" have turned out to be left-wing hacks or partisan groups like the Southern Poverty Law Center (SPLC) that receive funding from affiliates or directly from corrupt left-wing social agitators like George Soros.

In fact, like never before in American history, social media continues to censor those of us who refuse to bow down before the high priests of divisity and the Left. They hate our religions but fervently worship their own golden asses that continually proselytize over social media and cable news. Their overarching belief, like the teachings of the prophet Muhammad, must be unquestionably accepted or there will be dire consequences. The overarching myth that forms the foundation for "the religion of the Left" is the belief in something called "systemic racism."

The missionaries from the Left have made it the fastest growing religion in the world. Its message that you are a victim of systemic racism and your country should be damned has metastasized throughout society and is killing our education system at all levels.

The DOJ must deal forcefully with the dangerous social media and high-tech monopolistic abuse; like drug dealers, they push addictive, poisonous victimization and diversity myths on those looking for a quick feel-good high, without considering the deadly consequences of their actions.

With the Biden administration rapidly repopulating the swamp and the Black lagoon, Big Tech will feel safe to parrot left-wing myths while continuing to censor those of us who see behind the curtain. Congresswomen Alexandria Cortez OC the former bar maid and current pinup girl for radical insanity is calling for even more censorship. After all, big-tech and the fake news deserve pay back for being the major reason Joe won. Congress is already opening the visa program to provide unlimited foreign labor from China and India an open door to take good, high-paying tech jobs. Along with the fake news, Big Tech successfully carried pompoms and played softball with Joe on those rare occasions his handlers let him out of his basement. In a move reminiscent of banana republic dictators they have successfully censored anything from the credible witness to the global Biden corruption that was scandal breaking just before the election. Joe's role in the Obamagate spying and the Russian collusion hoax was also buried along with the historical Trump accomplishments. *Do you now believe it is very obvious that Google is using its monopolistic influence peddling a biased left-wing viewpoint and is no longer an objective search engine? If not yet, do a search about the danger of teaching White Privilege in elementary school, liberal bias or Black Lives Matter rioting, or revolutionary goals.*

Why this bias?

Like Twitter, Facebook, Apple, and other malignant high tech and social media monopolies, Google's naïve, tech savvy, politically correct, socially unjust left-wing monoculture covey has no clue of the damage they are helping to unleash on America. How sick it is that Obama and the Democrats are pushing for even more censorship of speech. They call anything they or their victimization and divisity mob disagrees with "hate speech" and plan to work with their left-coast, high tech soldiers to continue to crush dissent. Despite the Obama administration's anemic two-term achievements, corruption, divisive racism, and their spying on and colluding to undermine the incoming Trump administration, he is the darling of Big-Tech. They think he is a cool guy who they can relate to and have poured millions into his pocket and naively promoted his dangerous agenda while gleefully squashing his mainstream opponents.

Returning fire in an early round of America's Cultural Revolution

While not condemning the nightly riots by the BLM Marxists and ANTIFA anarchists, the Democrats, business, Big Tech, and media become totally unhinged by rioting in the Capital by Trump supporters. Unfortunately for the thousands of peaceful protestors, a small group of these people along with a few BLM and ANTIFA troublemakers breached the Capital giving excuse to repress the basic rights of millions of Trump supporters.

Trump people are rightly concerned that his historical accomplishments could be reversed by the radical Left and their axis of evil allies in the political, media, and oligarch class. What are good people to do when charges of rampant voter fraud, reverse racism, Biden corruption, pro-criminal anti-police policies and destructive nonsensical China virus lockdowns are being censored by the gang protecting the incoming Biden administration?

The historical hatred of Trump is now getting as bizarre as the digging up your enemies after they have died to accuse them of wrong doing, put them on trial, and punish them again, as was done in London in the 1600s. With only a few days before his leaving office, the do-nothing Democrats along with their business eunuchs and high-tech marshmallows are out for revenge against Trump and his supporters.

How is this for bizarre! While there are plenty of strange myths on the Left about President Trump, the "cult of MAGA" delusion would assure an immediate and long stay in an insane asylum. There are nut cases who believe in their soul that all Trump voters need deprogramming, and are planning how best to do that. Some stoned leftist Twitter twits on the lunatic fringe have regurgitated up this bile for some time, but it's now accepted enough that a member of the Democratic National Committee is spouting it.

David Atkins, a member of the DNC's California convention, became the latest poster boy for Biden administration's historical radical lunacy when he implied that the 75 million proud Americans who voted for Trump were basically a cult.

"No seriously...how *do* you deprogram 75 million people? Where do you start? Fox? Facebook?" he wrote in a Tuesday tweet. "We have to start thinking in terms of post-WWII Germany or Japan. Or the failures of Reconstruction in the South."

No seriously...how *do* you deprogram 75 million people? Where do you start? Fox? Facebook?

Does this scarily sound similar to the Mao's reeducation camps or those China is using today against the Uyghur?

Bring out the clowns

Starting out with another ridiculous impeachment dog and pony show, the Biden administration looks like it will be a reflection of its bumbling, corrupt, empty suit leader. Indeed, Trump's historical accomplishments that really helped everyday people are felt as hurtful zingers when compared to the almost zero accomplishments of the divisive corrupt Obama/Biden days.

Big business once again highlighted its total disdain for our constitution and values as a steady stream of businesses are cutting off business with the Trump organization or halting political contributions to Republicans. Included on this Hall of Shame, Blue Shield, Amazon, and Marriott were among a growing list of companies suspending donations to Republicans.

President Donald Trump has lost access to most of his social media megaphone.

The overpaid, severely brainwashed snowflakes at tech giants Facebook, Google, and Microsoft said they will call for Trump's removal from office. Alphabet is calling on YouTube executives to take further action against President Donald Trump. Employees said the company's unwillingness to de-platform the President will result in further misinformation and potential violence. YouTube says it's accelerating its enforcement of voter fraud claims against President Trump and others.

These naïve spoiled woke workers formed a company-wide minority union earlier in the week and claimed more than 400 active members; Alphabet has more than 130,000 full-time employees. The letter grade from this global management consultant to the PC Alphabet eunuchs for being too willing to change their diapers or allow temper tantrums from these brainwashed crybabies is an F. *Is social activism by the naïve brainwashed employees in the job description for Big Tech companies and sports jocks? Shut up, dribble or code!*

Nearly every major tech company has taken some action against President Trump's accounts.

Twitch and Snapchat disabled Trump's accounts. Shopify took down two online stores affiliated with the president. Facebook and Instagram banned him from posting for at least two weeks. Twitter froze Trump out of his account one day before reinstating him the next dayonce he deleted problematic tweets. TikTok is redirecting hashtags like #stormthecapitol and #patriotparty to its Community Guidelines to reduce discoverability as it also removes content. Reddit says it's taking action on reported violations of its content policies, which prohibit the incitement of violence.

There will be a cost for Big Tech misusing their monopoly power, and the 70 plus millions who voted legally for Trump will not accept their voices being censored and eliminated in the marketplace of ideas. Technology will try to contain a mounting backlash against their social media sites, with shares of Twitter Inc. and Facebook Inc. falling in early trading; and rival platform, Parler, is suing for being forced offline. As Trump fans migrated to the uncensored upstart, the Google and

Apple monopolies dropped the platform from their app stores and Amazon has booted the network from its servers, taking the site offline completely.

Political posturing about tech firms has quieted during the transition, but the existential crisis that these firms have created remains unchecked. Even faced with opposition on both sides of the aisle, the oligarchs—those five tech giants that now constitute *the world's five wealthiest companies*—continue to rapidly consolidate economic, cultural, and political power on a scale not seen for over a century. Senior employees of tech giants such as Facebook, Google, and Twitter are preparing to join President-elect Joe Biden's administration amid a digital crackdown on President Trump's supporters.

The companies are purging their platforms after Wednesday's Capitol riot and break-in by Trump supporters, in the name of preventing more violence. But many fear potential government-sanctioned censorship and surveillance akin to the post-9/11 Patriot Act, which federal authorities secretly interpreted as allowing for the dragnet collection of domestic call records.

Big Tech aides pouring into the Biden White House and federal swamp will give the companies access to decision-makers, including the president, potentially conflating the policies of the large companies and the government. The influx also could influence other policies, including anti-trust actions and the future of Section 230 legal protections. Already, a mob of Big Tech vets are helping review appointments for Biden's transition office and followed him into office.

Finally even some in the left-wing are beginning to realize that the brainwashed Big Tech monoculture has stepped in the doo doo with their banana republic type censorship. Liberal journalist Glenn Greenwald, who's reporting on whistleblower Edward Snowden's 2013 mass surveillance revelations won a Pulitzer Prize, tweeted, "History moves quickly. The 9/11 attack was 20 years ago. That means nobody under 35, maybe 40, has a real political memory of it. Liberals begging corporations to censor 'extremist' speech. Emotions exploited to demand quick new anti-terrorism laws & powers? The same dynamic."

The American Civil Liberties Union's senior legislative counsel Kate Ruane said, "We understand the desire to permanently suspend [Trump] now, but it should concern everyone when companies like Facebook and Twitter wield the unchecked power to remove people from platforms that have become indispensable for the speech of billions — especially when political realities make those decisions easier."

Journalist Michael Tracey, a past supporter of socialist Vermont Sen. Bernie Sanders, wrote, "The new corporate authoritarian liberal-left monoculture is going to be absolutely ruthless — and in 12 days it is merging with the state. This [is] only the beginning... The real 'threat' at this point is crazed oligarchs + politicians using the 'crises' to consolidate power."

He added: "Notice that the threat of 'violence' Twitter says justifies their political purge never applies to traditional forms of state violence — Trump's tweets announcing bombings or assassinations were never seen as necessitating some disciplinary intervention in the name of 'safety'."

Before the November 3rd election, Republicans rallied in October to repeal Section 230 of the Communications Decency Act following Twitter and Facebook censorship of *The Post's* reporting on documents from Hunter Biden's laptop, which appeared to link the elder Biden, then the Democratic presidential candidate, to his son's work in China and Ukraine.

Twitter claimed without evidence that Hunter Biden's documents may have been hacked, although the records were sourced from a Delaware computer repairman who provided documents indicating the equipment was legally abandoned. Neither Hunter Biden nor the Biden campaign denied their authenticity. Facebook said it was throttling article distribution pending "fact checking," but later relented.

The Senate Judiciary Committee held a November hearing on censorship of *The Post's* reporting, with Republicans accusing tech giants of censoring truthful information out of political bias while some Democrats pushed for additional censorship.

Trump has waged continuous efforts throughout his administration to repeal Section 230 in an effort to curb online censorship and political bias by tech companies. In December, he vetoed the annual defense spending bill because Congress did not repeal Section 230, citing it as a matter of national security and election integrity. Democrats will hold the White House, Senate, and House under Biden, though historically both Biden and House Speaker Nancy Pelosi (D-Calif.) backed repeal of Section 230, which gives companies immunity for third-party content.

Big Tech and the Left's motives and goals, unlike Trump's, are rarely transparent. *Are the Dems going to pack the court?* Indeed, as we all have experienced with online advertising, they can be just low down sneaky. For example, inexplicably the day before the election, our Amazon Echo device for the first time turned itself on for the whole day; perhaps to spy on what we were saying and listening to. The usual Amazon excuse for these illegal activities is that they only listen to improve the system. This of course is complete nonsense. Using such devices for electronic spying is a dangerous abuse of privacy and, along with rampant search engine/social media censorship, should be criminally prosecuted.

Most of these techie social warriors are not aware that, like the "Manchurian Candidate," they are thoroughly brainwashed. In all fairness, most of these pawns of victimization and diversity flimflammers were too young to watch how the Black con games started and were played so well in Silicon Valley. They never watched the king of Black hustlers and Godfather of the "victimization and divisity" gang, Jessie Jackson, in action. Indeed, the sham he started still continues to spread like cancer through Silicon Valley and the country.

Big Brother's Media Brothers

My fear about the world after a Biden victory is already proving even much worse than I thought. Did you know: before the election, a whistleblower CEO and Biden insider, Tony Bobulinski, released a public statement on Wednesday evening backing up the reporting of the *New York Post* from last week and claiming that he personally witnessed Democrat presidential nominee former Vice President Joe Biden discussing business deals with his son, Hunter Biden.

It is already so historically bad that besides a *Wall Street Journal* editor calling the press "lapdogs," even a Progressive journalist Jordan Chariton slammed corporate media for ignoring the ongoing scandal surrounding Hunter Biden's laptop in a scathing Twitter thread that blasted MSNBC, CNN, *The New York Times*, and *The Washington Post* for selective censorship.

"The corporate media—and Twitter/FB—are still crickets as Hunter Biden's biz partner confirms the emails in @nypost story are real," Chariton wrote in response to a Fox News report that Tony Bobulinski—who was listed as the recipient of an email published by The New York Post that appeared to detail a business arrangement involving a Chinese company and members of the Biden family—confirmed the email is "genuine" and provided more information regarding Biden's role in the deal.

Did you know that during the election campaign over 90% of media coverage was negative to Trump? This in spite of his historical achievements in his first term in economic, security, and peace deals that have him nominated for five Nobel prizes. Biden on the other hand, has received over 60% positive coverage even with numerous unscripted blunders and serious credible corruption charges against him.

Chapter 2
LEFT-WING MYTHS

"The trouble with our liberal friends is not that they're ignorant; it's just that they know so much that isn't so."

Ronald Reagan

"He's naked!"

Hans Christian Andersen in "The Emperor's New Clothes"

Myth: Systemic Racism

Everyone is entitled to their opinion but not the facts!

"Systemic Racism" is the most dangerous <u>myth</u> and slogan for the brainwashed Left in America's Cultural Revolution. The cause of most of the brainwashing of Americans can be traced to the fact that almost all segments of society swallowed the poisoned fruit from this artificial tree at some time. Can you give me one example of systemic racism that you observed in the past decade? *Did you come up with police targeting Blacks? Facts disproving that hoax will soon follow in this chapter.*

Did America elect a Black President for two terms and did we currently elect a Black woman as Vice President? In fact, the only systemic, institutionalized racial discrimination making news lately in the U.S. concerned Harvard's discrimination against Whites and Asians being pursued by the Justice Department. Indeed, this form of reverse racism against Whites and Asians is the real problem rather than racism against Blacks. This led Sheriff David Clarke, a Black man, to make several elephant-in-the-room observations in *The Hill*.

First: the media love stories of race so much that they sprint to unfurl the "breaking news" banner before knowing the facts. It seems facts don't matter, or more precisely, facts are inconvenient if they can use the story as a political bludgeon to smear all conservatives and Republicans as racists.

The process works like this: First, liberal media outlets instantly parachute in to cover the story from the scene. Live coverage and interviews play on emotions, since the facts are murky at best. Anchors earnestly remind viewers "race is an explosive issue in America."

These "news" reports are followed by coverage of race hustlers calling for a "national discussion on race." Provocateurs demand that all White Americans engage in self-flagellation, confess to false accusations of harboring racist feelings, and admit that America is racist to the core.

Like Pavlov's dogs, many Republican politicians begin rushing to the nearest camera to flaunt their racial sensitivity. Should they not do this soon enough; the Left will spin their delay into indisputable evidence of the politicians' acceptance of racism.

This is what the liberal media did to President Trump following the melee in Charlottesville. They convicted him as a supporter of white supremacy simply for having the wisdom to wait until facts emerged. They declared his statement too little, too late.

After a black cadet at the Air Force Academy's preparatory school made the accusation that someone had written racist words on the dorms of other black cadets, the entire Academy came under a cloud of suspicion by school superintendent Lt. Gen. Salveria. He assembled all cadets and made them record him on their cell phones as he made the ritual display of racial sensitivity at a highly public news conference. This was too good an opportunity for Superintendent Salveria to miss: He could exercise the reflex for racial 'wokeness' rather than exercising the discipline to wait until the investigation was complete.

Now that the facts are in and the incident has been discovered to be a hoax, it will be interesting to see if he calls a follow up news conference, gathers all cadets, and makes them record his apology for having rushed to judgment in indicting them as racist. I wouldn't hold my breath.

In the case of the (fake) racist graffiti incident in Manhattan, Kansas, an entire town came under a cloud of suspicion. It caused everyone to suspect their neighbor wrote those derogatory words on the accuser's automobile. One false police report damaged the psyche, image, and morale of an entire city and its residents.

Yet, after two local law enforcement agencies with assistance from the FBI determined the incident a hoax, they decided criminal charges "would not be in the best interests of the citizens of Manhattan," the *Kansas City Star* reports. This is insane. The hell it wouldn't be in their best interest! It would allow the people of Manhattan to feel vindicated after being painted as racists.

How did the law enforcement agencies arrive at that conclusion? The director of the county police himself stated the false police report "had a decidedly negative impact on the community."

And when did the FBI begin allowing itself to be lied to? (Don't answer that, James Comey.) Do we allow false accusers to commit a criminal act and escape accountability? Not prosecuting a crime encourages others to commit similar offenses.

Identity politics and a culture of victimhood have caused these pathological behaviors. Everyone is encouraged to feel aggrieved (everyone except White and Asian males). If no feeling exists, fantasize and make one up.

We can be sure of one thing: The stories of fraud will not get anywhere near the coverage that the initial accusations did. That is sad. These race-hate instigators should be plastered all over TV just like Dylann Roof was. But since the facts don't advance the narrative that America is irredeemably racist, liberal media will take a pass.

The facts show that systemic racism in America continues to be so rare today that there is a need to make it up. Jussie Smollett and Bubba Watson, with the help of fraudsters, made up libelous stories to keep the systemic racism lie alive. Al Sharpton and other "civil wrongs" leaders taught them how to do it. Sharpton, an MSNBC commentator, visited the Obama White House probably more than anyone outside the administration; he used to dress like a pimp at the time he fabricated a story about police involvement in raping a young girl.

These race-baiters use still warm coals of the many fake systemic racism flare ups. We have all watched in horror as, again, our cities burned after racial flames are fanned by the hot air blown by fake news and social media. The burning and looting by BLM ignites the combustible diversity squeaky wheel extortionists. These modern-day carpet-baggers scream their demands on CNN and MSNBC and get rich with lucrative but ludicrous training and other community pork projects.

Racism in America is on life support at best. That is a good sign for America but not for the victimization and diversity extortionist that tragically have made it a foundation of the Biden platform.

Reverse Discrimination

The disgusting current and future reality is growing systemic racism not against Blacks but against Whites and Asians. A recent survey revealed that a startling number of White Americans—believe that they are the targets of discrimination. Other studies have corroborated the results of this survey.

Myth: Racist Cops Killing Blacks

The false charge of systemic racism and its corollary racist cops killing Blacks is most often raised after a cop kills a black criminal in the line of duty. These are myths that have caused untold death and destruction to our cities. *Do you have another example of "systemic racism" besides the cops killing Blacks myth? Do you know this divisive myth forms the basis of one of Biden's top platform agendas?*

Since I followed BLM for years since their funding by George Soros, I knew these Marxists are virulent racists and anti-Semites, out for trouble under the false banners of social justice and systemic racism. Moreover, I followed how the new "divisity"/victimization industry grew using those threadbare themes to extort billions from corporations and government. I followed all the players; con men like Al Sharpton, who recently led the large MLK event in D.C., all the way from the days he dressed like a pimp and concocted a story about cops raping a black girl. I covered Jessie Jackson's lifetime of lies and extortion as well as the criminal behavior of those in the Congressional Black Caucus which I cover later in this book.

I have seen this "police unjustly killing Blacks" con game many times before, but it still sickens me watching Blacks and the Left burn, loot, riot, and disrespects our flag and anthem. They often use the killing of a black criminal and their slogan "Black Lives Matter." But for these revolutionaries nothing could be further from the truth. Did you ever hear a word from any of the well-funded, Biden supported, domestic terrorists about the three dozen black children killed by Blacks since the killing of Floyd George rioters? Or that Chicago experienced its highest murder rate in 28 years this August, almost all black-on-black shootings? Daily, the lazy media parrots dangerous reverse racist lies and propaganda to stir up the masses, rather than clearly and simply stating the **facts:**

A recent rash of over-hyped coverage of cops shooting Blacks continues to fuel their narrative that racist white police officers are hunting down innocent black men. This has caused uproar and an excuse for Black Lives Matter and left-wing agitators like Antifa to burn, loot, and destroy our cities.

This lie is supported by a naïve brainwashed public, social media and fake news, and social media monoculture that provides justification for their deadly mayhem. The myth is amplified daily by Black and left-wing politicians, Hollywood "looney-tunes," dumb jocks that kneel for the national anthem, and the fake news media.

But the statistics, brought to light by the superb work of Heather Mac Donald and others, tell a different story. *Are you open to facts that will shatter this deadly myth?*

You know of course, police do not go looking for people to shoot. In shooting situations, police are confronting crime suspects, the majority of whom are armed. As Mac Donald notes, there were 7,407 black homicide victims in the United States in 2018, the last year for which final numbers are available. **Assuming a comparable number in 2019, the nine unarmed men killed in police shootings would represent just 0.1 percent of black homicides.** In stark contrast, she asserts, **"a police officer is 18½ times more likely to be killed by a black male than an unarmed black male is to be killed by a police officer."**

More Whites and Hispanics die from police homicides than Blacks. According to Mac Donald, 12 percent of White and Hispanic homicide deaths were due to police officers, while only four percent of Black homicide deaths were the result of police officers. "If we're going to have a 'Lives Matter' anti-police movement, it would be more appropriately named 'White and Hispanic Lives Matter'," says Mac Donald.

Presenting facts like this from the President's bully pulpit might get some Black sports players to stand up for America but could get white players to take a knee since more Whites are killed by police homicide than Blacks. Moreover, I'm about to prove **police shooting an unarmed Black is a very rare event.**

Like this year, many people viewed 2015 as a year of reckoning for police, with continued scrutiny of the use of deadly force spurring momentum for reform. **In reality, however, almost all police shootings of Blacks were justified by the circumstances. That point is clearly reflected in the number of police officers who were convicted on murder or manslaughter charges for fatally shooting a civilian in the line of duty. In 2015, that number was <u>zero</u>.**

And that's not unusual. No officers were convicted on such charges in 2014 either. In fact, since 2005, there have only been 35 officers convicted of murder or manslaughter in fatal on-duty shootings. In the 10-year period from 2005 to 2014, when perhaps 10,000 Americans were killed by the police, only 153 officers were even charged, a meager *1.5* percent, according to data provided by Philip Stinson, a professor of criminology at Ohio's Bowling Green State University.

The tiny number of convictions in fatal police shootings looks even smaller when you consider just how many cases the criminal justice system considers each year. Although there are no reliable government statistics on civilians killed by police, data compiled independently in 2016 by outlets like *The Guardian* and *The Washington Post*, or civilian tracker *Mapping Police Violence*, have led to estimates of roughly 1,000 deadly shootings each year.

Of that total, prosecutors and grand juries around the nation each year have determined that around five of these cases involve misconduct worthy of manslaughter or murder charges. In the end, the criminal justice system typically concludes that only around one shooting each year is consistent with manslaughter or murder. ***This means the overwhelming majority of police shooting cases are ultimately determined to be justifiable homicides, in which deadly force was used lawfully***; often in what police say was an effort to protect an officer's safety or to prevent harm to the public.

The inability to convict police on murder or manslaughter charges for fatal on-duty shootings contrasts, however, with a recent increase in prosecution. In 2015, 18 officers faced such charges, a significant increase from an average of around five officers each year over the preceding decade.

Expect more charges to be filled against cops as overzealous radical prosecutors with support from George Soros affiliates, fake news media, minority and left–wing politicians, and greedy civil rights activist lawyers (including those reverse racists lawyers who populate the Civil Rights Division of the DOJ) look to blame cops and make martyrs of the perpetrators to help extort money for themselves and the families of the street thugs that were killed.

But given that George Floyd was unarmed, let's consider unarmed people killed in such encounters. **Such unarmed decedents were twice as likely to be White as Black in 2019**—i.e., 19 unarmed Whites, nine unarmed blacks. As Ms. Mac Donald observes, this ratio is not stable and there is some looseness in what the media define as "unarmed." The "unarmed" label is literally accurate, but it frequently fails to convey highly charged policing situations.

In a number of cases, if the victim ended up being unarmed, it was certainly not for lack of trying. At least five black victims had reportedly tried to grab the officer's gun, or had been beating the cop with his own equipment. Some were shot from an accidental discharge triggered by their own assault on the officer. And two individuals included in the *Post's* "unarmed black victims" category were struck by stray bullets aimed at someone else in justified cop shootings. If the victims were not the intended targets, then racism could have played no role in their deaths.

In one of those unintended cases, an undercover cop from the New York Police Department was conducting a gun sting in Mount Vernon, just north of New York City. One of the gun traffickers jumped into the cop's car, stuck a pistol to his head, grabbed $2,400, and fled. The officer gave chase and opened fire after the thief again pointed his gun at him. Two of the officer's bullets accidentally hit a 61-year-old bystander, killing him. That older man happened to be black, but his race had nothing to do with his tragic death. In another collateral damage case, Virginia Beach, Virginia, officers approached a car parked at a convenience store that had a homicide suspect in the passenger seat. The suspect opened fire, sending a bullet through an officer's shirt. The cops returned fire, killing their assailant as well as a woman in the driver's seat. That woman entered the *Post's* database without qualification as an "unarmed black victim" of police fire.

Mac Donald examines a number of other instances, including unarmed black men in San Diego, CA, and Prince George's County, MD, attempting to reach for a gun in a police officer's holster. In the San Diego case, the unarmed black man actually "jumped the officer" and assaulted him, and the cop shot the man since he "feared for his life." Mac Donald also notes that there was an instance in 2015 where "three officers were killed with their own guns, which the suspects had wrestled from them."

Blacks and the Left riot and disrespect our flag and anthem, and the lazy media parrots dangerous reverse racist lies and propaganda to stir up the masses, rather than clearly and simply stating the facts: *Since June 2007, out of approximately 10,000 police shootings, only five white police officers have been imprisoned for killing someone black.* While there is no definitive resource that catalogs police killings by race, *The Root* (an English language online magazine of African American Culture) looked at data from 2007 to 2017 and found only three cases of a white police officer serving time for killing an African American (in one case, three officers were charged with killing a 92-year-old grandmother).

Myth: George Floyd–clearly killed by cop

The George Floyd killing continues to be the cause célèbre for providing slogans and visual support for the current systemic racism narrative that innocent, unarmed black men are murdered by cops. Again, face validity comes into play. Remember, face validity is when something appears to be true but really isn't.

Seeing the video of a cop with his knee on Floyd's neck had almost everyone including me believing a cop was killing an innocent black man but it turns out that is not the case. But as I learned from past episodes that served as excuses for rioting and other deadly criminal behavior; I wait for the facts to come in and let the justice system run its course. This rule was reinforced for me in the Floyd case, when I was reminded that a well-known, unethical, radical left-wing politician Keith Ellison is the Minnesota AG and prosecuting the murder case against the cop. Like the historical infamous suppression surrounding the massive "Bidengate" corruption case, Ellison, Big Tech and the fake news media are suppressing vital information in the Floyd case. It took lots of digging to even find out that this latest martyr of BLM and the Left was also a drug-addicted career criminal, who had been arrested for felony home invasion. During that crime he stuck his gun into the woman homeowner's stomach.

But what is much more important and troubling is the cause of his death is being suppressed by Google and the media. **Did you know that Floyd had a "fatal level of Fentanyl" in his system?**

New documents filed in the George Floyd case give information about the Hennepin County Medical Examiner's findings in Floyd's autopsy. Notes of a law enforcement interview with Dr. Andrew Baker, the Hennepin County Medical Examiner, say Floyd had 11ng/mL of Fentanyl in his system. If he were found dead at home alone and no other apparent causes, this could be acceptable to call an OD. "Deaths have been certified with levels of 3," Baker told investigators. Moreover, new documents say Floyd had a "heavy heart" and at least one artery was approximately 75% blocked. *How much death and destruction could have been avoided if the facts came out immediately and we had an honest press?*

Myth: Jacob Blake–innocent man shot by cops

In the case of Jacob Blake, the mob, the Left, and the fake news are trying to do the same thing. Few are highlighting that at the very least, this guy had a warrant for sexual assault, trespassing, and domestic abuse. None of this of course would have happened if guys like him were taught to obey the law and not violently resist arrest. Indeed, this guy continued to resist even after being tased. Most important and clearly heard on the tape is that he was told to "drop the knife" at least twice. Blake finally admitted he did indeed have a knife in his hand. *Did you support the rioters or are you allowing the justice process to play out?*

Myth: Kyle Rittenhouse–White Supremacist kills innocent protestors

With regard to the 17-year-old white Kyle Rittenhouse, who shot two BLM rioters in Kenosha; thankfully, the truth will eventually come out. Rittenhouse was guarding the boarded-up establishment of a friend that had been attacked by BLM the night before. My prediction is that he will eventually be found innocent by pleading self-defense. Bottom line, he was chased by the BLM mob and after he fell was attacked by a guy (with a record as a sex offender) who was trying to grab his gun when he was on the ground. The other "victim" was about to bash his head in with a large skate board. There is no question about him fearing for his life. Therefore, he was justified by Wisconsin law to defend himself from possible death or severe bodily harm. *Did you let the mob and fake news influence your views about this case? Is this an example of systemic racism hoax coloring the facts?*

Of course, when he is free or given a lesser sentence, the Left and BLM mob will follow up on their Marxist pledge to destroy America, mistakenly thinking these idiots can try to rebuild it better with their failed radical policies. We all can see these failed policies playing nightly in the continuing decline of once great cities; all of course run by progressives. Expect more crime in these cities under a Biden administration, since he praised BLM and has nothing bad to say about the Antifa terrorists.

Did you know that Antifa rioters are now painting "fuck President Biden" signs on the walls in Portland? These radicals do always eventually eat their own. *Do you understand that these are committed revolutionaries intent on destroying America?*

Criminals over Cops

How sick is it for Biden, Obama, and the dumb 'I hate America' NBA and other jocks to support criminals over cops? What would they have done if someone with a knife was threatening them; as recently happened with another black man whose recent killing sparked more of the looting game? Facts mean nothing to these idiots or their accessories, the fake news, immoral exploiting sponsors, and the biased brainwashed monoculture in the social media.

Tragically, this sick anti-American chapter can be traced to the media once again not verifying a story and ignoring facts. Indeed, they created a mythical rich hero out of some dumb jock who knew almost nothing about police brutality, aka Colin Kaepernick. I watched on local Bay Area TV when he took one of his first interviews after his first kneel down episode. He was asked by the local reporter about what he experienced to make him do this. To paraphrase, he told about an incident while he was at UNLV where a security guard on campus was rude to a friend he was with. I remember thinking at the time that it seemed like much to do about nothing. But then he added; his girlfriend's family was Muslim and he did not like that the U.S. was fighting Muslims in the Middle-East. The bottom line: he was showing off to his girlfriend and her family by disrespecting our country with his kneeling and knew almost nothing about police/black interaction.

I was fascinated watching how the media left-wing and diversity cons always searching for evidence of systemic racism (which is as elusive as proof of UFO's) worked with the media propaganda machine to mold him into the symbol of deadly police/black interaction. To his credit, this low IQ showoff has made millions, is now idolized by the left-wing and victimization celebrities; the eunuchs playing, running, and sponsoring professional sports; as well as the brainwashed puppets marching in lock step in the big social media firms. The Left, including our former Black President, Joe Biden, and his most radical Black VP, still will not acknowledge how transparent and ludicrous playing the systematic racism card is. Why should they if the brainwashed who voted for them still believe it?

Like many of us, I don't turn on sports to watch dumb spoiled jocks like Lebron James disrespect my country or some team put on a segment on revisionist Black history that features some anti-American Black radical. They have killed the game for many of us as the dismal ratings for the NBA this year prove. *Isn't it time to boycott the teams and their sponsors who perpetuate the racial myths and prevent the facts that show clearly that cops do not target blacks and indeed the opposite is true?*

Win or lose it's a good pay day

However, the facts do eventually come and in almost every case the police action is found justified and the cops involved are found innocent in a court of law. Even so, the criminal victims' families often supported by victimization and "divisity" extortionists like Sharpton and Jessie Jackson still get millions in compensation. They also get a piece of mandated (by the oversupply of civil rights lawyers) nonsense PC police training courses from their buddies in the new lucrative "divisity" and victimization.

The victimization and divisity vultures flying around Minnesota know it can be a big payday if you're Black and your death involves the police, even if the cop is

54

eventually proved innocent as they usually are. For example, Michael Brown died in Ferguson, Missouri, when he was shot several times by white police officer Darren Wilson, while trying to take the officer's gun. The incident transformed the city into a war zone after a grand jury chose not to indict Officer Wilson. However, later the City of Ferguson agreed to settle a wrongful death lawsuit with Brown's family for $1.5 million.

Trayvon Martin was shot to death by George Zimmerman, only after attacking Zimmerman. Zimmerman, like Wilson, was found innocent; nevertheless, the Martin family received a settlement believed to be in excess of $1 million.

The city of Baltimore and its black mayor received a failing grade globally as riots, looting, vandalism, and a well-publicized witch hunt involving the officers involved unfolded after Freddie Gray's arrest. Gray, who had been arrested more than a dozen times, died in a police van. All charges were dropped against the officers involved in his arrest. But unbelievably, the city settled for $6.4 million.

Crowdsourced memorial funds for the families of Mr. Floyd; Ahmaud Arbery, who was gunned down this year in Georgia; and Breonna Taylor, who was killed by the police inside her home in Louisville, KY, have amassed more than $23 million. The Floyd memorial broke GoFundMe's record for most contributions, with nearly 500,000 people contributing.

Con-on man!

Blacks make up only a quarter of the total number of people killed in police shootings annually, a ratio that has held steady since 2015. The reigning canard, however, is that this 25 percent figure proves racism since African Americans make up just 13 percent of the U.S. population.

But as we know from the 'color the facts' strategy in The Great Con, it is just one more example of face validity; it seems to make sense until you look at the obvious reason why a higher percentage of Blacks are killed by police than their representation in the general population. **It's simple! Blacks commit disproportionately more crime. Indeed, they commit much more crime than any other race.**

Mac Donald points out that Blacks "commit 75 percent of all shootings, 70 percent of all robberies, and 66 percent of all violent crime" in New York City, even though they consist of only 23 percent of the city's population.

The 2013 FBI Uniform Crime Report, a compilation of annual crime statistics, shows that black offenders killed 90 percent of black victims; 14 percent of white victims were killed by black offenders; yet only 7.6 percent of black victims were killed by white offenders. Blacks also made up 42 percent of all cop killers whose race was known. **Blacks are less than 13 percent of the national population, but according to the U.S. Department of Justice, they accounted for 52.5 percent of homicide offenders from 1980 to 2008.**

"Officer use of force will occur where the police interact most often with violent criminals, armed suspects, and those resisting arrest and that are in Black neighborhoods. Such a concentration of criminal violence in minority communities means that officers will be disproportionately confronting armed and often resisting suspects, in those communities, raising officers' own risk of using lethal force," writes Mac Donald.

More facts to dissolve the racist cop targeting Blacks myths:

Black and Hispanic police officers are more likely to fire a gun at blacks, than white officers. This is according to a 2015 Department of Justice report about the Philadelphia Police Department, and is further confirmed by a 2015 study conducted by the University of Pennsylvania where criminologist Greg Ridgeway determined that black cops were 3.3 times more likely to fire a gun than other cops at a crime scene.

Blacks are more likely to kill cops than be killed by cops. This is according to FBI data, which also found that 40 percent of cop killers are black. According to Mac Donald, the police officer is 18.5 times more likely to be killed by a black person than a cop killing an unarmed black person.

Despite the facts, the anti-police rhetoric of Black Lives Matter and their leftist sympathizers have resulted in what Mac Donald calls the "Ferguson Effect," as murders have spiked by double digits in 36 of the 50 biggest cities in the U.S. as a result of cops being more reluctant to police neighborhoods out of fear of being labeled as racists. Anti-police rhetoric has deadly consequences: in 2019, 48 cops were victimized by fatal shootings. This year on July 13, the 32nd officer was already killed marking a 28% jump over the same period last year.

While African Americans are involved in two times more police shootings than their percentage of the population would seem to warrant, they commit 53 percent of murders and 60 percent of robberies—well over *four times* their percentage of the population. The political establishment would have you assume this statistical disparity is caused by institutional racism that myopically beams police attention onto black men. But we know the statistics accurately reflect reality *because crimes get reported by victims*—a large percentage of whom are black (also outstripping their share of the overall population).

If you just focus on interracial crime, though, Mac Donald (writing this time in the *City Journal*) has crunched those numbers. "Between 2012 and 2015, blacks committed 85.5 percent of all black-white interracial violent victimizations." This, she qualifies, excludes interracial homicide. *Powerline*'s Paul Mirengoff fills in that blank: "Blacks commit around 70 percent of black-white interracial homicides." For this, he draws on FBI crime statistics for 2016. They show that, of 776 black–white homicides, blacks committed 533 and whites 243.

The most dangerous threat to the African-American community in America is not cops. It is liberals. The United States is not institutionally racist. The political system, the criminal-justice system, and academe overflow with political progressives. The notion that they would tolerate racism in their institutions would be laughable if sensible people were encouraged to think about it rather than mindlessly accept it. Nor could we conceivably be "unconsciously" racist. Let's put aside that to *discriminate* is to choose, and that, where it exists, racial discrimination is a conscious state of mind. The reality is that our institutions of opinion are so obsessively racialist; no one in America has the luxury of being unconscious about racism.

Myth: America Is Always Wrong

George Orwell commented that the left-wing intelligentsia of his time was "markedly hostile to their country," and that what distinguished left-wing newspapers was "their generally negative, querulous attitude." Nothing has changed!

Today's Left is a self-hating, spiteful group undergoing a mental breakdown. Symptoms are manifest in many areas. For example, sociologist Dana Fisher from the University of Maryland found that of hundreds of protesters in multiple cities, participating in the recent protests, are extremely dissatisfied with the state of democracy. Just 4% of respondents said they were "satisfied with democracy," the author reported. Moreover, 70% of millennials say they will vote for a socialist. *Do you get it yet? They are so brainwashed that they don't like democracy but support socialism?*

Moreover, the propaganda has even brainwashed most White Americans to say racism is a "big problem" in their country. The study found that people consistently reported being motivated to participate in the protests because of (mythical issues summarized by the empty slogans of America's Cultural Revolution) police brutality, racial justice, and equity. But the findings also showed that Trump was a key factor in motivating people to take to the streets. In Washington over a weekend, for example, 45% of respondents cited Trump as their motivation for participating in the demonstrations and 100% of protestors said they were Biden supporters. *To summarize, 96% of protestors interviewed are dissatisfied with democracy and 100% are Biden supporters. Moreover, 70% of millennials support socialism. Do you see how these brainwashed millions who believe socialism is better than democracy supported Biden?*

In other countries, the government, people, and press inflate virtues of their nation but downplay the vices. In the United States, it's just the opposite. The Left would like the world to believe that America stands for killing innocent Blacks, being racist in hiring and education, putting minorities in jail without due process, and putting illegal immigrant kids in cages.

Thankfully, the American silent majority can see through the left-wing media fog of national self-hate. We value being American, and are proud of our country's courage against murderous and deranged evil dictators now and in the past. When it comes to aid, immigration, and equal opportunity, we know that we are the most generous nation that ever existed. We marvel at our country's continuing record of achievements in medicine, science, technology, and commerce. We stay silent and allow the minority squeaking wheel to get more oil than deserved or earned.

Myth: Right-wing evil is black and white but Left evil is gray

The Left sees evil in terms of shades of gray when it comes to issues like terrorism, which they believe is the result of victimization and occupation. Terrorists are often called freedom fighters. People like Maduro, Castro, Soleimani, Farrakhan, Dubois, Hitler and organizations like Isis, Hezbollah, Hamas, BLM, and Antifa are seen as complex. They may sometimes do evil things, but they are always excused by the Left as justifiable while White America is viewed as simply evil. Indeed, killers of innocent people, particularly if they are Black, are never seen by the Left as purely evil people. It is embarrassing to listen to the left-wing intelligentsia and media, coolly and calmly give logical, well-thought-out, but misleading and factually wrong, reasons for every terrorist thought and action including 9/11. Some leftists have gone so far as to say the people killed indiscriminately in the World Trade Center were not innocent victims; however, those Afghans killed accidentally while the U.S. fights terrorists are.

It is infuriating that left-wing media tries to obscure the simple truth that these terrorists represent the very essence of evil. Indeed, for the Left, the only truly bad, evil people are people on the Right, who they see in black and white terms. Not even the President of the United States, with his millions of supporters who love and respect our country, has any redeeming qualities. *Have the inmates taken over the asylum?*

Myth: America Doesn't Care About the Rest of the World

The little traitor and so-called American Taliban, John Walker Lindh, sent a letter to his mother questioning her loyalty to America. Lindh wrote asking what America had ever done for anybody. The Left, like Lindh, believes that the answer is "not much."

The truth that the brainwashed Left doesn't want to discuss is that America has given well over $500 billion in aid to foreign countries since World War II. No other country comes close. This year alone the budget for foreign aid is over 52 billion dollars. Today, the U.S. manages foreign assistance programs in more than 100 countries around the world through the efforts of over 20 different U.S. government agencies. These investments further America's foreign policy interests on issues ranging from expanding free markets, combating extremism, ensuring stable democracies, and addressing the root causes of poverty, while simultaneously fostering global good will.

In addition we recently passed the Coronavirus Aid, Relief, and Economic Security (CARES) Act contains $1.15 billion for the Department of State, USAID, and other international initiatives. While the U.S. government is concerned with controlling the virus at home, it has continued to support its foreign partners and allies during this time. Secretary of State Mike Pompeo announced $500 million in humanitarian and economic assistance for countries combating Covid-19, though likely much more funding is needed.

Unbelievable as it sounds, the anti-American, anti-Trump, do-nothing but teardown, left-wing brainwashed counterculture found another opportunity to denigrate the country for our foreign aid assistance though we give much more than any country in the world.

"The United States' commitment to global development does not look good compared with that of other wealthy countries—and it's likely to get worse. According to an annual index released Tuesday by the left-wing Center for Global Development that ranks 27 of the world's wealthiest countries, the U.S. scored dead last on foreign aid contributions and quality—despite being the largest donor in dollar amount. That's because in 2017, it allocated a mere 0.18 percent of its gross national income for development assistance. That is well short of the

0.7 percent that wealthy countries have committed to strive for since 1970. (Only seven countries met or exceeded that target in 2016.)

"Not only that, but by the measures of the index, American aid is also poor quality. When the index assessed aid given directly to recipient countries, the U.S. performed below average on every measure of quality (efficient use, transparency, building up institutions in recipient countries, and reducing their administrative burden."

What is disturbing is the Left pushing to give aid to their favorite nations—those that express their gratitude by chanting "Down with America" and burning our flag. These actions of course are also associated with our own darlings in the American Left.

Myth: The Rest of the World Knows What They are Talking About, and We Should Care What They Think

From my world travels, I've learned that the knowledge most foreigners have about America is consistently wrong. Often, the political fringe and controlled media biased views about the U.S. are dismal and self-serving at best. Watching BBC and other foreign news channels interviewing almost entirely left-wing or anti-Trump media figures during the election felt like piling on the over biased 90% negative coverage Trump received by all but two networks in America.

But for some reason, the Left thinks that what the rest of the world thinks about us is very important and relevant. They think global debating organizations like the UN, where most members hate America but like the funds it supplies are better than Trump's America First policy. *Taking off your rose color glasses; will you agree Biden's open borders, Green New Deal, and free everything for illegals and all America is more than enough to bankrupt the U.S. without adding the rest of the world into our sinking lifeboat?*

The U.S. did the right thing by getting rid of John Kerry's terrible Iran's nuclear accord though it is still supported by our "friends" in Europe. The Trump administration, to their credit, does not change values just because the global majorities of brainwashed, uninformed, prejudiced people have different values and morals. Trump would never have been nominated for five Noble Peace Prizes if his bold, decisive actions needed approval from the UN and EU debating societies.

Moreover, I'm a life-long conservationist and give a talk called *Health of the Planet*. My conclusion about the Paris Climate Accord is that it is more a socialist global wealth distribution scheme that was designed to severely hurt American business and taxpayers than a realistic environmental approach to climate change. *Did you know, without fanfare or media coverage, the U.S. has significantly reduced carbon emissions under Trump while having the best economy in U.S. history for all income levels and all minorities?*

The U.S. morals and values have been the global gold standard for decades. But perhaps the Left could offer some foreign example of a more moral country or a better economic model than capitalism. Would they like us to be like Greece whose socialist policies and unions have doomed the country to the economic toilet? Perhaps a communist country should be our model. Maybe the largest left-wing country, Communist China, could be a model? That could work if you are one of the corrupt elites like those who paid the Biden gang millions for influence. They could care less if China's economic growth tips the global environment into a global disaster. How about Bernie's and Obama's socialist hero, Cuba? Perhaps they will share their Swiss bank accounts, valued at more than the Queen of England's, with his struggling people. Venezuela's Maduro is another leftist pinup boy that is re-making the democratic country of Venezuela into his own banana republic dictatorship.

Has there ever been a foreign left-wing leader whose verbose verbiage translated into anything positive? I objectively cannot think of a better country in the world then the U.S. of A. If the Left disagrees, let them move to that new country ASAP. If they can't come up with a better country, they must stop playing their no-win game of trying to destroy this country with asinine words and actions. The simple truth is that the masses are now brainwashed asses that believe and spit up whatever the media prepares for them, and nothing they serve up is good for the health of the country. *Will the country move even further left with a Biden presidency and having the most radical senator in Congress as V.P.? Are you ready for a socialist experiment in the U.S.?*

Myth: White Privilege

To understand why and how the charge that there is systemic racism in the U.S. happened, I needed to research its origin. My first observation was that those who are most associated with "White Privilege" education tend to be White academics: Tim Wise, Robin DeAngelo, Paul Gorski, and Peggy McIntosh, author of the 1989 article, "White Privilege: Unpacking the Invisible Knapsack." One of the reasons McIntosh's piece is so powerful is that it rings true for many people even without much hard data or facts; it is again what we psychologists call "face validity." If you are promoting an unproven agenda or conducting brainwashing, this is what you really want. The hope is to engage you at an emotional level. That is why the systematic racism charge, like the myth of bias and police targeting blacks, is defended with blind faith and emotion **but not with facts**. These "social justice warriors" are not data driven by facts but rather by re-branding subjective, touchy feely, pseudo academic mush.

Indeed, the more emotion and temper tantrums, the less you need facts to make your case. It seems the must-see useful resource to "educate" white people on racism is the Lee Mun Wah film *Color of Fear*. The film takes place in a setting similar to a small men's group therapy session. A white liberal and various minorities express their fears and distaste for America. The other White American who believes in the strange principle that all people are equal. This most basic American value is targeted by subjective slights and fears these hyphenated American crybabies say they feel in "White America." Give me a break—like someone would prefer living less fearful in Black run cities where the vast majority of all crime happens.

The star of the show is a black man who does not accept America's societal norms. He doesn't accept societal values like what is the proper attire for work. Not surprising, Roosevelt Thomas one of the successful exploiters of the victimization and divisity con game, said something like, 'Don't think Blacks should be on time; it's a "White thing". Meanwhile, the Smithsonian had to take down a list of disturbing "White values" such a "hard work."

The black guy in the film wants America to know how angry and pissed off he is at Whites and our country by throwing an award-winning temper tantrum on set. But sadly, I learned nothing new from him since I see this type of kicking and screaming out of control child behavior by Blacks burning and looting our cities nightly. But this "I left my meds at home" nonspecific rant seems to stimulate the woke marshmallows who graduated from hyphenated feminist 'Hate men 101' and 'Black studies: Hate Whites' courses who are all too willing to goose-step with BLM and Antifa with their torches and burn down our progressive run cities. Indeed, such human passion with a lust of violence will allow Black Marxists and their co-dependent brainwashed radical Left Gestapo to continue their power play to overthrow our country. Meanwhile, the brainwashed liberal eunuchs in academia, high tech censors, and the fake news media provide academic and financial support and cover to this puerile out-of-control dysfunctional behavior.

The disgruntled black guy film reminded me of being on a safari in Africa where we heard a loud bellowing and watched as trees across the river from us were being toppled. The guide informed us that it was a rogue elephant angrily looking for a herd to disrupt. He explained that growing up without the strong social bond of the community and without the wisdom and leadership of a male role model; these rogues become an out-of-control danger to themselves and others. I see a similarity with the kicking and screaming looters and rioters ravaging our cities and beginning to cause havoc in our suburban communities. Indeed, with three quarters of African American families headed by single women, there are very few male role models and fewer good ones. We see the results with the disproportionately high crime rate for Blacks in America.

How to Play the White Privilege Con Game

Congress 90% White - President & VP 100% White - Current POTUS cabinet 91% White - Top Military advisors 100% White - People who decide what TV shows we see 93% White - Which books are published 90% White - Teachers 83% White - Full time College Professors 84% White - Owners of football teams 97%White.

Robin DiAngelo, one of the perpetrators of the White privlege hoax, uses the above table to help promulgate this myth. With so many important power players being White there must be an obvious bias against Blacks. Therefore we social warriors should sue, boycott, and harass until Blacks are equally represented. This is how the con begins. *But by now hopefully you will recognize this shell game as another of the color the facts strategies "The Great Con" uses to perpetuate the myth of systemic racism*

The con assumes that these discrepancies are based on the color on one's skin. This of course is complete nonsense as there are dozens of other variables at play. The most obvious is that Blacks do much worse in academics than Whites and that limits their career options. Indeed much of this racist White privilege nonsense is to lower standards and expectations for Blacks. For example, the first categories are elected or selected officials. Using her distorted logic that color of their skin determined their positions, how did Obama serve two terms if Blacks don't represent the majority of the electorate and color of his skin decided the election outcome? Moreover, did his children attend Ivy League schools only because of their skin color or were other factors at play?

The next categories relate to media, sports, and teaching. The people who achieved the power to make decisions in these areas may predominately be White but like in other sectors of the economy, such as hiring and admissions decisions, disproportionally favor Blacks and women often over usually more qualified white applicants. Indeed, if Ms. DiAngelo had biracial children, I bet they would list themselves as Black if applying to Harvard or any other schools. In fact, the only bias being currently prosecuted by the DOJ in school admissions is against Yale and others for discrimination against Whites and Asians.

As for owners of football teams or any other corporation, anyone including rich Blacks can make a bid to buy a team. What is biased is the "Rooney Rule" that forces an owner of a team to interview a Black candidate for coaching positions. It makes as little sense as requiring the coach to have a required proportion of Whites, Asians, women, Hispanics, and little people on every team rather than those that will perform best. *The point is that there are many reasons Whites are in position of power but today none of them have anything to do with systematic racism. Indeed, with five decades of global management consulting, I've learned people make decisions that will be most profitable and advantageous for them and their business.*

Myth: Critical Race Theory

In his speech at the National Archives Museum, the President posited that using critical race theory (CRT) as a framework to consider the history of the U.S., including its use of slave labor, encourages "deceptions, falsehoods and lies" by the "left-wing cultural revolution."

"Students in our universities are inundated with critical race theory," he said. "This is a Marxist doctrine holding that America is a wicked and racist nation, that even young children are complicit in oppression, and that our entire society must be radically transformed. Critical race theory is being forced into our children's schools, it's being imposed into workplace trainings, and it's being deployed to rip apart friends, neighbors, and families."

Scholars who work with CRT, however, say it has become an indispensable and widely accepted tool for properly understanding the state of the country. Following the memo from the Office of Management and Budget, American Association of University Professors President Irene Mulvey called on faculty and administrators to "condemn this ban" on critical race theory.

"Critical race theory represents an important body of such expertise and President Trump's recent attack on it is a naked attempt to politicize our national reckoning with racism and a new escalation in the assault on expert knowledge," Mulvey wrote. Our universities need a complete housekeeping when, divisive, hateful anti-American, unproven theory developed by reverse racists and biased left-wing radicals becomes "expert knowledge." It is not! This exercise in mental masturbation is, however, very dangerous propaganda that belongs in the waste bin of history with "race theory" published in the 1920s by some of these same universities and professional journals to study such idiotic topics as phrenology or "The Negro: Is He a Biological Inferior?" Such pseudo intellectual pap like CRT can be found in the "Red-Book" that was used for brainwashing and intellectual justification of Maoist atrocities; and Mein Kamph did the same for the unspeakable horrors unleashed by Hitler. *CRT is spreading like wild fire in our schools. What are you going to do to stop its devastating spread?*

OXFORD - THE FIGHTBACK HAS BEGUN

The eunuchs leading and the radical idiots teaching in our brainwashed, reverse racist American universities get a failing grade from independent thinkers. Here is what an A plus response looks like from a real scholar, University Chancellor Patten. His letter is a response from Oxford University to Black students attending as Rhodes Scholars—who are demanding the removal of the statue of Oxford benefactor, Cecil Rhodes.

Interestingly, Chris Patten (Lord Patten of Barnes), The Chancellor of Oxford University, was on the "Today" programme on BBC Radio 4 yesterday on precisely the same topic. *The Daily Telegraph* headline yesterday was "Oxford will not rewrite history." Patten commented, "Education is not indoctrination. Our history is not a blank page on which we can write our own version of what it should have been according to our contemporary views and prejudice."

Dear Scrotty Students,

Cecil Rhodes's generous bequest has contributed greatly to the comfort and well being of many generations of Oxford students – a good many of them, dare we say it, better, brighter and more deserving than you.

This does not necessarily mean we approve of everything Rhodes did in his lifetime – but then we don't have to. Cecil Rhodes died over a century ago. Autres temps, autres moeurs. If you don't understand what this means – and it would not remotely surprise us if that were the case – then we really think you should ask yourself the question: "Why am I at Oxford?"

Oxford, let us remind you, is the world's second oldest extant university. Scholars have been studying here since at least the 11th century. We've played a major part in the invention of Western civilization, from the 12th century intellectual renaissance through the Enlightenment and beyond.

Our alumni include William of Ockham, Roger Bacon, William Tyndale, John Donne, Sir Walter Raleigh, Erasmus, Sir Christopher Wren, William Penn, Rep. Adam Smith (D-WA), Samuel Johnson, Robert Hooke, William Morris, Oscar Wilde, Emily Davison, Cardinal Newman, Julie Cocks. We're a big deal. And most of the people privileged to come and study here are conscious of what a big deal we are. Oxford is their alma mater – their dear mother – and they respect and revere her accordingly.

And what were your ancestors doing in that period? Living in mud huts, mainly. Sure we'll concede you the short-lived Southern African civilization of Great Zimbabwe. But let's be brutally honest here. The contribution of the Bantu tribes to modern civilization has been as near as damn it to zilch.

You'll probably say that's "racist." But it's what we here at Oxford prefer to call "true." Perhaps the rules are different at other universities. In fact, we know things are different at other universities. We've watched with horror at what has been happening across the pond from the University of Missouri to the University of Virginia and even to revered institutions like Harvard and Yale: the "safe spaces"; the #blacklivesmatter [BLM]; the creeping cultural relativism; the stifling political correctness; what Allan Bloom rightly called "the closing of the American mind."

At Oxford however, we will always prefer facts and free, open debate to petty grievance-mongering, identity politics and empty sloganeering. The day we cease to do so is the day we lose the right to call ourselves the world's greatest university.

Of course, you are perfectly within your rights to squander your time at Oxford on silly, vexatious, single-issue political campaigns. (Though it does make us wonder how stringent the vetting procedure is these days for Rhodes scholarships, and even more so for Mandela Rhodes scholarships.)

We are well used to seeing undergraduates – or, in your case, postgraduates, making idiots of themselves. Just don't expect us to indulge your idiocy, let alone genuflect before it. You may be black – "BME" as the grisly modern terminology has it – but we are colour blind. We have been educating gifted undergraduates from our former colonies, our Empire, our Commonwealth and beyond for many generations. We do not discriminate over sex, race, colour, or creed.

We do, however, discriminate according to intellect. That means, inter alia, that when our undergrads or post grads come up with fatuous ideas, we don't pat them on the back, give them a red rosette and say: "Ooh, you're black and you come from South Africa. What a clever chap you are!" No. We prefer to see the quality of those ideas tested in the crucible of public debate. That's another key part of the Oxford intellectual tradition you see.

Chapter 3
DIVERSITY BECOMES "DIVISITY"

"If we are to guard against ignorance and remain free, it is the responsibility of every American to be informed."

Thomas Jefferson

It is time to topple the idol on top of the victimization and extortionist/left-wing totem pole. That is the misguided belief that diversity is strength. In order to protect our country and society, we must see diversity as the divisive threat and danger that it has proven to be. By using divisive diversity or what I call "divisity" as their weapon of choice, the high priests of diversity have made billions as they have successfully infiltrated our legal, media, governmental, political, business, financial, cultural, and most importantly, our educational sectors. Their success continues to come at great cost to our country's well being.

 Many of America's Blacks have strayed way too far off Martin Luther King's trail to the mountaintop. They have instead been rolled down the less strenuous hill toward victim-hood. Indeed, recent generations brainwashed by teachers and others grow up believing that they live in a hostile, alien nation. Encouraged by corrupt leaders to act like dysfunctional children, many Blacks have learned that they can get what they want by stomping their feet and throwing temper tantrums at all forms of authority. And government has allowed them to do just that, time and again. For example, instead of responding firmly to nightly burning, looting, and other criminal actions in Democratic run cities and states like Philadelphia, Pennsylvania; Seattle, Washington; Portland, Oregon; and New York; so-called progressive leaders at all levels continue to look for excuses to rationalize the causes of minority crime, poor school scores, and job performance. Moreover, politicians have allowed the might of powerful government agencies and departments such as the Department of Justice to be usurped by minority leaders, for use as weapons to bully businesses, schools, and media; and now even the Oscars, like other organizations, are willing to lower standards so minorities are given recognition and opportunities based on their color and sex.

In next chapters, I deconstruct how extremists, demagogues, and extortionists hijacked the civil rights movement and the basic good will of all the American people in order to benefit themselves and to promote their radical ideology. In the name of diversity, we have damaged the very foundations of our great institutions and values, brainwashed a whole generation of our youth, and silenced public outrage.

WHO IS TO BLAME?

In January 1961, I watched the inauguration of John F. Kennedy, our youngest president ever. He brought a vital energy and enthusiasm that was contagious. His rallying cry, "Ask not what your country can do for you, but what you can do for your country," inspired young people to participate in the world's greatest democracy and mold a new vision of the future. JFK brought the Peace Corp into being, and was immensely popular at home and abroad. He even promised us the moon! But before JFK could lead us to a world of peace and prosperity for all, he was assassinated. For many of us, the killing was a rude awakening from a collective hopeful American dream.

My World in the 1960s

I heard the news about the Kennedy assassination while I was working as Employment Supervisor for Coca-Cola Bottling Company of New York. I was devastated because I knew what a rare person JFK was and that the world had lost a great leader.

As a newly degreed Industrial Psychologist at the time, as I previously mentioned, I prided myself on my objectivity and my professional use of testing and interviewing tools to hire the best people for this NYSE-listed company. After a period of interviewing and testing, I found a good applicant for an accounting supervisor job. He was Black, but I didn't give it a second thought. Perhaps I should have.

I brought the candidate to the accounting manager's office. The manager's secretary said that the manager would be right back. I left the test results, my extensive interview form, and the applicant with the secretary. On my way back to my office, I stopped walking because I heard someone yelling behind me. As I turned around, I saw the red-faced accounting manager throw the candidate's paperwork at me and scream, "When you hire one of them, then I will!" I was quickly learning that by presenting a Black candidate, I had crossed an unacceptable boundary.

The elderly chairman of Coca-Cola Bottling of New York rarely strayed from his office, which occupied the whole fourth floor of the building. So, you can imagine my shock the next day when this red-faced old geezer threw open my door and stomped into my office. "You're Jewish. You know how to talk to them. Make them go away!" he shouted. The "them" he referred to was a group from the Urban League who were picketing the Coca-Cola headquarters because of the incident the day before.

I quickly walked downstairs and talked with the demonstrators, explaining that I was the person who had recommended the applicant, and was I ashamed and disgusted at what had transpired. After they understood that I was a recent hire and was attempting to change this ingrained culture, they began to see me as an ally. I accepted their invitation to become a member of the New York Urban League Job and Economic Development Committee, and they agreed to abandon their protest against Coca-Cola.

Later on, at one of the Urban League committee meetings, a problem surfaced. A number of black applicants had failed a test required to get jobs in the then-racially closed airline industry. Being a testing maven, I asked what test was given. It was the Bennett Mechanical Comprehension Test that I also used as part of my standard test battery. I then asked which scoring scale was used, and received some blank stares. I explained that there were scales for those with two years of high school, high school graduates, and those with a college education. Upon checking, we learned that the HR person at TWA was using a college scoring scale for Blacks and a high school scoring scale for Whites, when both groups had only high school educations. Faced with that information, it was amazing how willingly and how quickly TWA and the other airlines began to hire Blacks.

The point of this history is to show by example that in the early 1960s, there was real discrimination and I am proud to having done my part in ending it. Blacks were indeed being discriminated against. Most black people were poor and often faced discrimination in employment, including the despicable practice of putting racial notations on application forms. (Our government now requires similar notations to promote Affirmative Action.)

Black leadership, at that time, included great people like Roy Wilkins, who welcomed the continuing gains the civil rights movement was making, and welcomed the White liberal power base that was at the forefront of the movement. The Jews, who made up a large percentage of the civil rights movement, felt particular kinship with the movement; their children were also being discriminated against when they applied to universities, businesses, and country clubs throughout the U.S.

By 1973, I was working as Assistant to the President, for a brilliant, liberal businessman and political aspirant involved in many worthwhile causes, including civil rights. As his assistant, I participated in numerous benefits and committee meetings, and did so enthusiastically. However, at one of these meetings a subtle change occurred that would alter history. Few understood that the hot air being vented by the speaker would mushroom into such a damaging storm.

I cannot remember the date, but the speaker was Stokley Carmichael, Chairman of Student Non-violent Coordinating Committee (SNCC). As he spoke, the crowd, which was split between Blacks and Whites, cheered his fiery rhetoric. I had also been cheering, but at some point, became aware of a dramatically different tone and theme.

The focus of the talk shifted to the need for a Black power movement to create awareness among Blacks of their ability to change their own circumstances, without reliance on the White power structure. Though there was some logic to his argument, his tone and words made me feel defensive, unwelcome, and confused at a gut level. Carmichael's SNCC position paper confirmed his "Whites not welcome here" attitude.

> "No matter how much money you make in the Black community, when you go into the White world you are still a nigger. Any white person who comes into the movement has concepts in his mind about Black people, if only subconsciously. He cannot escape them because the whole society has geared his subconscious in that direction... One white person can come into a meeting of Black people and change the complexion of that meeting. If Blacks feel intimated by Whites, then they are not liable to vent the rage they feel about Whites in the presence of Whites. This is not to say that Whites have not had an important role in the movement. In the case of Mississippi, their role was very important in that they helped give Blacks the right to organize, but that role is over, and it should be. The charge might be made that we are racists but Whites that are sensitive to our problems will realize that we must determine our own destiny."

Carmichael used the term "Black Power" to label the movement that he was advocating.

While most of the white liberals just continued cheering, my gut and my objective mind were once again telling me that something was changing very dramatically. The bottom line was that many people, Black and White, felt that the civil rights movement was achieving significant economic, social, and political liberation. But some black radicals, disgusted with the slow pace of reform, decided to speed things up through in-your-face confrontation rather than cooperation. Indeed, once again in world history, a subtle new belief system was about to spin out of control with enormous consequences to society, but few people understood that at the time it began. *Were you aware of this time, when black radicals and criminals overthrew moderate, sane black leaders and their white liberal partners in the civil rights movement (such as me), and virulent irrational black discrimination against Whites and America began?*

The Black Revolution

Black Muslims

Among the most outspoken black people who changed the "civil" rights agenda was Malcolm X, formerly Malcolm Little. He was a guy in trouble with the law. This Black Muslim extremist demanded not only equality, but also a Black revolution, as a response to the oppression and inequality black people experienced. Malcolm X looked at the history of the Black people in America and pointed out how the country was still suffering from a slave mentality on the part of both the White establishment and Blacks' thinking. Malcolm somehow identified with the Muslim faith, although the Quran condones slavery, and Arabs had long been the major slave traders in Africa.

Black Panthers

Eldridge Cleaver made the issue literally black and white. "All of us must take a stand for or against the freedom of your people. You must be with your people or against them. You are either part of the solution or part of the problem." In his book, *Soul on Ice*, Cleaver aired Black grievances against White society; and like Malcolm X, pointed out that Black anger was rooted in hundreds of years of psychological oppression by Whites. Cleaver went on to become the Minister of the Black Panther Party.

Huey Newton, along with Bobby Seale, embraced the teachings of Malcolm X and founded the Black Panther Party, which is when the counter-culture enemies of America began their ongoing guerrilla war. "We have two evils to fight, capitalism and racism. We must destroy both racism and capitalism," said Newton. Their agenda was nothing less than revolution!

To protect Blacks from alleged police brutality, the Black Panthers advocated arming Black people with weapons with which to defend themselves. Cleaver made that clear when he said, "No force can stop us from achieving our goal. If it is necessary to destroy the U.S. of America, then let us destroy it with a smile on our faces." This radical group is re-emerging as the New Black Panther Party as the armed wing of Black Lives Matter (BLM). Both these groups openly state their intentions to get what they want or they will destroy America. More discussion about BLM will be found later in the book.

Furthermore, Cleaver's attempt to destroy the morale of Black troops in Vietnam was a blatant act of treason that was never pursued by authorities.

> I am the Minister of Information of the Black Panther Party, and I am speaking to you for the Party, but I want to put a personal note into this because I know you niggers have your minds all messed up about Black organizations, or you wouldn't be flunkies for the White organization – the USA – for whom you have picked up the gun... Either quit the army, now, or start destroying it from the inside... You need to start killing the racist pigs who are over there giving you orders. Kill General Abrahams and his staff, all his officers. Sabotage supplies and equipment, or turn them over to Vietnamese people... You should start now weeding out traitors amongst you. It is better to do it now than to allow them to return home to help the pigs wipe us out.

The Panthers' preaching of revolution and armed struggle was a very credible threat to American society and is even more so today with spineless Democrats' defund the police efforts. They were well organized, highly motivated, well-armed, and trained. And unfortunately, like today, the new tough talk appealed more to the gut of the Black masses and their revolutionary zombie followers than the slow, steady gains, and the reasoned and inclusive work of the civil rights movement. Indeed, a *Wall Street Journal* poll of four metropolitan areas in the late 1960s indicated that a clear majority of Blacks strongly supported both the goals and methods of the Black Panthers.

Their supporters were happy to parrot some of the irrational nonsense of the revolutionary group. Many of these radicals are now highly paid professors in public universities and Democratic politicians. Their party line included:

- Exemption of all Black men from military service
- Freedom for all Black men in all jails

- A UN plebiscite for a Black colony, with the purpose of determining the will of the Black people as to their national destiny
- Forty acres and two mules as restitution for slave labor and mass murder of Blacks

The angry Black rhetoric can still be heard in today's rap and the in-your-face racial slurs BLM screams at white seniors peacefully sitting in restaurants or through loud speakers as they try to sleep in the suburbs. *Have you heard one word from the Democrats denouncing this racist "Black KKK" for burning, looting, and attacking the police and the public nightly in blue states? Do you think these opportunistic criminal offenses will stop when they are not prosecuted or even condemned? Are you beginning to understand?*

It quickly became the chorus of other groups looking to overthrow the status quo. The Young Lords Party Platform sounded a similar note to that of the Panthers for a Puerto Rican/Latin audience.

"In every way we are slaves of the gringo... Our Latin brothers and sisters, inside and outside the U.S., are oppressed by amerikkkan (sic) business. All the colored and oppressed people of the world are one nation under oppression... No Puerto Rican should serve in the U.S. Army against his Brothers and Sisters, for the only true army of oppressed people is the people's army to fight all rulers... The time has come ... for revolutionary war against the businessman, politician and police."

The unrealistic Black Panther Platform of 1966 helped set the stage for the acceptance of closed and hyphenated groups such as African-Americans, Asian-Americans, and Arab-Americans, who identify themselves first by race, national origin, religion, and gender, and rarely as proud Americans. Our country could now be symbolized as a tattered patchwork quilt, rather than the melting pot that turned immigrants and natives into the steel, built America's businesses, and fought fascism. *Moreover, as rational thought is being silenced by political correctness, the minority squeaky wheel whines on, always demanding more oil to quiet its shrill sound.*

Though those Black Panther leaders were eventually either killed or incarcerated, they managed to inspire many Blacks, other ethnic and protected groups, and their left-wing supporters, to continue to angrily fight, disrespect, and undermine the greatest democracy the world has ever known. The class warfare and victim mentality that still permeates the black community spread to the new left-wing, Hispanics, disabled, LGBT, and Women's Rights movement. Despite their hugely, disproportionately high crime rates, out of wedlock births, welfare rolls, and terrible academic performance they never take responsibility but rather continue to blame America.

Moreover, our brainwashed children are now being taught to respect and legitimize radicals such as Malcolm X. Malcolm X didn't mince words. "I'm not an American!" he sputtered. "America is a nightmare! America practices slavery! The white man is the common enemy!" Naturally, *Time* magazine heralded him during Black History Month. And let's not forget other radical troublemakers, such as Eldridge Cleaver and Bobby Seale, who are now presented as role models to our brainwashed students. These radical views are reinforced in black churches that preach Black Liberation theology that tries to combine Marxism and God. But like mixing oil and water, it doesn't work. *Do remember Obama swallowed this dangerous mix for years, as he listened to his Reverend Wright. Another proponent of this anti-American anti-Semitic poison is an Atlanta Reverend running in the hope of turning the Senate blue.*

I have watched with horror as our schools celebrated the schism, they call diversity, not seeing that it rips apart the moral fabric that binds us together as Americans. While minority groups are using "divisity" as a weapon to slice the American whole into separate, angry, unmanageable pieces, many of us long for the togetherness of the cohesive and proud country that was propelled by the vibrant energy of President Kennedy. He spoke of a new generation of Americans, participating in the world's greatest democracy to create a new vision of the future.

The Tattered Patchwork Quilt

Though Kennedy's legacy and dreams have long faded, the seeds of irrationality, reverse discrimination, anti-Americanism, anti-Semitism, blackmail, negativity, diversity, threat, and extortion sowed by the Black extremists around the same time continued to sprout weeds and are reseeding in another generation. As radical and revolutionary dialogue and action were being introduced and accepted by a large percentage of the population, the whole USA, rather than just a few individuals, Southern states, or specific businesses, is now seen as the enemy. I watched as cancerous Black reverse racism permeated the North, at a time when we should have been celebrating how racism against Blacks was declining dramatically in the South and the rest of the country.

Part of the Kennedy legacy was his call for Congress to bring forth civil rights legislation. Lyndon Johnson, a master politician fearful of Black tension and aware of the need to eliminate discrimination, passed the Civil Rights Act of 1964. The Civil Rights Act was groundbreaking legislation, aimed at ending all forms of discrimination based on race, color, gender, religion, and national origin.

Title I of the Act guarantees equal voting rights. Title II bans discrimination in public accommodations involved in interstate commerce. Title IV calls for the desegregation of schools. Title V of the Act establishes a government agency, the Equal Employment Opportunity Commission (EEOC), to enforce the provisions that prohibit discrimination by employers dealing with the Federal Government or interstate commerce. Title VII deals with discrimination in employment and Title IX requires equal school spending in athletics for women.

Congress also debated the issues of racial preferences and proportional representation. The result of the debate was the adoption of **Section 703(j) of the Act, which states that nothing in the Act "shall be interpreted to require any employer ... to grant preferential treatment to any individual or group because of race ... of such individual or group" in order to maintain a racial balance.**

Senators Clark and Case, who steered that section of Title VII through the legislative process, left no doubt about Congress's intent in their statement at the time.

Any deliberate attempt to maintain a racial balance, whatever such balance might be, would involve a violation of Title VII because maintaining such a balance would require an employer to hire or refuse to hire on the basis of race. It must be emphasized that discrimination is prohibited to any individual.

I've covered this section in the last chapter but I can't overstate its importance to understanding how the Act is being abused by giving racial preference to minorities; it could not be clearer! Do you now understand now, how illegal, immoral, unproductive all this race, sex, color based, and other advantage in hiring and admission in government, business, and our schools are? Do you realize how brainwashed we have to become to think hiring or admission based on color, sex, etc., is OK?

Like so many best intentions, few of us who celebrated the passage of the Civil Rights Act realized how it would be bastardized into a weapon of mass destruction. No one would have guessed that it would someday be used to legitimize reverse discrimination against Whites and Asians, or to have quotas based on skin color and race used as a substitute for picking the most qualified person for the job, board of directors, or for admission to school. Moreover, no one could have predicted that black politicians and leaders of the EEOC, and other government agencies, would misuse the legislation to help them extort business, media, and associations with deep pockets.

It is no wonder that Latinos, Asians, Arabs, women, LGBTQ, and the handicapped have expropriated the Black approach to dealing with society and the government for themselves. The U.S. is at war with itself, as cooperation has given way to confrontation, and irrational thinking has replaced logic in race relations.

Solidifying Mediocrity and Reverse Discrimination

For a brief, shining moment, the principle of colorblind justice was recognized as the law of the land. But all too soon, that principle was thrust aside by the Nixon administration, to make way for a system of race-based entitlement. The critical events took place during the Nixon Administration when the so-called Philadelphia Plan was adopted. It became the prototypical program of racial preferences for federal contractors.

In February 1970, the U.S. Department of Labor issued an order that the Affirmative Action programs adopted by all government contractors must include "goals and timetables to which the contactor's good faith efforts must be directed to correct ... deficiencies in the utilization of minority groups."

This construct of goals and timetables clearly envisioned a system of proportional representation in which group identity would be a factor—often the decisive factor—in hiring decisions. Embodied in this misguided bureaucratic verbiage was a policy requiring that distinctions in treatment be made on the basis of race. This is an anathema to all the American values we hold dearly and against what I and others fought for in the civil rights movement.

This language has allowed a newly protected class to become reverse racists and use fear of our own government's equal opportunity laws to bully fearful executives and administrators. They successfully seeded their diversity apostles into the power positions in our schools, government, and businesses. They, in turn, follow the party line and hire, promote, and contract with their less-qualified insider buddies. Later in this chapter, I will highlight the Boeing case, where race rather than performance or experience determines hiring and pay grade.

The Bad Guys Are Now the Good Guys

Minority criminals and illegal aliens are now seen as victims that should be given voting rights healthcare, schooling, childcare, support, and other benefits—some not available to law-abiding citizens. Gangster illogic has become chic to the Left. This dystopian logic states that we (minorities) are victims of society, so if we commit crimes on society, we should not go to prison. We (minorities) should not be profiled, though statistically we are much more likely to commit crimes. I'm looking at a description of a suspect who stabbed a 14-year-old girl after stalking her. Nowhere is the race of this suspect mentioned, because the local police and newspaper find that it is more important to be politically correct than to take dangerous criminals off the street.

Because minorities are more heavily represented in prison (in 2018, the imprisonment rate of black males was 5.8 times that of white males, while the imprisonment rate of black females was 1.8 times the rate of white females), their cheerleaders contend that there must be something unfair about the system. They do not consider the obvious fact: those minorities commit much more crime and if they are ever prosecuted, they end up in prison. Dah!

Google Whitewash

If you need to see another of the multitude of examples of blatant left-wing Google bias, try to search the percentage of Blacks committing major crime like murder, rape, and armed robbery in the U.S. What comes up instead is their selection of left-wing sites offering opinion and cover by their left-wing pantywaist friends and similar smoke screens and excuses for black incarceration.

As mentioned earlier, Google is no longer an objective "search engine" but instead has become a sewer line filled with whitewash to cover the simple facts such as Blacks and illegals commit a disproportionate majority of our crime. Moreover, in spite of or perhaps aided by Google fronting for them, the impact of Blacks blaming others for their bad decisions and getting advantage based on their color rather than merit is to degrade their race, themselves, our country, and our founding values.

We need to have DOJ step in and break up or at the very least take away Section 230 which protects the owners of any "interactive computer service" from liability for anything posted by third parties. The idea was that such protection was necessary to encourage the emergence of new types of communications and services at the dawn of the Internet. These companies, rather than play a role as objective non-biased interactive computing services, decided instead to be brainwashed puppets of the Left. They have become dangerous monopolies promoting nanny state propaganda over objectivity. *How can a brainwashed student finally get the facts if Google, Twitter, and Facebook are all part of the racketeering efforts to hide or shape the truth and perpetuate left-wing myths?* Finally, how sad to watch the destruction of our legal system as the oversupply of lawyers, many paid by our government, tries to prove the one creed that all prisoners share: that they are innocent.

Teen Idle

Other blessings to society from the diversity idol include minority pop gangster culture idols that are foul mouthed and inarticulate, with large gold chains, diamonds, and other "bling," and who wear baggy pants that are great for concealing weapons. These ignorant losers, who extol drugs, nice asses, and violence while playing with their genitalia on TV, have been allowed to become role models for our children. For example, Netflix, with board members and associates like the Obamas and Prince Harry, promote shows like *Cuties* where girls as young as eleven shake their booties and perform their best imitation of their slut-like role models. In her book *Think: Straight Talk for Women to Stay Smart in a Dumbed-Down World*, author Lisa Bloom reveals that 25 percent of young American women would rather win *America's Next Top Model* than the Nobel Peace Prize.

Many of our youth say that their role model is either from Hollywood or the sports arena and compare themselves to images they see of celebrities. Among those girls, almost half said that celebrity images make them feel dissatisfied with the way they look. Therefore, appearance is among teenagers' top concerns, teen girls in particular.

Following rap gangsters; shallow, unscripted Hollow-wood brain-dead, empty vessels; and the all-star team of irrelevant dumb jocks who think mother is a two-syllable word; helps provide the manure necessary to grow new generations of brainwashed noxious weeds on weed.

Indeed, our youth are like Pinocchio who, after a time of out-of-control indulgence on Pleasure Island, was slowly turned into an ass by unscrupulous profiteers. Signs of our youth becoming jackasses abound. For example, could you imagine the most searched person on Google in 2019 was Antonio Brown, the free-agent wide receiver? Brown, 31, played one game with the New England Patriots before he was suspended from the team while the NFL investigated his behavior following several sexual misconduct allegations. Brown also got into Twitter fights with the NFL and made controversial posts on Instagram. In 2018, Demi Lovato, a pop star you probably never heard of beat out Meghan Markle and Brett Kavanaugh during a year rocked by celebrity cheating scandals, controversial YouTube stars, and the #MeToo movement. Lovato made headlines after she was hospitalized for an apparent drug overdose. The hospitalization was just weeks after the singer released a song called "Sober."

What has happened to all those consumer companies? They take pride in their social responsibility programs, yet promote these losers and their reverse racist, anti-American agenda to help them to reach target demographic audiences. To stop this madness, we must boycott the sponsors and the programs that are polluting future generations.

The Sorry State of Black Leadership

Jessie Jackson

Jessie Jackson, in my personal opinion, is the worst of the black leaders. His ego, need for control, greed, and stamina keep him looking for the next mark or opportunity to exploit. He uses his high profile to promote racial division, and to support the American haters at home and abroad for his own enrichment and promotion. He gets credit for developing "The Great Con," which has developed into a multibillion-dollar business for generations of Black victimization and divisity extortionists. He should also be credited with doing more to divide our country and brainwash a generation than any other corrupt black leader.

We have reviewed his greed earlier but his chutzpah, inflated ego, and self-serving opportunism continue to both amaze and scare me. He was as obvious when he tried to costume his addiction to headlines, respectability, and money with his colorful poetic preacher rhetoric. This hypocrite, known to have a mistress, counseled President Clinton after the Lewinsky affair. Jackson and Clinton did have something in common, according to Ken Timmerman, author of Shakedown—they are both compulsive liars.

Timmerman outlines lies about Jackson's athletic and academic achievements, as well as the spin regarding his actions during the assassination of Martin Luther King. For example, Timmerman reports that Jessie Jackson was not on the balcony when King was killed, when Jackson and his camp have tried to show a picture of Jackson up on the balcony with King. The picture in question was actually taken the day before. It was in fact a publicity shot.

Though never elected, this troublemaker often goes over the President's head to get his unwelcome oar into foreign policy areas. It appears that if he can embarrass the U.S. and get a few bucks while visiting a foreign dictator, like Omar Khadafy in Libya, it is all the better. His meetings at the United Nations with Kofi Anon to discuss Iraq undermined our State Department. His visit to Castro's buddy, Hugo Chavez, provided support for this anti-U.S. radical. Jackson also tried to influence how Venezuelan oil is distributed and priced in the U.S. He showed up to direct the flow of billions of Federal funds to storm-ravaged New Orleans. Like the Black Caucus, Jackson was quick to assign racially motivated blame for the way the disaster was mishandled. Lately, he even suggested that attacks on Barry Bonds' records are also racially motivated, rather than caused by alleged steroid use.

Jessie Jackson Accused of "Racketeering" by Top Black Businessman

One of America's wealthiest African-Americans, asked by Jessie Jackson to assist with Jackson's "Wall Street Project," said that the tactics used by the civil rights leader amounted to "racketeering." Harold Doley Jr., a broadcasting executive rated as one of the country's 100 wealthiest African-Americans by a newsletter covering Blacks on Wall Street, said that he was the victim of intimidation at the hands of Jackson. Doley is fighting the Federal Communications Commission's efforts to block the sale of his television stations.

After initial exuberance about Jackson's stated goal of "making corporate America look more like America from the entry level to the board room," Doley became disillusioned. Jackson, who seems to believe he has an inalienable right to get a piece of someone else's pie, went after the multi-trillion-dollar pension fund industry. He sought legislation that would require that 10% to 15% of the nation's pension funds be brokered or managed by minority firms. Doley, like most standup people, disapproved of the methods Jackson employed in persuading the pension industry to aid minorities. "What worried me was the way he operated, dealing with those veiled threats," Doley stated.

He soon realized that Jackson was actually "directing an enormous income from pension [funds]," by channeling them to "roughly ten firms that qualify." Doley doubted that most Americans knew "that they [were] paying and putting money in Jessie Jackson's coffers to the tune of $170 million in commissions a year, 10% of which is going to Jackson." These antics might seem all too familiar to those who have followed Jackson's career.

Al Sharpton

A quarter-century after a black teenager falsely accused an innocent white man of rape; she has begun paying reparations for her slander. The man who rocketed to fame on her falsehoods is still at it. If ever there was a case of racial injustice it was the case of Tawana Brawley and Steven Pagones, except the roles of victim and perpetrator were reversed in the parallel universe of the racial grievance industry. The master of that universe is Al Sharpton.

Pagones is not as well-known as George Zimmerman, nor is he likely to be now, given the media's subservience to that grievance industry. But 25 years ago the former New York prosecutor was accused of rape by Brawley, then just 15 years old. Sharpton, the man who demanded justice for Tawana as she told her blatantly false story, is the man who now demands justice for Trayvon Martin, the teenager shot by neighborhood-watch volunteer Zimmerman, who was found not guilty of second-degree murder in what a jury ruled was legitimate self-defense.

As the New York Post reports, Tawana Brawley has finally started payment on a defamation judgment awarded Pagones. He sued Brawley and her handlers, including Sharpton, alleging the story that she was abducted and raped by a gang of white men, including Pagones, was a hoax. A grand jury, which heard from 180 witnesses over seven months, concluded in 1988 that the entire story was indeed apocryphal. Brawley's advisers in the infamous race-baiting case, the Rev. Al Sharpton and attorneys C. Vernon Mason and Alton Maddox, have already paid, or are paying, their defamation debt—at least the monetary part. Sharpton has never paid in human terms for the damage done to Pagones' life, which quickly unraveled, even as Sharpton's career as a race-baiting hustler pushed him forward to his current job as an MSNBC commentator. Pagones' marriage collapsed, and he left his job as a prosecutor.

Sharpton has made a career of racial incitement. He once called Jews "diamond merchants" and described whites moving businesses into Harlem as "interlopers." He helped incite three days of anti-Semitic rioting in 1991 in the Crown Heights neighborhood of Brooklyn, turning a tragic traffic accident into a riot where two people died and more than 100 were wounded. Then there was Freddy's Fashion Mart in Harlem in 1995, subject to the Sharpton campaign to drive out "interlopers." To scare the Jewish owner away, Sharpton turned a tenant-landlord dispute into a racial conflict, resulting in arson of the store and seven deaths.

Pagones, who now works as a private investigator, has said he'd forgive Brawley's debt if only she would apologize and admit the truth. Brawley has not and says she will not. Nor has Sharpton, who's been rewarded with an MSNBC forum to spew his racially divisive venom. And the mainstream media only yawned. Sharpton long ago should have been mocked and shunned, if not incarcerated. That he has not been is the ultimate injustice here.

I listened intently as naïve CNN Barbie Doll Paula Zhan, in her best drama queen voice, seriously announced to straight man sheep-in-Wolf's-clothing Blitzer that there would be a special on the serious topic of racism in America. But then I fell off my chair laughing, when unbelievably, she stated that the two experts selected to discuss the problem were the we-deserve-no-respect duo of Jessie Jackson and Al Sharpton. Having people, who some have labeled as being compulsive liars, hypocrites, and racist profiteers discuss racism, as CNN does consistently, is as useless as plastic vegetables in a soup kitchen. Some people seem to enjoy watching low IQ graduates of "I hate White men and America" hyphenated courses do their "what a racist country we live in" comedy routine. "I cry all the way to the bank for racial justice" is one of their favorite song and dance numbers.

Indeed, for Al Sharpton, the business of racial justice has been very lucrative—his compensation has grown fourfold since the Black Lives Matter movement was founded, tax records show. Sharpton and his tax-exempt National Action Network 501(c)(4) organization have been fierce opponents of "threats to racial justice" since the tragic death of Trayvon Martin in 2012. The death of Martin was only the beginning in a long line of tragedies to which Sharpton and his network have brought national media attention, becoming in the process among the most outspoken critics of police brutality. It has become somewhat of a business model for Sharpton—and very lucrative at that.

Since 2013, Sharpton's compensation at NAN has risen dramatically along with NAN's revenues. In 2014, Sharpton was paid $412,644—a more than 70% increase over the previous year—and NAN's total revenues approached $7 million. (NAN's average annual revenue in the preceding three years was $4.4 million). NAN's most recently available financial report is for the year 2018, and it lists Sharpton's salary as $1,046,948—a four-fold increase from 2013. NAN's revenues in 2018 were $7.3 million—its highest ever.

In 2018, a similar organization, Color of Change, received $8,173,663 in total revenue and paid its president $320,857. That same year, Sharpton received over $1 million—more than triple the amount Color of Change paid its leader and more than eight times what MoveOn.org paid its highest earner.

According to NAN's website, Sharpton founded the organization in 1991. It now has 93 chapters across the United States and hosts radio stations in Birmingham, Cincinnati, Detroit, Tallahassee, and Washington, D.C. NAN's 'about page,' titled "No Justice, No Peace," lists seven areas of action: criminal justice reform, police accountability, crisis intake and victim assistance, voting rights, corporate responsibility and pension diversity, youth leadership, and bridging the digital divide.

This year, Sharpton led NAN's "Get Your Knee Off Our Necks" march in Washington. The march was on August 25th to coincide with the 57th anniversary of Dr. Martin Luther King's famous "I have a dream" speech at the 1963 March on Washington. *Do you agree Sharpton would have been an embarrassment to MLK?*

But seriously, these men and their pompous, ignorant apprentices in government, academia, and Big Tech belong near the top of a list of the most dangerous racists in the country. Instead of having the balls to confront race-baiting hypocrites and profiteers of the reverse discrimination game, MSDNC, ABC, CBS, and CNN bend over backwards to provide these corrupt agitators a platform to attack the true victims of racism; White and Asian America. By legitimizing rather than strongly condemning black racists like BLM, the fake news networks continue to be major contributors to the moral decline of this country. Programs that continually brainwash a naïve public by making heroes of black racists bear a major responsibility for completely reversing our moral compass and negatively impacting the future of our society.

Representative Maxine Waters

Maxine Waters understood the power of reverse discrimination and cronyism early on, as a legislator in California. I once sent a proposal in response to a request for a small business consulting opportunity. On follow up, I was told I that would have to hire a black person to lead the project. I explained that a woman in my office would lead it, and it was at best only a two-person job. I was told that my bid would not be considered. Outraged, I asked who came up with this stupid policy. I then heard the name of Maxine Waters for the first time. I asked that she call me regarding this matter, and she did get back quickly. When I explained how unfair and wasteful the policy was, she commented, "That's tough," and then she hung up. I have watched her on cable TV with the Congressional Black Caucus, and was reminded of the French saying what roughly translates to "those who assemble resemble." Waters is in her element with this poor excuse for Black leadership.

Black lawmakers providing shade in the case against Maxine Waters, one of the most corrupt people in Congress, shook the congressional ethics system to its foundations. The longest-tenured African-American woman in Congress, Waters is accused of arranging a 2008 meeting with Treasury Department officials to help steer financial-bailout funds to a minority-owned bank in which her husband held a stake. Soon after the meeting, Treasury gave the bank $12 million. Her punishment was being appointed chair of the US House Committee on Financial

Services which regulates the banks. *The wolf now controls the sheep and their bales of money.*

Like career criminals, lifelong corrupt politicians like Waters and Joe Biden are unrepentant masters of using the old "razzle dazzle" to hide their crimes. "Aunty" Waters is currently accused of giving a million dollars of campaign contributions to her daughter; while puppet President Joe appointed a law partner colleague of his corrupt pervert son's defense lawyer to head DOJ's criminal division. Come on man! *Did you ever believe we would experience such examples of public corruption in this country?*

Waters is also a vicious race-baiter whose comments to constituents to harass members of the Trump administration wherever they are gave shade to the BLM and Antifa Gestapo attacking peaceful Trump supporters, including children and the elderly in scenes reminisced of Hitler youth harassing Jews in Germany. Add the banning of books, including one about the worrying rise in the teenage girls who, along with their friends, are deciding to change sex, and you see more evidence of the danger of the fascist Left.

The Black Caucus

How sad it was for me to watch as the opportunistic cabal of black leaders wielded the ax of discrimination with the same frenzy as the white racists of antebellum times. Greedy members like their white counterparts' nose their way into the free-flowing pig trough of public money to find opportunities for families and friends; they will, however, get all the pork they want from Nancy Pelosi if Biden wins. Why isn't the Black Caucus speaking out against the tobacco, junk food, and alcohol companies that prey on the nation's young and old alike?

Could it be because Anheuser-Busch, Heineken USA, Miller Brewing Company, PepsiCo, Philip Morris, R.J. Reynolds, and Coca-Cola give big dollars to the Foundation, and Ms. Tina Walls of the Miller Brewing Company sits on the board of the Black Caucus Foundation? This "Foundation" provides the Caucus with a way to get its cut of the corporate and Fannie Mae hush money pie for its pet projects.

A disproportionate share of Congressional ethics violation cases have been brought against Black Caucus members.

Emanuel Cleaver, a Methodist minister and the chairman of the Congressional Black Caucus, stood up and began searching his desk for a Bible. Cleaver wasn't looking up a particular verse or Psalm. He grabbed the Good Book for emphasis.

He wanted to hold it in his hands as he declared, with a firm shake, that the way Congress investigates the ethics of its own lawmakers is horribly broken. *This is yet another example of Blacks not taking responsibility for their own actions, but rather looking for lame excuses for bad behavior using both "The Great Con" numbers game as well as the never seen equivalent to the Abominable Snowman fable, the myth of systematic racism.*

Cleaver said, "The facts speak for themselves." Indeed, they always do—like the reason more Blacks are in jail is simply that they commit more crimes. Why they are not in positions requiring academic achievement is also no mystery; studies continue to show Blacks perform lowest of all races on tests like the SATs. *The facts speak but they are drowned out by lame excuses from the squeaky wheel minorities for bad behavior and poor outcomes. Do you agree?*

The facts say this: African-Americans make up 10 percent of the House, but as of the end of February, five of the sitting six named lawmakers under review by the House Ethics Committee are Black. The pattern isn't new. At one point in late 2009, seven lawmakers were known to be involved in formal House Ethics inquiries; all were members of the Congressional Black Caucus. An eighth caucus member, Rep. Jesse Jackson Jr. of Illinois, had also been under investigation, but his probe was halted temporarily while the Justice Department undertook an inquiry of its own. Here are a couple of the many corrupt Black Caucus candidates that deserved a perp walk at that time.

Representative William Jefferson

Court papers documented a videotape of this Louisiana Democrat accepting $100,000 from an FBI informant. Instead, of condemning this betrayal of his office, the Black Caucus and Congressional leaders Nancy Pelosi and Dennis Hastert initially came out in support of the alleged crook, even after the "frozen assets" were found in the representative's freezer.

Representative John Conyers

Aide Deanna Maher recapped allegations that Dewayne Boyd, a former top aide to John Conyers, used Conyers' congressional office to obtain a fake passport after being convicted of fraud, making false statements, and government theft in 2004. Sentenced in 2005 to 30 to 46 months in prison, Boyd fled to Ghana before being recaptured and extradited to the United States. Moreover, Conyers' Congressional aides sent letters to the House Ethics Committee and to the FBI alleging that they were forced to babysit and chauffeur his children. Conyers must agree with Mel Brooks, who said, "It is good to be the king."

Conyers tried to do more damage to our country by introducing legislation against racial profiling. This would have played right into the hands of Islamic terrorist supporters in the U.S., who play the racist card to try to loosen up security at our airports for their terrorist buddies.

All told, about one-third of sitting black lawmakers have been named in an ethics probe during their careers, *according to a* National Journal *review.*

Only two members of Congress have been formally charged with ethics violations in recent years and have faced the specter of public trials—Reps. Charles Rangel of New York (censured) and Maxine Waters of California (investigation ongoing). Both are black.

Those are the facts, as Cleaver said. The question is why so many African-American members have been in the ethics spotlight. In interviews with more than a dozen members of the CBC, an unsettling thread emerges: They feel targeted. There could be no other explanation, many said, for what they see as disproportionate treatment at the hands of ethics investigators. They describe a disquieting reality of being black in Congress today: a feeling that each move they make is unfairly scrutinized. "We all feel threatened," said Rep. Hank Johnson, a Georgia Democrat, as he sat by the fireplace off the House floor. "If the only reason that you would suffer a complaint is because of your skin color that is a cause for concern."

It is a grave accusation: Could the congressional ethics process, ostensibly safeguarded by professional staff members and by a bipartisan structure that allows nothing to move forward unless Democrats and Republicans agree, be singling out African-Americans? Not likely; but what is of course happening is another example of what I call the "color the facts" strategy. *Do you agree other explanations are more likely?*

Perhaps more ethical issues arise within the Black Caucus than within the House as a whole. Many of its members occupy safe seats, after all, and have been in Washington for decades. Maybe some of them grew too comfortable or insulated, and they failed to track changing ethics standards. Whatever the reason, the disparity has had a profound effect on African-American legislators on Capitol Hill. "People walk around on eggshells," Cleaver said, "doing everything they can to avoid attention without retreating from the work that is front of us."

Like their efforts to blame the police for the fact that Blacks commit a disproportionate amount of the nation's crime, and are therefore subject to more attention by the judicial system, they look for excuses for the unwanted attention they are getting from the Congressional committees charged with policing ethics violations. In both cases they would like to delegitimize these law enforcement activities calling them a "police force out of control."

Since its inception, the office has recommended that the Ethics Committee undertake further investigations in 26 cases involving sitting House members. Twelve of those have targeted African-Americans, including Rangel, Waters, and Jackson.

The steady drumbeat of allegations and accusations has damaged the image of the Congressional Black Caucus, which likes to mislabel itself "the conscience of the Congress." More accurately they are "the 'hood' for Congressional corruption." As a result, African-American lawmakers have been in a cold war with the office almost since its creation in 2008. They've met privately with investigators, complained to their Godmother, the daughter of a former Baltimore Godfather, Nancy Pelosi, who dispenses pork for kissing her ring and unquestioning loyalty. Indeed, this dispensing of pork in the form of pet projects that enrich themselves and their friends is at the heart of the Democratic Party. Look how the Bidens and so many other Democrats somehow became multi-millionaires on government salaries. With the blessings of their Godmother they introduced legislation to curb its powers to police their corruption. When Rep. Marcia Fudge, D-Ohio, introduced a measure in 2010 to shrink the office's authority, her bill had 19 cosponsors, all of them fellow members of the Black Caucus. A year later, when African-American Rep. Melvin Watt, D-N.C., pushed on the floor to slash the office's funding by 40 percent, 25 of the 29 Democrats who voted with him on the failed measure were Black.

The office is "like a police force out of control," said Rep. William Lacy Clay Jr., a Missouri Democrat whose father was a founder of the Black Caucus, adding that the disparity reflects larger law-and-order issues that plague African-Americans. "What the process mirrors is our criminal-justice system," he said. "Look at the fact that African-Americans make up about 12.5 percent of the total national population, but we are much higher in the percentages in prisons and on parole and under criminal investigation, and all that." *You should recognize the Big Con numbers racket by now as your brainwashing rinses down the drain. Do you see it now?*

Omar Ashmawy, chief counsel to the Office of Congressional Ethics, bristled at the suggestion of any bias in the office's approach. Three of his four investigating counsels are minorities. His chief deputy is African-American. And one of the office's eight board directors is a former CBC chairwoman.

"Anybody who would make that accusation is not living in the real world," said Ashmawy, who is Arab-American.

The Washington swamp plays the race card and the Ethics panel folds its hand

The Ethics panel formally charged Waters with violating House rules in mid-2010. But by last summer, the inquiry was frozen; a special counsel, D.C. lawyer Billy Martin, a prominent African-American attorney whose past clients have ranged from Monica Lewinsky to Michael Vick was recruited after allegations surfaced of improper communication between investigators and GOP committee members. Two committee aides who had led the Waters probe have been placed on indefinite leave. The panel's then-staff director, in a memo first published by *Politico*, accused them of making racially insensitive remarks. Later every Republican on the Ethics Committee, and the top Democrat, recused themselves from the case at Martin's recommendation. *These Waters it seems are too hot to touch; is it politics over justice?*

Black lawmakers who have chafed under ethics reviews seem almost giddy at the turn of events. Rangel, for one, could barely muzzle his pleasure when asked about the imbroglio. "The Ethics Committee is presently under investigation," he said with a grin.

Growing Too Comfortable

But the question persists: Do African-American members simply commit more ethical lapses? "Nobody wants to say that, because as soon as you do, you're accused of being racists," said Melanie Sloan, executive director of Citizens for Responsibility and Ethics in Washington, a watchdog group. Sloan said it anyway: "The black caucus really does have more ethics problems."

Sloan said she empathizes with those innocent lawmakers who feel targeted. But, she said, plenty of African-Americans have been guilty of bending the rules. For the past six years, at least one black lawmaker has graced her group's list of the "Most Corrupt Members of Congress." Last year, five out 19 were black. One former fixture on that list, African-American ex-Rep. William Jefferson, D-La., is in prison after the FBI raided his home in 2006 and found $90,000 stashed in his freezer.

Some of the current targets of probes don't present the most sympathetic of profiles. Richardson has seen a constant churning of staff and one former aide's resignation letter, since made public, called her office "toxic and hostile." The California lawmaker is facing her second ethics investigation, this time over whether she forced aides to "volunteer" for her campaign; the first probe cleared Richardson of receiving preferential treatment from her mortgage lender.

Another current target, Rep. Alcee Hastings, D-Fla., was impeached and tossed off the federal bench by Congress in 1989 in connection with a $150,000 bribery case when he was a judge. Recently, he has been tied to two ethics probes, the first as part of a group of lawmakers—some of whom are White—accused of pocketing per diem allowances (he was cleared) and another alleging that he sexually harassed a staffer. The Federal Election Commission once levied a fine of $63,000 against another black lawmaker, Rep. Gregory Meeks, D-N.Y., after he billed his campaign treasury more than $6,000 in personal-trainer expenses, among other things. He is currently under the microscope for failure to disclose a $40,000 payment he said was a loan.

Sloan argued that the Caucus's ethics woes stem in part from job security. African-American members so often represent safe districts and serve for so long that bright moral lines become obscured, she said. A 2010 survey by the University of Minnesota showed that black lawmakers hold 22 of the 50 safest House seats. Indeed, most of those entangled in ethics reviews are long-in-the-tooth, notably Rangel (who took office in 1971), Waters (1991), Hastings (1993), and Jackson (1995). Richardson, elected in 2007, is an exception.

Yvonne Burke, who serves on the OCE's bipartisan board of directors and chaired the Congressional Black Caucus in the 1970s, also suggested that some veteran members' long tenure could explain the disparity—but for a slightly different reason. "I think members who are there for a long period of time may not keep up with the rules," such as financial-disclosure laws that have tripped up numerous lawmakers, including Rangel, she said. Burke adamantly insisted that race has no part in the office's probes: "I can say that very comfortably."

Outside Influences

No single case has ensnared more black lawmakers than a 2008 trip to the Caribbean island of St. Maarten. As lawmakers boarded planes for the three-day beachside conference, Flaherty, camera in hand, was close on their heels.

Flaherty, president of the National Legal and Policy Center, a conservative watchdog group, showed up at the meeting, snapped some photos, and handed the exclusive on a corporate-funded junket to the *New York Post*. (House rules forbid business interests from picking up such tabs; the corporate sponsors of the

Caribbean conference hung their banners from the rafters.) The story spread to other media, and soon the ethics watchdogs in Congress had sunk their teeth into a full-blown investigation. Along the way, Flaherty offered up his pictures, audio recordings, and a copy of the program to help make the case.

All told, investigators probed six black members for two different island jaunts. All but one was ultimately cleared of knowingly receiving a corporate-paid trip. The exception was Rangel, whose staff was proven to have known that corporations were footing the bill; he was admonished.

Corruption and Black/left-wing favoritism will be rampant as the Sharpton, Jackson, Waters, and other black cons continue to be taken care of by the low life left-wing eunuchs running their failed city and state government. The divisty conmen have found a perfect puppet in Joe Biden. Even before his inauguration they have him out supporting asinine, illegal anti-American programs sure to line the pockets of these extortionists, including giving COVID relief money only to black and women owned businesses. This type of insanity is a sure sign that the Biden administration will not close America's deepening divide but will force it into two camps as divided as those in our Civil War.

Enough is enough; good natured Middle Americans and now the naïve suburban women will finally realize they were indeed duped and as brainwashed as the Cultural Revolution generation under Mao. Hopefully there will still be enough legal means left to throw these greedy power grabbing bums out of office before complete chaos ensues.

Already there are troubling signs in the picks 'empty suit' Biden is considering for his cabinet. He is bragging that it is the most diverse cabinet in history. That is true, but picking by color and sex has made it the most radical and unqualified in our history. For example, considering a CEO for a Soros funded organization into a top cabinet post will successfully complete the megalomaniac's lifelong sinister plot to infect all sectors of society with his cancerous radicalism. Biden apparently intends to hire a man called Patrick Gaspard. Gaspard was Barack Obama's political director, then U.S. ambassador to South Africa. Most recently, though, and this tells you everything, Gaspard has been the president of the Open Society Foundations, funded by George Soros.

As Tucker Carlson highlighted, "in Patrick Gaspard, George Soros has found someone as radical as he is. Three years ago, South Africa's ruling party, the African National Congress, endorsed a plan of taking land from farmers based on skin color without compensating them. They called it land reform. Neighboring

Zimbabwe had already done this under its bloodthirsty lunatic leader, Robert Mugabe, and promptly became the single poorest country in the world, killing a lot of people in the process."

"No sane person thought or thinks this was a good idea. But Patrick Gaspard thought it was a great idea. As the former ambassador to South Africa, Gaspard wrote an op-ed in the U.K.'s *Sunday Times* newspaper endorsing this and sucking up to the criminally incompetent and corrupt ANC government:"

"Ah, more equity, just like in Zimbabwe. Gaspard added in many forums that anyone who disagreed with both this point of view and land reform generally was, of course, an irredeemable racist. Gaspard later said that he found the South African constitution superior to America's constitution, and George Soros would no doubt agree with that. But would many South Africans agree with that? How many have fled that country in just the past 10 years?"

"Patrick Gaspard doesn't care. Like George Soros, he is an ideologue. For him, as for all ideologues, outcomes are far less interesting and far less important than theories. So you won't be surprised to learn that Patrick Gaspard was once a community organizer, that he once worked for failed New York City Mayor David Dinkins, and that he remains personally close to current Mayor Bill de Blasio. New York City is collapsing, but as far as Patrick Gaspard is concerned, it's collapsing for the right reasons..."

A natural course of radicals trying to overthrow America with their idiotic venom and actions will be the development of right-wing with a militia to balance the BLM, ANTIFA, and other left-wing paramilitaries. This is the story of left-right revolution that has played out over history. But the U.S. has been spared of these tragic confrontations since our break from Britain.

Your vote began this domino effect. It is your future; I'm near the end of mine. As a successful futurist for five decades, I owe it to future generations to share my insight.

We Have Silenced the Good Hearts and Minds of America

The majority of Americans have bottled up their anger and become silent, for fear of saying something that would go against our government-protected classes. Indeed, the Cato 2017 Free Speech and Tolerance Survey, a new national poll of 2,300 U.S. adults, finds that 71% Americans believe that political correctness has silenced important discussions our society needs to have. The consequences are personal—58% of Americans believe the political climate prevents them from sharing their own political beliefs. These include those who risk losing their job if they challenge left-wing dogma. *No wonder the Trump voters remain silent when contacted by pollsters.*

Democrats are unique, however, in that a slim majority (53%) does not feel the need to self-censor. Conversely, strong majorities of Republicans (73%) and independents (58%) say they keep some political beliefs to themselves. They are the "silent majority" that made Trump the President.

Brainwashed college students becoming a 'silence free speech' Gestapo.

It's not just "Berzerkly" aka the University of California at Berkeley where surprisingly large numbers of U.S. college students believe that violence and shouting are acceptable methods to prevent people from saying things. Fifty-one percent of all U.S. college students believe shouting is an acceptable response to free speech, and one in five (19 percent) believe violence is an acceptable response, according to results from a national survey of 1,500 students in 49 states and D.C.

An Arizona State University student is suing for being fired from her university radio job over her tweet about Jacob Blake's criminal record. The divisity puppeteers use their naïve wooden–headed Big Tech and media puppets to prevent the truth from coming out about black criminals like Blake, and Floyd, who committed a felony household invasion where he stuck his gun into a woman's stomach, rather than stand up for the victims of these losers.

Fifty-three percent of survey respondents said colleges should "create a positive learning environment for all students by prohibiting certain speech or expression of viewpoints that are offensive or biased against certain groups of people" rather than "create an open learning environment where students are exposed to all types of speech and viewpoints, even if it means allowing speech that is offensive or biased against certain groups of people." Meanwhile, Harvard is losing more class as it continues on its suicide mission. The school seems intent on killing off the last remnants of diverse thought and further lowering their falling academic reputation by abandoning truth, to instead just acquiesce to the demands of the radical Left cancer that is killing discourse for brainwashing. The latest papal bull is a petition circulating in the Harvard University student body that seeks to ban Trump administration officials from teaching, speaking, or attending the institution because of their association with the president. The petition represented the latest attempt to punish Trump associates. Students are also demanding that the university does not associate with a Trump alumnus. *Harvard and other colleges have been censoring conservative viewpoints. Do you think this is a good thing?*

Chapter 4
THE GOVERNMENT GETS INTO THE ACT

"A government big enough to give you everything you want is a government big enough to take from you everything you have."

Gerald Ford

"The nine most terrifying words in the English language are: I'm from the government and I'm here to help."

Ronald Reagan

The bloated Federal government has unleashed a rat's nest of lawyers, causing a plague that is destroying our businesses and economy. Using its legitimacy as an arm of the Federal government, the Equal Employment Opportunity Commission (EEOC), which grew out of the landmark Civil Rights Act of 1964 and was intended to help prevent discrimination against Blacks, has instead become the home base for reverse discrimination against Whites.

Government lawyers have helped Jesse Jackson and other opportunists successfully use threats and intimidation to achieve large cash settlements and force employment of Blacks from deep-pocket organizations throughout the country. These organizations are willing to pay off black leaders and their cadre of lawyers and consultants in order to prevent spurious boycotts, lawsuits, demonstrations, and other problems.

EEOC

The EEOC is one of most dangerous organizations in America. It has done irreparable damage to our businesses, schools, and government institutions. I first became aware of the EEOC when, as the head of Labor Relations for a New York company, I was asked to appear before the Commission regarding a complaint by an employee who had recently been fired. The employee, a Hispanic union member, was let go after several months of the normal grievance process, and with the agreement of the union. His argument was that he was discriminated against because he was Hispanic. I explained to the Commission members that this claim was nonsense, because about three-quarters of our union employees were Black or Hispanic.

The logic of my argument should have produced a win for my company; it was instead a no-brainer that highlighted that the all-minority panel consisted of no-brainers. The EEOC insisted that we had discriminated, and that we must rehire the troublemaker with back pay. These irrational, one-sided, unjust rulings, I was learning were the rule rather than the exception with the EEOC. The legacy of this worthless department continues today.

The Equal Employment Opportunity Commission can be extremely aggressive. Anyone who has ever been targeted for an EEOC investigation knows just how intimidating it can be responding to requests for information, knowing that the agency has a reputation of engaging in wholesale fishing expeditions for violations that may have nothing to do with the initial complaint.

Case in point, EEOC initiated an investigation of the McLane Company after an employee filed a complaint alleging sex discrimination. But rather than focusing on that employee's claim EEOC, began requesting information about many other employees, and began investigating potential age discrimination issues. Yet at the end of the day, when the employer objected to certain requests for information, a federal district court sided with the employer—refusing to enforce EEOC's subpoenas because it thought the agency's requested information was not relevant to EEOC's claim of age discrimination.

This is where things got interesting because the Ninth Circuit Federal Court of Appeals overturned that decision—so as to force the employer to comply with EEOC's subpoena. Unfortunately, that's usually the end of the road in a case like this. But in this case the McLane Company managed to convince the U.S. Supreme Court to take the case. And the Supreme Court handed-down a decision holding that the Ninth Circuit had exceeded its authority in reversing the District Court's decision.

The victimization and divisity business con men need to keep the systemic racist hoax alive in order to keep extorting billions from easy corporate marks. They know very well that real discrimination has disappeared and they must look at even any perceived subtle slight, the statistical studies con, anecdotal stories for the legal vultures to find any meat left on the bones to pick at. The overpopulation of lawyers in the EEOC **bull**pen provides justification and profits to share, by using government resources to keep this charade going, by reaching their quota of EEOC charges, Office of Federal Contract Compliance Program (OFCCP) enforcement actions and Title VII lawsuits.

Discrimination cases are used by the divisity cons to demonstrate that discrimination is alive in the workplace. Finding discrimination against Blacks in America is a supply and demand problem. Therefore, EEOC witch hunts to find something or someone to bitch about are critical and take creativity, since real discrimination in America dried up years ago. If you can't find any discrimination but the demand for examples is so high, then just make it up. This is now called "Smolletting," a term for making up discrimination claims. This term is of course named for Jussie Smollett, who wanted the publicity of being a victim and a chance for another hoax to hurt Trump, enough to hire foreigners to act in a staged racial attack against him by "White Supremacists."

Indeed, as proposed "CAREN Law" in San Francisco exemplifies, the reality is that Blacks are already treated like fragile glass, given benefits not available to other races and over-protected from discrimination by existing laws and policies in every segment of society. If a woman was home alone and called 911 to report the suspicious behavior of a black man near her home in San Francisco, under CAREN Law (the name Karen is now a social media racial slur stereotype, used against middle aged white women) she could be prosecuted and sued by that man. Moreover, California's governor recently signed a measure making the crime a misdemeanor punishable by jail time and a fine. New York approved legislation allowing the victims of racist 911 calls to sue. This is happening at a time when our prisons are being emptied due to "justice reform" and China virus fears which is producing a record high spike in crime in progressive run states.

I'm 80 years old and in all my years I've never met a single White Supremacist. Indeed, I watched as a small-time low life racist, like David Duke, a former KKK leader became legendary in the media. This is because his type is as rare in the U.S. as the Tasmanian devil is in Australia. There is however an overpopulation of black radicals, like former Black Panther leader Bobby Rush, spreading their divisity cancer in Congress and our public universities; yet not a word is mentioned about them.

Protect Illegal Aliens

When Ida Castro, a Latino female, became EEOC chair, it was the Hispanics' turn to swing with the EEOC paddle and try to break apart an American piñata, filled with jobs and cash payoffs just waiting to fall into what the Federation for Immigration Reform (FAIR) called "unclean hands." She quickly sought protection for the undocumented workers who illegally entered the country while thousands who followed the law waited for a chance to immigrate legally. Her policy called for the undocumented workers to be entitled to wrongful termination, back pay, damages, and legal costs. According to FAIR, this policy "appears to be sanctioning people who have unclean hands, people who break our laws willingly and knowingly, and people who are bidding down the wages of all Americans."

Payoff for Not Speaking Our Language

If you're still not convinced that the EEOC should be shattered and swept into the dustbin of history, the following cases will change your mind.

A private Catholic university in San Antonio, Texas did a tremendous favor for its Hispanic housekeepers when it told them to speak English on the job—not because the workers learned to speak the language of the U.S., but because the EEOC then helped the housekeepers win a $2.4 million legal settlement. Note that 71% of the students at the University of the Incarnate Word are minorities. Their tuition dollars now line the pockets of people who couldn't bear the thought of speaking English.

In this case, it didn't matter that it is legal for employers to have English work rules; in this wacko world, the EEOC insisted that there was a violation of the 1964 Civil Rights Act on the grounds that they discriminated against people on the basis of their national origin. Similar language case boondoggles have shot up 500% over the last few years. It is another one of the typical EEOC cases where everyone loses except the people who should have.

Here is another case of how the bloated cadres of EEOC lawyers waste taxpayer money looking for discrimination when there isn't any. It is as dangerous as a fireman who is an arsonist. ProEnglish, the nation's leading official English advocacy group condemns the federal Equal Employment Opportunity Commission (EEOC) for suing a private American company for firing employees over their inability to speak English in the workplace. ProEnglish is also offering assistance to Wisconsin Plastics Inc., which the EEOC falsely accuses of violating

Title VII of the Civil Rights Act, which prohibits discrimination based on "national origin."

"The EEOC is acting illegally and is abusing its statutory authority by prosecuting employers like the Green Bay-based Wisconsin Plastics which require employees to communicate in English," says ProEnglish Executive Director Robert Vandervoort. "By filing this latest lawsuit, the EEOC is not only violating the rights of employers to run their businesses, it is also violating the rights of employees to work in a safe, non-threatening work environment."

"Since the fired workers were of Hispanic and Asian origin, the EEOC claims there is a close connection between language and 'national origin,'" Vandervoort continues. "But in the 21st century a person's primary language is rarely an essential national origin characteristic."

"In 40 years of court cases there has not been a single ruling supporting the EEOC's interpretation that was ultimately upheld, or which is controlling: not one supports the EEOC's language equals national origin notion. To cite just one example, a few years ago the EEOC settled its lawsuit against the Salvation Army that left the Army's English-on-the-job policy intact. The courts have long recognized an employer's right to set conditions of employment, including what employees can say on the job—a right, by the way, PROTECTED by Title VII of the Civil Rights Act," Vandervoort concludes.

Biden's candidate for top EEOC post is an ignorant racist

Biden's destruction of America is happening at an accelerated pace I could never have predicted. Further proof that the inmates will be running the insane asylum and that a degree in chocolate donuts from any community college is better than a Harvard education.

Joe Biden's pick to run the Justice Department's enormously powerful Civil Rights Division, Kristen Clarke, says her job is simple: End hate. But like so many in her victimization and divisity world, Clarke is actually an enthusiastic purveyor of hate. She will be the equivalent of the "Grand Wizard," the leader of the KKK for the BLM and victimization/divisity extortionists. Some examples of Clarke's extreme wacko racist theory were uncovered by a Tucker Carlson investigation. They uncovered shocking statements that Clarke made while attending Harvard as an undergraduate. In 1994, Clarke wrote a letter to *The Harvard Crimson* in her capacity as the president of the Black Students Association to explain her views on race science.

"Please use the following theories and observations to assist you in your search for truth regarding the genetic differences between Blacks and whites [sic]," Clarke wrote. "One: Dr Richard King reveals that the core of the human brain is the 'locus coeruleus,' which is a structure that is Black, because it contains large amounts of neuro-melanin, which is essential for its operation.

"Two: Black infants sit, crawl and walk sooner than whites [sic].

"Three: Carol Barnes notes that human mental processes are controlled by melanin — that same chemical which gives Blacks their superior physical and mental abilities.

"Four: Some scientists have revealed that most whites [sic] are unable to produce melanin because their pineal glands are often calcified or non-functioning. Pineal calcification rates with Africans are five to 15 percent [sic], Asians 15 to 25 percent [sic] and Europeans 60 to 80 percent [sic]. This is the chemical basis for the cultural differences between blacks and whites [sic].

"Five: Melanin endows Blacks with greater mental, physical and spiritual abilities — something which cannot be measured based on Eurocentric standards."

Do you now understand why the EEOC is such a dangerous racist threat to our country and why this bloated worthless crib for featherbedding lawyers looking to stir up trouble must be eliminated?

As Carlson noted, the above is not an editorial from the *Final Call*, Louis Farrakhan's free newspaper. That is a direct quote from the person Joe Biden is about to put in charge of this country's civil rights laws.

Even at Harvard, crackpot virulent racist theories like that were considered deranged and dangerous. After an outcry on campus, Kristen Clarke suggested that she didn't necessarily believe what she had written.

Just a month later, however, Clarke invited the noted Trinidadian anti-Semite Tony Martin to speak on campus. Martin, then a professor at Wellesley College, was the author of a self-published manifesto called "The Jewish Onslaught." In it, Martin chronicled the "escalating Jewish onslaught" against Black people.

For Martin's fans like Kristen Clarke, his speech at Harvard did not disappoint. He attacked both Jews and Judaism as a religion. Martin, who retired from Wellesley in 2007 and died in 2013, spent his final years giving speeches to Holocaust denial organizations on topics such as "tactics of organized Jewry in suppressing free speech."

Kristen Clarke strongly approved of Tony Martin, telling *The Crimson*: "Professor Martin is an intelligent, well-versed Black intellectual who bases his information on indisputable fact." According to Kristen Clarke, Tony Martin's anti-Semitism was based on "indisputable fact."

Kristen Clarke has never shed these views. They've simply become more sophisticated. Just last year, Clarke was fighting for the crudest kind of racial discrimination in college admissions, saying it was "madness" for the federal government to take the side of Asian applicants who had been denied college admission on the basis of their skin color.

Do you support putting such idiotic anti-Semitic, anti-white, anti-Asian, Black low lives in power positions in our government and universities? Biden does!

If you are *still* not convinced that the EEOC and the quota business should be shut down and padlocked, the following case might shock you.

Boeing

Boeing, the huge aerospace and government contractor with over $18 billion in contracts, was brutalized by the growing quota industry to aggressively exclude non-minorities. **The aerospace giant spent $1.3 billion on race-based and gender-based programs, to ensure that Boeing's employment policies specifically favor minorities in hiring and promotions.** Moreover, Boeing suppliers and subcontractors must be in the correct race, gender, and ethnicity classes in order to do business with the aerospace giant. *Do you think picking suppliers based on race and gender is fair or the smart way to purchase?*

Our bloated, duplicative, wasteful Federal government sends no fewer than three huge federal agencies to monitor Boeing's employment practices regarding selected minorities: the U.S. Department of Justice, the U.S. EEOC, and the U.S. Department of Labor. This virtual army of tax-supported lawyers and analysts combs through Boeing's personnel files to verify the total number and pay scales of each of the following categories of Boeing preferred employees and suppliers: Black, Asian Pacific-American, Sub-continental Asian-American, Hispanic-American, Native-American, and females of any ethnicity.

In their analysis of Boeing's "enforced diversity," the U.S. Department of Labor does not take into account seniority or years of service. As a Federal contractor, Boeing must prove to the Federal bureaucracy that it has hired the correct proportions for all of these preferred races, ethnic, and gender classes, and that they have been paid the same as their White counterparts, regardless of performance or seniority. Got that! Preferred races get paid the same as Whites regardless of seniority and performance. *Are you beginning to understand how wrong this is from a moral and business perspective? These are the reverse racist policies your Biden vote will perpetuate.* The government also requires Federal contractors such as Boeing to aggressively ensure that people of the "correct" race and gender are their suppliers and subcontractors ("correct" is a code word for Blacks and other protected minorities).

Race and Gender-Motivated Lawsuits against Boeing

Since 1997 alone, at least five discrimination lawsuits have been filed against Boeing on behalf of Black, Asian, and female employees. Boeing chose not to contest the two largest suits, and instead agreed to pay a total of almost $20 million to settle disputes. *This again is how the "Big Con" works so well for the divisity extortionists with the help of the EEOC Gestapo and "social warriors," aka brainwashed pawns.*

In response to a lawsuit filed by Black Boeing employees (Staton v. Boeing), Boeing settled for $15 million in January of 1999. Jesse Jackson figured prominently in brokering the $15 million deal. It has been reported that his various tax-exempt organizations "profited handsomely from his interference." In fact, Boeing Chairman and CEO, Phil Condit, made a point to announce the settlement in a joint news conference with Jesse Jackson. However, on November 26, 2002, the U.S. Circuit Court of Appeals ruled that the method of distributing the $15 million among the individual plaintiffs, as well as the compensation to be paid to the lawyers, was suspect, and sent the case back to the District Court for review.

Women and minorities won a second settlement for $4.5 million in November 1999, in a case concerning alleged pay disparities among female and minority workers. The settlement was agreed to after the U.S. Department of Labor launched no fewer than ten burdensome and contentious audits of Boeing's pay practices around the country. *Do these cons cutting up these huge companies remind you of vultures eating a whale carcass or hyenas attacking a defenseless elephant?*

Also, as part of the deal with former President Bill Clinton's Department of Labor, Boeing must collect and report race and gender data on anyone who merely expresses an interest in working at Boeing and not just the people Boeing actually interviews. *Why not put up a sign outside the employment office those non-handicapped straight white males like those who built this company need not apply? Do you think hiring, promoting, and purchasing based on color and sex is better than using merit, experience, price, and quality for the company and the country?*

The U.S. Department of Labor's Office of Federal Contract Compliance Programs (OFCCP) analyzed Boeing's compensation data, and determined that some women and minorities were earning less than the median pay scale, as compared to white males in their particular jobs. The OFCCP analysis never took into account length of time on the job or how well individuals did their jobs. *Remember the Big Con only considers race and sex; not years of experience, skill level, or job performance. Of course, race or sex are non-factors that should have as much weight as whether you wear Jockey's or briefs for underwear. Are you beginning to understand how wrong, absurd, and racist these groups you may support are?*

These class actions by minority employees are significant for two reasons. First, the cases illustrate that the racial quota industry is able to exploit huge concessions and preferences from large employers. In virtually all cases of this type, the employer *never* goes to the expense of proving itself innocent in a court of law. **In fact, no major civil rights lawsuit of this type in the past decade has ever gone to trial!** Second, the dollar amount, both on the books ($15 million) and off the books (over $1.3 billion) is far larger than in other cases.

Boeing's concessions to the quota industry, as reported in the press, are: Employees must have worked at Boeing for at least one year to be eligible for awards, and since Boeing had previously bought McDonnell Douglas and Rockwell, the settlement also included former McDonnell Douglas and Rockwell employees. The black workers got a total of $6.65 million, while various attorneys involved were to receive $7.7 million. This contested amount is puny compared to the huge off-the-books payments.

Public records reveal that Boeing has made race-based payments of $1.3 billion to the quota industry. One wouldn't be surprised if this was done specifically to keep "Jessie James Jackson," as he has been called, and his gang (Department of Labor, EEOC, et al), off their backs.

A partial list of Boeing's off-the-books racial payments is:

- $800 million – In the first nine months of 2001 alone, Boeing boasted that it had issued $800 million in contracts and supply orders to minority and woman-owned businesses as part of their "Supplier Diversity Program."
- $500 million was reported for contracts to three minority-owned investment banks that have financial ties to Jesse Jackson's Chicago-based Rainbow PUSH coalition, for contracts to manage the company's pension funds and defined benefit trusts.

- $3.7 million was spent for equal opportunity and diversity training initiatives.
- $1 million was paid to the National Minority Supplier Development Council Business Consortium fund, which provided contract financing to certified minority businesses across America through a network of local participating certified lending banks and regional councils.
- $250,000 – For his Boeing intervention, Jackson reportedly received at least $250,000 for his CEF fund.
- $225,000 was reportedly paid to Boeing-appointed Rosalind Crenshaw, a supplier diversity specialist, who acted as Boeing's liaison to Jesse Jackson's Rainbow PUSH organization, with 25% of Ms. Crenshaw's salaried Boeing job being devoted to Rainbow PUSH activities.
- $150,000 – Four scholarships are provided annually by Boeing St. Louis for owners of minority businesses to attend the Kellogg School of Business and Northwestern University, and two scholarships are provided to attend the Minority Business Executive Program at the expensive Dartmouth University.
- $100,000 – Reportedly, Boeing "donates" hundreds of thousands of "off-the-books funds" to Jesse Jackson for sponsorship of Jesse Jackson fundraisers, conventions, and dinner galas.

One such dinner gala, a black-tie event for which Boeing had paid over $100,000 in sponsorship fees, raised an additional $2.1 million in a race-based shakedown of corporate America to support Jesse Jackson's Citizen Education Fund (CEF). The CEF is the fund from which Jesse Jackson cut a $40,000 check to his mistress, Karen Stanford, who bore his out-of-wedlock child.

The IRS subsequently ruled that Jackson's use of these tax-exempt funds to avoid a lawsuit was a permissible use of taxpayer funds! This is an example of how the virus carried by the diversity business moves back into the protection of a government agency once it has infected the host company, in this case Boeing.

These companies are paying to assure that they will continue to be ripped off. According to the *Seattle Times*, during Washington State's Initiative 200, a campaign to overturn racial preferences, Boeing contributed $50,000 to opponents of the initiative, who wanted to retain racial preferences in the state. In spite of Boeing's efforts, the voters, by an overwhelming majority, approved Initiative 200. Boeing's unnecessary involvement and support of the University of Michigan's use of racial quotas in admissions is another example of how the parasitic racial preference groups made Boeing their personal bitch, and used their cash machine to push their agenda.

As the Judicial, Legislative, and Executive branches, along with infected businesses and liberal media, try to legitimize these horrible wrongs, other groups also identifying themselves as victims literally begin to follow suit—lawsuit that is. Moreover, the left-wing/minority-dominated extremists at the EEOC expanded their sphere of influence, making areas such as sexual harassment a profitable growth business for their friends. Their success brought forth headlines such as "Ford settles harassment case for $7.5 million," making it the fourth-largest sexual harassment case in EEOC history.

Business Learns to Roll Over

The diversity business has spread like a cancer throughout many industries. Having a "diversity officer" to assure that minorities get a leg up when applying for a job or competing as suppliers is now the latest form of featherbedding and influence peddling offered by the "un-civil rights" mob to their "good fellows." Businesses who unquestionably give the most are called socially responsible for allowing part of their shareholder profits to be siphoned off to these unproductive leaches. I have watched over the years as the dangerous victimization and divisity puppet masters have infected the brainwashed monoculture of Silicon Valley. These rich monopolies fund the spread of reverse racist left-wing propaganda. Netflix employees for example, sent 98% of their donations to Democrats in 2016 and 99.6% in the 2018 midterm elections. These high-tech employees are working in a bubble that they themselves are about to break. Like so many employees and executives in Silicon Valley, they were working during the greatest economy in the history of the world for all income groups; Blacks, women, Asians, and Hispanics under President Trump before the China virus. These techies are totally brainwashed, naïve, and spoiled, but very well paid. They have little sense of the real world or history but, like windup toys, parrot left-wing and slogans created by divisity cons. How else can you explain that the biggest individual recipient of Netflix and most other Big Tech employee funds was socialist Sen. Bernie Sanders, whose radical policies are being adopted by the Biden mob? By far the biggest recipient of Netflix employee money has been the Senate Majority PAC, a political action committee that's "solely dedicated to building a Democratic majority in the U.S. Senate," according to its website.

An exception to the brainwashed eunuchs running high tech companies, and a hero of mine, is T.J. Rodgers. When Jessie Jackson tried to shake down T.J.'s company, his board originally said, "Don't make waves—go along to get along." Originally, he was going to adopt the "under-the-desk" reaction like the board wanted him to. But after listening to Jackson saying outrageous things on the radio, T.J. got ticked off. He challenged Jackson to a debate about the facts in Jackson's racial discrimination claims. Rodgers offered to hire any well-qualified black candidates Jackson sent him. But of course, it is not the needs of the black community in which "Me-first Jackson," as some call him in Chicago, is primarily interested. His close circle, however, does get its payoffs—beer distributorships for his sons and millions of dollars for about two dozen of his closest friends.

Author Ken Timmerman had a number of CEOs come up to him and actually tell him that paying Jessie Jackson $400,000 to $500,000 was the price of doing business. I guess it's cheaper than being involved in a lawsuit, but it is we, the shareholders and the consumers, that are being ripped off. Shame on the CEOs who don't have the balls to stand up against, what talk show host Geoff Metcalf calls extortion.

Business goes spineless - divisity cancer rapidly spreads

How could you have possibly escaped the brainwashing? As we have learned, like the China virus, it infected all sectors of your life including your workplace. Divisity cancer in the workplace is called "diversity training." In some of these training sessions, white employees are made to sit without responding as black employees bitch about trivial bullshit that bothers them at work and in America. There seems to be an oversupply of unhappy Blacks that would love to target their anger at white men. *What do you call a happy black man? The answer is a Republican.*

These trainings are often taught by black radicals who majored in the divisive hyphenated "I hate Whites" courses at our universities. As someone who was an organization psychologist and President of an American Society for Training and Development (ASTD) chapter, I know how dangerous such "sensitivity" training can be even when done by a licensed professional.

We recently heard about Starbucks putting 175,000 of its workers through this boondoggle training because of the arrest of two black men in one of their stores. As I have said, this nonsense has become a very big business for the affiliates of the victimization and divisity extortionists over the decades. For companies, paying off these cons through their training budget is better than having the EEOC sniffing around in their business. Sadly, there are not many executives with the balls like a T.J. Rodgers in America today. Indeed, nearly all the Fortune 500 companies do training and more than two-thirds of colleges and universities assure compliance with their anti-American left-wing radicalism. To assure that the American Cultural Revolution spreads its virus into the next generation, most freshmen will be put though some form of this brainwashing.

Thankfully, employers admit that these expensive programs are ineffective. Indeed, hundreds of studies going back decades suggest that anti-bias training doesn't reduce bias, alter behavior, or change the workplace. But it has developed into a business angry Blacks can make millions from. They are kept because of the worry about the optics and fear of litigation if they are dropped.

Mexicans want their part of the action

The Mexican American Legal Defense Fund (MALDEF) has immigration reform at the top of their legal agenda; they support immigration reform that includes a roadmap to citizenship. They see those opposed to illegal immigration, strong borders, and asking about citizenship on the 2020 census as part of a White wing conspiracy by Trump to advance a White nationalist agenda rather than what every country in the world does. They have expanded the extortion of big companies with lawsuits even for non-citizens. A left-wing judge decided that refusing to hire DACA recipients was discrimination by Procter & Gamble. In her ruling, U.S. District Judge Kathleen M. Williams expanded rights for people here illegally and made American companies also a target for more phony discrimination cases. "By asking 'are you currently a U.S. citizen or national' as a criterion for exclusion, the policy explicitly singled out non-citizens and subjected them to less favorable treatment," the judge wrote in the 40-page ruling.

To support their legal fishing expeditions it is good to have friends with deep pockets willing to pay protection money as a cost of doing business, as well as left-wing headed foundations that are all too willing to support causes that are destroying law and order and American values.

Some of the largest corporate/foundation contributors to this Latino organization in past years were:

- $100,000 – Anheuser-Busch Companies, Ford Foundation, The State Bar of California, University of Notre Dame
- $50,000 to $99,000 – Wells Fargo, AT&T Foundation, Bank of America, Disney Corporation
- Other contributors listed on their website are General Motors, AARP, BP, SBC, Ford Motor, and Fannie Mae

With such strong support for illegal and immigrant rights, the ridiculous growing trend of having to "press one" to speak English in America has become a way of life.

Forcing Diversity on the Media

Having planted people in power positions in business, educational institutions, and government, it is time for minorities to try to get more control of the media. The quota industry egotists would then have more airtime to spread their propaganda and to balance the rare negative media attention. Black leaders get on fair and balanced news programs to launch their transparent tactic of playing the race card as an excuse for unacceptable Black behavior.

We watched as Jesse Jackson called for widespread consolidation in the communications industry, saying that the "re-segregation of ownership" was a threat to democracy, when it really was a natural byproduct of competition, and industry consolidation as correctly characterized by Ken Johnson, the press secretary to Rep Tauzin.

Another Black strategy, when possible, is to bring the lambs to the lion's den. Why in the world did Boeing move its headquarters to Jackson's stomping grounds in Chicago? Moreover, FCC Chairman William Kennard appeared, bearing gifts, at a two-day conference in Chicago that was organized by Jesse Jackson. To rousing applause, Kennard told the conference that he would "complete a proceeding to explore new incentives for minority owners." But as Ken Johnson correctly warned afterward, "We do not believe it is within the scope of the FCC to dictate quotas for broadcasting licenses."

Jackson's Rainbow PUSH coalition previously announced that it would form a rating system to evaluate performance opportunities at media companies. Of course, one must always question Jackson's motives when he is backed by armies of tax payer-funded lawyer hit men in the Department of Justice and the Department of Labor, all drooling over alleged grievances about minority employment and job training.

NAACP President Mfume also used a challenging, confrontational style, calling TV programs an "outrage ... a virtual whitewash," because of the lack of minority representation. The need to write in more roles for minorities under court threat is pure chutzpah. How about counting the number of minority players on baseball, football, and basketball teams, and insisting that some black players be dropped because there seems to be a virtual blackball of white players? How about redirecting the disproportionate amount of NFL philanthropy from Black colleges to White-only universities?

Who is going to stand up to this absurd illogic, and throw this extortion, protection, and numbers racket onto the rubbish heap of history? *Can anyone say quota?*

Where is it written that we must have a quota of minorities, often less qualified, in every segment of business, education, media, trade group, foundation, and government? What has happened to the concept of equality and competition? The U.S. becomes a very scary place when our basic values are under threat.

Affirmative Action

Discrimination is treatment or distinction based in favor or against a person, group, etc, by promoting a system of race-based entitlement. Affirmative Action is keeping America from evolving into a colorblind society where people are judged by their abilities rather than the color of their skin. *Do you agree with Martin Luther King's dream that we want every child to be judged on their talent and content of their character, not by their skin color or Affirmative Action?*

Affirmative Action is a system of racial preferences and quotas that denies opportunity to individuals solely because they are not members of a preferred race or ethnic group. By locking deserving Whites and Asians out of schools to make room for minorities with much weaker records, Affirmative Action exacerbates racial divisions.

Affirmative Action is in fact a smoke screen for discrimination. In Europe, it is called "positive discrimination," but even the judges continue to rationalize its use. "A racially diverse and ethnically diverse student body produces significant educational benefits such that diversity constitutes a compelling government interest," wrote Judge Patrick Duggan in his justification of the University of Michigan's use of racial preferences in its admissions policy.

In actuality, Affirmative Action is primarily a powerful force for perpetuating preferential treatment and discrimination based on race, sex, ethnic origin, or some other approved badge of victimization. It does not assure equality of opportunity, but rather judicially enforced equality of outcome. As Ken Smith wrote in the *Washington Times*, "Skin color quotas are just quotas by another name. Henceforth, judges will be looking over the shoulders of school administrators to determine when the skin color bonus is too high or perhaps not high enough."

In a federal lawsuit filed in Massachusetts in 2014, a group representing Asian-Americans is claiming that Harvard University's undergraduate-admissions practices unlawfully discriminate against Asians. The suit poses questions about what a truly diverse college class might look like, spotlighting a group that is often perceived as lacking internal diversity. The court complaint quotes a college counselor at Hunter College High School who was reporting a Harvard admissions officer's feedback to the school: Asian students weren't admitted, the officer said, because "so many" of them "looked just like" each other on paper. *Do you agree that there would be uproar if such a racially insensitive statement was made against Blacks?*

The lawsuit alleges that Harvard effectively employs quotas on the number of Asians admitted and holds them to a higher standard than Whites. At selective colleges, Asians are demographically overrepresented minorities, but they are underrepresented relative to the applicant pool. Since the nineteen-nineties, the share of Asians in Harvard's freshman class has remained stable, at between sixteen and nineteen per cent, while the percentage of Asians in the U.S. population more than doubled. A 2009 Princeton study showed that Asians had to score a hundred and forty points higher on the SAT than Whites to have the same chance of admission to top universities. The discrimination suit survived Harvard's motion to dismiss and is currently pending. Notice the disparity between scores used was presented only between Asians and Whites to avoid the real issue which is that Asians would have to score 450 points higher than Blacks to get into Harvard. *Do you think this is fair or a perfect example of reverse racism?*

When the *New York Times* reported the Justice Department's Civil Rights Division was internally seeking lawyers to investigate or litigate "intentional race-based discrimination in college and university admissions," many people immediately assumed that the Trump Administration was hoping to benefit Whites by assailing affirmative action. The Department soon insisted that it specifically intends to revive a 2015 complaint against Harvard filed with the Education and Justice Departments by sixty-four Asian-American groups, making the same claim as the current court case: that Harvard intentionally discriminates against Asians in admissions, giving Whites an advantage, again avoiding the elephant in the room: Black affirmative action programs. The treatment of Asians will frame the next phase of the legal debate over race-conscious admissions programs.

Just last year, the Supreme Court upheld the constitutionality of the University of Texas at Austin's affirmative action program, which, like Harvard's, aims to build a diverse class along multiple dimensions and considers race as one factor in a holistic review of each applicant. Justice Kennedy, writing for the majority, approved of a university's ability to define "intangible characteristics, like student body diversity, that are central to its identity and educational mission." The cover your ass phrase "intangible characteristics" echoes the sort of language that often describes the individualizing or leadership qualities that many Asian-American applicants, stereotyped as hard-working achievers with high test scores, are perceived to lack. The complaint against Harvard highlights the school's history of using similar language to describe Jewish students nearly a century ago, which led to a "diversity" rationale designed to limit Jewish enrollment in favor of applicants from regions with fewer Jews, such as the Midwest. If diversity of various kinds is central to an élite school's mission, an Asian may have to swim upstream to be admitted. *Do you agree that the diversity of thought is what is most missing in our universities?*

The U.T. affirmative action case was brought by a white student and financed by Edward Blum, a white Jewish conservative who is also financing the lawsuit against Harvard. For Asian-Americans—the majority of whom support affirmative action—being cast in the foreground of the affirmative action debate can be awkward and painful. Affirmative action has consistently been a "wedge" issue, and groups such as Asian American groups have opposed attempts to use Asian students as the wedge in conservative attacks on affirmative action that may harm Black and Latino students. Some simply would rather deny that race-conscious admissions procedures are disadvantaging Asians at all to avoid confronting a complicated dilemma.

Years back, the University of Michigan's own expert studies confirmed that the value of ethnic diversity is slight; the University was just trying to get a racial mix for its own sake. This is illegal. Why should an individual be required to give up a chance to attend a state-run school solely because their skin color is not right for the current racial mix? Thankfully an Appeals Court struck down an admissions plan that resulted in a 15-year-old white girl being denied admission in favor of lower-scoring Black and Hispanic students. It should be made clear that school officials lack the authority to assign students by race to achieve a desired racial mix. To remedy growing racism against Whites and favoritism for Blacks, Michigan voted for Proposal 2, which would add this language to the state constitution.

The state shall not discriminate against, or grant preferential treatment to, any group on the basis of race, sex, color, ethnicity or national origin in the operation of public employment, public education, or public contacting.

Tragically, these words, which were once the foundation of the civil rights movement and our country's laws, are unacceptable to the "civil wrongs" puppet masters, who spent $3 million in their unsuccessful attempt to defeat the measure by using sick ads like this one on Detroit radio.

If you could have prevented 9/11 from ever happening ... would you have? If you could have prevented Katrina from ever happening ... what would you have done? On November 7, a national disaster headed for Michigan ... the elimination of affirmative action. And on November 7, there's only one way to stop this disaster ... by voting no on Proposal 2.

When will young people stop being puppets of the left-wing and the civil rights con men, and realize that their naïve support of Affirmative Action will negatively impact their lives and generations to follow? Why bother continuing an illegal, immoral, and divisive program when the Educational Testing Service expects college enrollment to swell over the next 15 years with Black, Hispanic, and Asian students accounting for 80% of the growth? Indeed, for the first time in history, public school students in the U.S. are majority-minority. *Since Whites are now the minority in our schools and discriminated against in admission, should they be made a protected class, and be given all the racial preferences currently offered to other former minorities?*

Dummying Down our Universities

Education officials worry that the minority newcomers will not be sufficiently prepared for the rigors of higher education. How do the NAACP and other minority organizations like the University of California Latino Eligibility Task Force respond to the fact that Blacks and Latinos don't perform well on College Board Tests? They employ the part of "The Great Con" I call the "color the facts" or myth of bias strategy, which again highlights the differences between Whites and these "protected" groups.

The con, as you have learned from the business examples, goes like this: first they hire an expert booster, who they know will support their position. The expert then prepares a slick statistical presentation of the obvious. Scores for Blacks, Latinos, and American Indians were drastically lower than those of Whites and Asian-Americans. They then play the victim card and present a series of lame, illogical excuses for the poor performance of minorities that would be laughable if the problem wasn't so serious.

For example, the Director of the *Princeton Review* attributed lower test scores by minorities to stereotypes that result in a self-fulfilling prophesy: minorities' fear of tests resulted in their avoiding them, waiting until the last moment to prepare, and not preparing adequately. Thus, the NAACP wants the importance of the College Board tests reduced, rather than having minorities compete fairly with other students, who cared more, studied longer, and got better grades.

Grade Inflation

Another reason the minority establishment wants to abolish testing is that exit exams rightly expose grade inflation as a cruel hoax. Just ask Shanika Bridges-King. "Being valedictorian, it didn't mean anything," she told about her time at Bryn Mawr to the *Boston Globe* recently. As part of a series of exposés, reporters spent a year tracking down the city's public high school valedictorians from the mid-2000s to learn how their lives had turned out. "I didn't understand anything I read. I didn't know how to write. I felt like I was disabled in this elite environment." Yet Bridges-King graduated at the top of her class at The English High School in Boston. Her statement is upsetting, yet not really surprising, due to an all-too-common problem at low-income high schools nationwide: Inflated grades that wrongly and harmfully signal to graduates—even valedictorians—that they're ready for college.

"I felt like I wasn't prepared to be there," claimed Jose Barbosa, who attended Boston University after finishing at the top of his class at the Jeremiah E. Burke High School, also in Boston. "I was massively unprepared," said a valedictorian of East Boston High School and recipient of a full scholarship to Northeastern University. "I felt like Hyde Park High School did nothing, really, to prepare you for a school like Boston College," according to a valedictorian of The Engineering School in the Hyde Park Education Complex.

The sad fact is that America's high school education is broken. Over the past year, stories have cast suspicion about the stratospheric graduation rates reported in several states including Alabama,. California, Georgia, Florida, Maryland, Minnesota, New Jersey, Texas, and Washington, D.C According to a September 2018 Fordham study "rising high school grade point averages have been accompanied by stagnant SAT, ACT, and NAEP scores." That's true just about everywhere in America. In North Carolina, the median grade in affluent high schools in 2016 was a B; in less affluent schools, it was a slightly lower B-. Pressure to boost graduation rates and grades is often due to school accountability policies. But so do complex motivations that range from being a popular teacher to concern for the future well-being of struggling students. It's these impulses that lead to the misplaced belief that lowering expectations, for Blacks and other non-achieving minority students, is a victimless misdemeanor; perhaps a socially just, noble act.

It does not however, improve the education of young Blacks to be awarded unearned diplomas. Indeed, grade inflation continues to degrade societal norms when these unqualified students are given a backdoor for getting a college degree. To get students who academically don't belong in college through the system, most schools offer courses like Black or feminist studies. These worthless brainwashing courses are increasingly being pushed on all students. They are taught by radicals that hate America and teach the many reasons to hate successful non-handicapped straight white men; those who had to get ahead by merit not skin color. A degree majoring in chocolate donuts has more credibility and value than these hyphenated courses aka "bitch sessions." Their schools are lying to them and us about what they've accomplished. This most harms the most vulnerable among them—and it needs to change.

Yet the hot air policy winds are blowing the other way. The easiest way to check inflated grades is via external exams, but states run by spineless blues state eunuchs, fearful of the divisity and victimization extortionists, are rushing to get rid of those—and colleges are pushing to make admissions SAT-optional. That might help the children of privileged parents who are pushing for their children to look even better to the admissions teams at the colleges from which they'll almost surely graduate. But it won't help poor and minority kids like those valedictorians in Boston. These kids' dreams are being killed by naïve liberal kindness.

The Bias of Low Expectations

Those who need color and sex to get ahead, rather than merit, need to continue to want to lower standards to change competition in their favor. Their accomplishments on the Left in academia, business, and fake news would have us believe that a chain of failure has continued for Blacks uninterrupted and is caused by slavery that came to our shores 400 years ago; therefore, we should continue to have low expectations and treat Blacks like special needs children. Like so much the brainwashed believe however, this too is not true.

As Thomas Sowell, a black man, has pointed out in his article *"Patterns of Black Excellence,"* there is a tradition of black achievement that dates to well before the civil rights era. **From the post-Civil War era to the 1950s, pupils at some leading all-Black schools in Atlanta, New Orleans, Brooklyn, and Washington, D.C. more than held their own against white high school students. This was despite run-down facilities and fewer teachers in some of the schools. Sowell credits teachers' high expectations of black students for these scores, rather than bowing to the excuses for poor performance, as is often the case today.**

As in the past, it is better not to lower standards. Studies show that black students from low-income families benefit dramatically from schools where standards are set high, more personal instruction is involved, and teachers are held accountable. This was the conclusion of a report issued by the Education Trust organization. The group took a close look at 366 elementary and secondary schools where students performed above average on math and reading tests in spite of poverty levels that qualified them as Title I schools, eligible for Federal assistance. The success factors included teachers and staff who were held accountable and increased time allotted for reading and math.

The Mismatch Effects

The so-called "mismatch effect" happens when a school extends to a student a significant admissions preference—sometimes because of a student's athletic prowess or legacy connection to the school, but usually because of the student's race. The students find themselves in a class where they have weaker academic preparation than most of their classmates. Students who would flourish at, say, San Jose City College or Sonoma State, instead find themselves at Stanford, where the professors are teaching to the "middle" of the class, introducing terms and concepts at a speed that is unnerving even to the best-prepared student. Predictably, unprepared students fall behind from the start and become increasingly lost as the professor and their classmates race ahead. Grades on tests and papers put them at the bottom of the class. Worse, the experience may well induce panic and self-doubt, making learning even harder.

Now assume that you and other students who joined you at the bottom of that class are Black and everyone else was Asian or White. This only reinforces the stereotype that Blacks are weak students.

Giving small preferences to Blacks are not much help in admissions. But contemporary racial preferences used by selective schools—especially those extended to Blacks and Native Americans—tend to be extremely large, often amounting to the equivalent of hundreds of SAT points.

At the University of Texas, the typical black student receiving a race preference placed at the 52nd percentile of the SAT; the typical White was at the 89th percentile. In other words, Texas is putting Blacks who score at the middle of the college-aspiring population in the midst of highly competitive students. This is the sort of academic gap where mismatch flourishes. And, of course, mismatch does not occur merely with racial preferences; it shows up with large preferences of all types.

Research on the mismatch problem was almost non-existent until the mid-1990s; it has developed rapidly in the past half-dozen years, especially among labor economists. To cite just a few examples of the findings:

- Black college freshmen are more likely to aspire to science or engineering careers than are white freshmen, but mismatch causes Blacks to abandon these fields at twice the rate of Whites.
- Blacks who start college interested in pursuing a doctorate and an academic career are twice as likely to be derailed from this path if they attend a school where they are mismatched.
- About half of black college students rank in the bottom 20 percent of their classes (and the bottom 10 percent in law school).
- Black law school graduates are four times as likely to fail bar exams as are Whites; mismatch explains half of this gap.
- Interracial friendships are more likely to form among students with relatively similar levels of academic preparation; thus, Blacks and Hispanics are more socially integrated on campuses where they are less academically mismatched.

Given the severity of the mismatch problem, and the importance of diversity issues to university leaders, one might expect that understanding and addressing mismatch would be at the very top of the academic agenda.

But in fact it is a largely invisible issue. With striking uniformity, university leaders view *discussion* of the mismatch problem as a threat to affirmative action and to racial peace on campuses, and therefore is a subject to be avoided. They suppress data and even often ostracize faculty who attempt to point out the seriousness of mismatch. (See, for instance, the case of UT professor Lino Graglia, who was condemned by university officials after he observed that Black and Mexican-American students were "not academically competitive" with their White peers.) We believe that the willful denial of the mismatch issue is as big a problem as mismatch itself.

A powerful example of these problems comes from UCLA, an elite school that used large racial preferences until the Proposition 209 ban took effect in 1998. The anticipated, devastating effects of the ban on preferences at UCLA and Berkeley on minorities were among the chief exhibits of those who attacked Prop 209 as a racist measure. Many predicted that over time Blacks and Hispanics would virtually disappear from the UCLA campus.

And there was indeed a post-209 drop in minority enrollment as preferences were phased out. Although it was smaller and more short-lived than anticipated, it was still quite substantial: a 50 percent drop in black freshman enrollment and a 25 percent drop for Hispanics. These drops precipitated ongoing protests by students and continual hand-wringing by administrators, and when, in 2006, there was a particularly low yield of black freshmen, the campus was roiled with agitation, so much so that the university reinstituted covert, illegal racial preferences.

Throughout these crises, university administrators constantly fed agitation against the preference ban by emphasizing the drop in undergraduate minority admissions. Never did the university point out one overwhelming fact: *The total number of Black and Hispanic students receiving bachelor's degrees was the same for the five classes after Prop 209 as for the five classes before.*

How was this possible? First, the ban on preferences produced better-matched students at UCLA, students who were more likely to graduate. The Black four-year graduation rate at UCLA doubled from the early 1990s to the years after Prop 209.

Second, strong Black and Hispanic students accepted UCLA offers of admission at much higher rates after the preferences ban went into effect; their choices seem to suggest that they were eager to attend a school where the stigma of a preference could not be attached to them. This mitigated the drop in enrollment.

Third, many minority students who would have been admitted to UCLA with weak qualifications before Prop 209 were admitted to less elite schools instead; those who proved their academic mettle were able to transfer up to UCLA and graduate there.

Thus, Prop 209 changed the minority experience at UCLA from one of frequent failure to much more consistent success. The school granted as many bachelor degrees to minority students as it did before Prop 209 while admitting many fewer and thus dramatically reducing failure and drop-out rates. It was able, in other words, to greatly reduce mismatch.

But university officials were unable or unwilling to advertise this fact. They regularly issued statements suggesting that Prop 209's consequences had caused unalloyed harm to minorities, and they suppressed data on actual student performance. The university never confronted the mismatch problem, and rather than engage in a candid discussion of the true costs and benefits of a ban on preferences, it engineered secret policies to violate Prop 209's requirement that admissions be colorblind.

The odd dynamics behind UCLA's official behavior exist throughout the contemporary academic world. The quest for racial sensitivity has created environments in which it is not only difficult but downright risky for students and professors, not to mention administrators, to talk about what affirmative action has become and about the nature and effects of large admissions preferences. Simply acknowledging the fact that large preferences exist can trigger accusations that one is insulting or stigmatizing minority groups; suggesting that these preferences have counterproductive effects can lead to the immediate inference that one wants to eliminate or cut back efforts to help minority students.

The desire to be sensitive has sealed off failing programs from the scrutiny and dialogue necessary for healthy progress. It has also made racial preferences a force for economic inequality: academically well-prepared working class and poor Asian and White students are routinely passed over in favor of Black and Hispanic students who are more affluent as well as less well-prepared.

The way racial preferences affect student outcomes is only part of the story. Equally relevant is the way the academic community has proved unequal to the task of reform—showing great resourcefulness in blocking access to information, enforcing homogenous preference policies across institutions, and evading even legal restrictions on the use of preferences. All of this makes the quest for workable reforms—which are most likely to come from the Supreme Court—both more complex and more interesting than one might at first suspect. *Much of my research about the "mismatch" issue came from an Atlantic article "The Painful Truth About Affirmative Action. Why racial preferences in college admissions hurt minority students -- and shroud the education system in dishonesty." by Richard Sander and Stuart Taylor Jr. October 2, 2012.*

Black Studies

Around the time of Malcolm X's rule, black students on college campuses were demanding classes that focused on Black history and minority studies rather than the traditional White version of history. This has made it difficult, if not impossible, to reverse the brainwashing going on in our schools or to fire the professors that are using these worthless programs as bully pulpits to pump their delusions of grandeur and one-sided anti-American extremist views at the expense of basic education.

In high demand by our public-supported colleges are former Black Panther criminals and left-wing radicals who, as professors, inculcate our impressionable students with their distorted views of history, making them social justice warriors' heroes against "the man." This educational system, which makes heroes out of criminals, encourages some of our best college athletes to make gang signs on national TV after winning championship football games. We were recently treated on TV to an overpaid Ivy League professor dressing like a pimp in support of his "brother" Harry Belafonte's right to call the President of the United States the world's greatest terrorist.

Going Backwards

It much easier to get ahead based on skin color over merit and hard work. With the assist of the bias of lower expectations, lowering standards, grade inflation, social indoctrination instead of math and English skills, lack of performance accountable for unionized teachers; failing Black education needs to find more excuses than White privilege for going in reverse at full speed.

The "divisty" cancer has spread down from our Ivy League schools to the Ivy prep schools. This will make it easier to mold the next generation of students into brainwashed zombies. The facility of the once prestigious Dalton School in NYC has proposed a list of idiotic, racist recommendations including: dropping high-level academic courses by 2023 if the performance of black students is not on par with non-blacks; requiring courses that focus on "Black Liberation" and challenges to white supremacy; overhauling the entire curriculum reading lists and student plays to reflect diversity and social justice themes; and hiring 12 full-time diversity officers and multiple psychologists to support students coping with race-based traumatic stress.

Isn't sad to see how quickly my dire predictions about our children's future are coming true? The puppet masters hiding behind a curtain labeled social justice will be quickly bringing their show to your community.

Quotas versus Quality in the Workplace

The reason for the decline in the U.S. worker correlates directly to the decline in our educational system. We are turning out high school students who can't pass a basic competency exam. Then we give them a free pass to college, where they double major in Hate America Revisionist History and Hyphenated Studies Programs. Minority recruiters then recruit these incompetents for employment. This is hardly a formula for success in the work place, or for the U.S. to compete on the global stage.

Sadly, the current black leaders do not have the character or moral strength or earned respect of someone like the late Roy Wilkins Jr. of the NAACP. In an encounter with James Farmer, the founder of the Congress of Racial Equality

(CORE), Wilkins summed up the traditional view of the civil rights movement, and how it differs from what is believed today.

I have a problem with the whole concept [Affirmative Action]. What you are asking for is not equal treatment, but special treatment to make up for unequal treatment of the past. I think that's outside the American tradition and the country won't buy it. *I don't feel at all comfortable asking for special treatment; I just want to be treated like everyone else.* Do you agree with me that Wilkins' response was the essence of fairness and American values that we should continue to fight for? It is a core principle for me!

Chapter 5
THE LEFT TURN

Democracy is only one generation from extinction.

Ronald Reagan

"They were not prepared for the storm today, so they have been thrown into great confusion. They do not possess a compass, for ordinarily when the weather is fine, they follow the old tradition and steer by the stars in the sky, without making serious mistakes regarding their direction. This is what we call 'depending on heaven for existence.'

But now they have run into bad weather so they have nothing to rely upon. It is not that they don't want to do well; only they do not know the direction and so the further they go the more mistakes they make."

Travels of Lao Can, by Liu E.   Beijing, China 1905

Mix the confrontational, militant, anti-American Black struggles of the early 1960s with the anti-war movement, the pot-smoking hippie lifestyle, modern-day anarchists, comedians turned pundits, authority-hating liberals, impressionable brainwashed students, day dreamers, unions, peace-at-any-cost politicians, do-gooders, Hollow-wood losers, remnants of the socialists and communists, militant subversives, ACLU lawyers, America-can-do-no-right professors, graying clergy misfits, overpaid Big Tech monoculture trying to be hip, and of course, advocates for women's liberation, illegal immigrants, gays, and welfare rights, and you will envision the myriad of faces carved on the totem pole of the new Left that will be toppled in this chapter.

HISTORICAL TIDBITS

The toxic mix that ignited and melted into the new Left in "Berzerkely," California in 1964 quickly mushroomed into a critical culture-changing clash. Cops, just returning from their battles with local black militants, drove onto the Berkeley campus to arrest a student at an illegal civil rights table. Hundreds of students trapped the cop car for two days, until hundreds of cops freed the car. A peacenik writer at the time, Michael Rossman gave the irrational but poetic rationale for using violence: "We're being roasted in the oven of our culture's violence."

The on-campus radicals quickly drew on the off-campus left-wing community, as well as the Black Panthers, and laid claim to a section of Telegraph Avenue near the university. The joining of this unholy trinity was another of those subtle events that changed history. There was a palpable and growing desire among the students and their community supporters to claim this piece of turf as the birthplace of an amorphous new culture that they wanted to grow and control.

On April 9, 1967, about 3,000 pot-smoking people, unmolested by police, closed the street and listened to music. Their laying claim to this piece of turf was accompanied by the shouts of the Black Panthers' revolutionary language, goals, and tactics. The Left quickly adopted this chic gang mentality, dress, and confrontational speech. Looking into my retro-scope, this moment in time was still another example of a subtle cultural change that would impact history, though at the time most Americans thought it was little more than a Berkeley freak show.

These idealistic, pot-smoking, middle-class peaceniks wanted to experience new paradigms and to create a more diverse, humane, creative, and joyous community, but they lacked the models for getting there. Across the country, many people experimented with utopian types of communities such as farm collectives, raising the level of free love, but growing little in the way of produce. Buddhist and Hindu-style teaching centers led by self-appointed gurus were also popular. But after the successful closure of Telegraph Avenue, the Left adopted the confrontational Black Panther approach to political action. At that moment and place, the mushroom culture that changed history and our society became deeply and permanently rooted in nonsensical manure. It was painful to watch the cultural vacuum suck up good middle-class kids and morph them into violent, hate-filled radicals.

The old left-wing in the academic community tried to portray the conflict in Vietnam and the establishment at home as two fronts of an imperial war.

Beginning with this warped premise, the New University Conference (NUC), an organization of radical faculty members and graduate students, labeled the Secretary of Health, Education, and Welfare (HEW) "a military officer in the domestic front of the war against people." Those heroic academics who disagreed with this nonsense were considered to be elitists who had "sold out" or been compromised.

Partisan political pronouncements by groups invoking the authority of their profession are treacherous exercises. They cast a chill on academic discourse by suggesting that there is a party line. This kind of politicization of academic professional groups is a fairly recent event in the United States, and can be blamed on the left-wing. Various left-wing academics disrupted professional meetings and developed organizations of radical faculty members like the NUC in order to "join the struggle for a democratized university and to radically transformed society." In 1969, at the American Sociological Association convention in San Francisco, around 100 students and faculty members took over the microphone, interrupting the keynote address by the association president, to conduct a memorial service for Ho Chi Minh, who had died a day before.

The same year, at the annual meeting of the American Historical Association (AHA), a "radical caucus" led by Staughton Lynd and Arthur Waskow attempted to have the organization pass an official resolution calling for American withdrawal from Vietnam and the end of "repression" of the Black Panther Party. Radical historian Eugene Genovese, who had become a national figure when he publicly declared support for the communist Viet Cong, led opposition to the resolution. He opposed the radical call for such a resolution as a "totalitarian" threat to the profession, and to the intellectual standards on which it was based. Genovese defeated the resolution with the help of H. Stuart Hughes, a Congressional peace candidate, who asserted that any anti-war resolution would "politicize" the AHA.

How and When the Left Took Control and the Brainwashing Began

The insights of Martin Kramer in his recent book provide an excellent example of a subtle event that has had, and will continue to have, mind-boggling implications to global society, but slipped completely under the radar of those who lived through the changes.

Kramer's example deals with the subversion of Middle Eastern studies. The way was cleared for academic revisionism in the Middle East studies establishment when the late Edward Said's **Orientalism** (1978) promoted his biased views. Said, a member of the ruling council of the late terrorist Yasser Arafat's PLO, quickly became one of the most powerful academics in America. Eventually he headed the Modern Language Association, the largest professional organization of academics, which had 40,000 members.

Months after the World Trade Center bombing, Said wrote an article for the *New York Times* with the revealing title "The Phony Islamic Threat." Said's title summarized the intellectual shift in Middle East studies during the previous decade. The new perspective infiltrating the field defined terrorist threats from Islamic radicals as expressions of "Euro-centric" or racist attitudes by their Western oppressors. *As I look up to the sky, I can't help thinking out loud again, "Yes, Uncle Tony, these academics really do believe that shit."*

Said bestowed academic license to the growing cadre of radical left-wing professors populating in the full range of phony, harmful, hyphenated culture departments (Latin-American, African-American, Asian-American, Islamic, and Women's Studies). They then argued that all previous scholarship, including that on the Middle East, was hopelessly biased because it had been written by White Europeans and was thus "racist**."**

How about this piece of Said's generalized bullshit for turning truth and our moral compass backwards? "All Western knowledge of the East was intrinsically tainted with imperialism." In one sentence, Said discredits all previous scholarship in the field, paving the way for its replacement by radicals like him. With the help of his left-wing academic allies, Said's extremist viewpoint created the climate and context for a revolution in Middle Eastern studies.

His views were reinforced by the pro "multi-cultural" attitudes of the university, as well as the racial preference policies in faculty hiring, and the widespread recruitment of political leftists and biased foreigners placed in history, human resources, administration, and all hyphenated culture departments. They would better serve the university by teaching fiction, since fiction is the basis for most of what is presented by these arrogant soapbox jockeys.

We must take back the control from the left-wing cabal of administrators charged with faculty hiring and student admission. Before the Said fiasco, "3.2% of America's Middle East area specialists had been born in the region. By 1992, nearly half came from the Middle East." This demographic transformation consolidated the conversion of Middle Eastern studies into Islamist/Leftist anti-Americanism. Eventually, objective professors with no axe to grind were replaced by anti-American Leftists. Left-wing radicals now constitute a teaching majority in hyphenated programs, and are the major reason that our students come out of universities sounding like Marxist wind-up toys, while those who still comprehend truth and morality are becoming an endangered species.

The Middle East Studies Association, the professional group representing the field, even refused to describe the perpetrators of the World Trade Center attacks as "terrorists," and preemptively opposed any U.S. military response. Georgetown professor John Esposito, a former president of the now infamous Middle East Studies Association, made his name by following Said's example. After disparaging concerns about Islamic terrorism as thinly veiled anti-Muslim prejudice, he was made a foreign affairs analyst for the Clinton State Department.

Georgetown University continues to provide a forum for Palestinian and other Arab propaganda. The Center for Muslim-Christian Understanding at Georgetown has been renamed for Saudi Prince Alwaleed bin Talal after he donated $20 million for the center. And while that may be just the tail, the dog appears to be moving away from its historic Catholic and Jesuit teaching philosophy too. Leaders say that the center now will be used to put on Islam workshops fostering exchanges with the Muslim world, addressing U.S. policy toward the Muslim world, working on the relationship of Islam and Arab culture, addressing Muslim citizenship and civil liberties, and developing exchange programs for students from the Muslim world. Although the University has a 200-year history of higher education based on its Christian founding, the Center's projects are now conspicuous because of the absence of Christian focus in the ten-year plan that has been posted on the Internet.

An objective measure of the magnitude of the damage caused by the academic earthquake that hit our universities is found in the fate of the celebrated Sproul academic freedom clause. This clause, written by the University of California president Robert Sproul for the Academic Personnel Manual, governs faculty behavior.

"Essentially the freedom of a university is the freedom of competent persons in the classroom. In order to protect this freedom, the University assumes the right to prevent exploitation of its prestige by unqualified persons or by those that would use it as a platform for propaganda... The function of the university is to seek and to transmit knowledge and to train students in the processes whereby truth is to be made known. **To convert, or to make converts, is alien and hostile to this dispassionate duty**. Where it becomes necessary in performing this function of a university, to consider political, social or sectarian movements, they are dissected and examined, not taught, and the conclusion left with no tipping of the scales, to the logic of the facts..." **Doesn't this make sense to you and is something any fair-minded person would support?**

In July 2003, the Faculty Senate of the University of California, by a 43-3 vote, removed this clause from the university's academic freedom provisions. **The Sproul clause was removed because it was in conflict with a course called "The Politics and Poetics of Palestinian Resistance," taught by a political activist who had been arrested for conducting illegal demonstrations on the Berkeley campus.** This candidate for my America's Academic Hall of Shame, Shingavi, issued a warning advising conservative students not to take the course—not a history or political science—but rather an English writing program required of all freshmen.

A secondary infection caused by yanking academic freedom out of the university is the corruption within the hyphenated studies programs. As always, the bloated University of California system is among the worst offenders. In the insulated playground called the University of Santa Cruz, a group of femmes fatales changed the Women's Studies Department to the Department of Feminist Studies. They use taxpayer money for the recruitment of students to radical causes. I can't help chuckling to myself when I read this nonsense, imagining the brew this coven of witches was drinking to come up with this crap.

"Employment Opportunities for Feminist Studies Majors: With a background in women and minorities' histories and an understanding of racism, sexism, homophobia, classism, and other forms of oppression, graduates have a good background for work with policy-making and lobbying organizations, research centers, trade and international associations, and unions. Graduates' knowledge about power relationships and injustice often leads them to choose careers in government and politics, because they are determined to use their skills to change the world."

The politicians and UC Regents who continue to piss our away our money on such divisive nonsense should be tarred and feathered, and made Into a May pole for these "Earth Mothers" to dance around.

The Left Agenda: Brainwash Students by Historical Revisionism

Another subtle act that swung our moral compass around and will continue to have a major negative, dangerous impact on future generations was the migration of 1960's radicals into our universities, where they politicized and polarized much of the academic curriculum and administration.

A new study by the National Association of Scholars found that college professors overwhelmingly donate to Democratic politicians instead of Republicans. The NAS data shows that American professors donate to Democrats instead of Republicans by a 95-1 ratio and that political contributions by faculty members were "almost exclusively to Democratic candidates and committees." The study, which gathered information from 12,372 professors across the United States, found the ratio between Democrat and Republican donations was most pronounced in the course areas of sociology, English, and anthropology.

When it comes to party registration, the difference between registered Democrats and Republicans was highest among assistant professors at a 10.5-1 ratio—compared to associate professors at 8.7-1 and full professors at 8.2-1.

The numbers are unsurprising to those following recent developments in higher education. A recent Harvard study found that only 35% of young Republicans feel comfortable sharing their political views on American campuses. *Remember something called the free speech movement? Do you agree that there is every kind of divisity except thought in our universities?*

In recent years, faculties at American colleges have also faced backlash and discipline for acting on their right-leaning beliefs. Shawnee State punished a professor for refusing to acknowledge a student's gender identity by using their preferred pronouns. University of Louisville fired Dr. Allan Josephson for criticizing the push for surgical transitions among youths with gender dysphoria. Wilfrid Laurier University admonished a teaching assistant for showing Jordan Peterson videos to her class. Additionally, an Evergreen State professor was sent death threats after refusing to leave campus during a "day of absence" in which white members of staff were asked to leave university premises.

"Universities justify their privileged position by claiming to be forums for the promotion of clarity, logic, and evidence. Yet their own policies, affecting millions, are too often defended with factual howlers, logical non sequiturs, and mindless boilerplate," wrote Harvard professor Stephen Pinker in 2018.

These losers, who I would never hire for a job in the real world, are the role models indoctrinating our children on high school and college campuses. We must organize the forces of rational thought to break into these academic fortresses, which are closely guarded by left-wing radicals and those who owe their existence to their affirmative action/victimization godfathers.

"In the first place, God made idiots," observed Mark Twain. "This was for practice. Then he made school boards." The San Francisco Board of Education abolishing the Junior Reserve Officers' Training Corps program (JROTC), which has been active in the city's high schools for 90 years, certainly supports Twain's view. Moreover, in an ongoing effort that will result in San Francisco continuing to turn out another generation of dumb, brainwashed, anti-American marching robots, and the city has decided to continue undermining our security, culture, and democracy from within. A local anti-war activist has donated 4,000 copies of *Can't Kick Militarism*, in comic book format, to the district.

According to Pete Hammer (who exemplifies Mark Twain's scorn for school boards), who approved it for use in the San Francisco Unified School District, this unabashedly biased left-wing look at the United States and its involvement in foreign wars throughout its history is a topic that a lot of teachers would have an interest in bringing into the classroom. Moreover, only 18% of universities require students to take even one course in American history. More absurd, less than one-third of the top 25 liberal arts colleges, top 25 national universities, and top 25 public institutions require U.S. history as a requirement for history majors.

To truly open the minds of our children, we need courageous teachers willing to stand up to these left-wing vampires and shine the light of commonsense. To save Western values and our country's truth and fairness, we must free future generations from the current anti-American, pro-radical syllabus. Parents must question why they shell out a small fortune to schools that have substituted left-wing propaganda for education.

The Vilest Anti-American Professors:

The following section names some of the top America-hating professors teaching at American colleges and universities. These vermin are infecting our students with a much more dangerous plague than the China virus. Their insane babbling, which sounds like what might be heard within padded cells, does not belong in any serious academic setting.

They are an insult to academia—the equivalent of what fake news is to real journalism. They are an embarrassment to our country and severely denigrate the reputation of any university stupid enough to employ such racists.

1. **Ward Churchill**- There was a lot of competition to become the poster boy for dangerous, radical left-wing academics, but we do have a whiner/winner. In many people's opinions, our winner could be University of Colorado Professor Ward Churchill, who wrote, among other things, that the people in the World Trade Centers deserved to die on September 11, 2001. They were, Churchill said, "little Eichmanns," comparing them to Adolf Hitler's right-hand butcher.

2. **Kevin Barrett**- Others have told me that a close competitor for my off-the-wall Professors' Hall of Shame is Kevin Barrett of the University of Wisconsin. This moron believes 9/11 was an inside job, and is able to teach his ridiculous views in an Islamic studies course. One might ask how a respected University would allow a dangerous view like that to be taught, when it reinforces and gives credence to the conspiracy paranoia beliefs of too many Muslims.

3. **Robert Jensen**- The eyes of Texas should be on University of Texas Professor Robert Jensen, who says, "The United States has lost the war in Iraq, and that's a good thing," and "I welcome the U.S. defeat ... its essential the American empire be defeated and dismantled."

4. **Kamau Kambon**- How about North Carolina State University's Professor Kamau Kambon? He has this to say: "We are going to exterminate white people because that in my estimation is only conclusion I have come to. We have to exterminate white people off the face of the planet to solve this problem."

5. **Sayed Rahmatullah**- Finally, Yale University seems intent on further tarnishing its fading reputation by actively recruiting the ex-Deputy Foreign Secretary/Ambassador for the Taliban for their freshman class. "I could have ended up in Guantanamo Bay. Instead, I ended up at Yale," he says. Though not yet a professor, this idiot fits perfectly with this list of lowlife losers.

In this election year, it is more important than ever to know and follow what our educators are saying about this fraught moment in American history. The following is David Horowitz's Top Ten America-Hating Professors teaching at American colleges and universities. Please visit his website at AmericaHatingProfessors.org for more information and to report an America-hating professor on your campus! These disgusting pseudo intellectual traitors are racist bigots that have done more damage to America and Western culture and values than the China virus did to world health.

David Horowitz's Top Ten America-Hating Professors teaching at American colleges and universities

#1: Nicholas De Genova, University of Houston

Nicholas De Genova is currently the chair of the Comparative Cultural Studies Department at the University of Houston, but he first made his mark as an America-hating academic when, as an assistant professor at Columbia University in the spring of 2003, he spoke at a rally against the just-launched Iraq War, calling for "a million more Mogadishus." De Genova was referencing the horrific carnage that resulted from a 1993 American military action in the Somali capital where 18 Americans and hundreds of Somalis perished.

The professor later attempted to clarify his remarks in a letter to the *Columbia Spectator*, writing that "imperialism and white supremacy have been constitutive of U.S. nation-state formation and U.S. nationalism," rejecting "all forms of U.S. patriotism" and declaring his desire to see "the defeat of the U.S. war machine." De Genova added, "My rejection of U.S. nationalism is an appeal to liberate our own political imaginations such that we might usher in a radically different world in which we will not remain the prisoners of U.S. global domination." In short, he wished for the defeat and downfall of the United States on the world stage. In the nearly two decades since his infamous statement at that anti-war rally, De Genova has not backed away from controversy—though his extreme and violence-abetting statements appear to have aided, rather than injured, his academic career.

In an article published in *Spectre* in June 2020, De Genova claimed that policing exists to enforce white supremacy. "In short," he declared, "policing in the United States is inextricable from the perpetration and perpetuation of racism." Later in that same piece, De Genova blamed police racism for the violent rioting and looting that occurred in the wake of George Floyd's death and condoned the rioters' destructive actions: "Confronted with the obscenity of law enforcement that repeatedly proves itself to be nothing less than torture and murder, the enraged response of aggrieved racially oppressed communities repeatedly finds itself with no other option than rioting and other forms of defiance toward the law." Professor De Genova goes on to claim that "most of what have been branded as 'riots' have, in fact, been veritable urban insurrections, albeit largely spontaneous insurgencies against the systemic violence of the racial state." *Are you also hearing this propaganda from the rioters? This slander is what our children are being taught about our great country. This dangerous Goebbels type propaganda gives academic license for radical thought and destructive actions being committed in our cities by a brainwashed generation.*

In another recent article, De Genova slanders President Trump as a White Supremacist and a fascist, writing "Trump's signature slogan, 'Make America Great Again'—becomes inseparable from a retreat into internecine racial tribalism: in short, White nationalism. And White nationalism, invigorated by an ethos of civil war, spells fascism." As a Marxist, De Genova believes that capitalism—the economic system that has enabled America to grow into the most powerful nation on earth—is inherently evil. He writes of the "endemic and irreconcilable struggle of capital, vampire-like, to cannibalize the creative energies of human life, and the struggle of human life against its objectification and alienation."

De Genova has also repeatedly made anti-Semitic remarks praising anti-Israel suicide bombers and bizarrely stating that "the heritage of the victims of the Holocaust belongs to the Palestinian people. The state of Israel has no claim to the heritage of the Holocaust." For his ardent desire to see the American military and American power go down in flames, De Genova belongs atop the list of the Top Ten America-Hating Professors.

#2: Joshua Clover, University of California-Davis

Joshua Clover is a Professor of English and Comparative Literature at UC-Davis and a self-declared communist who promotes the murder of law enforcement officers and sees life and property destroying riots as a legitimate means of political expression. Clover is the author of *"Riot. Strike. Riot.: The New Era of Uprisings."* He chooses to see riots as a positive good and has stated that they deserve "an adequate theory." He praises "moments of shattered glass and fire" because they interrupt "the grim continuity of daily life." While most Americans proudly use the phrase "from sea to shining sea" to portray the great promise and opportunity of the American nation, Professor Clover takes something entirely different from the phrase. "When you hear the phrase 'from sea to shining sea,' you would be forgiven for shivering at the destruction it signifies," he has written. "It comes with shivers because it arises from actual historical experience. It is a lyrical phrase that also means massive, brutal dispossession because that's how it went down; without that dispossession, no sea to sea, shining or otherwise."

Clover is also an extreme cop-hater who has called for murdering police officers. In a 2015 interview with SF Weekly he stated, "People think that cops need to be reformed. They need to be killed." He echoed these thoughts on Twitter, writing "I am thankful that every living cop will one day be dead, some by their own hand, some by others, too many of old age #letsnotmakemore" and "I mean, it's easier to shoot cops when their backs are turned, no?" When asked about these comments in 2019, Clover refused to backtrack. "I think we can all agree that the most effective way to end any violence against officers is the complete and immediate abolition of the police," he said. *Again, can you open your eyes and see how such libelous insane talk by someone being paid by California taxpayers could lead to the rash of cop killings and the 'defund the police' movement? Of course, the defund movement is opposed by the majority of Blacks who live in the neighborhoods most impacted, not in Davis.*

He justifies his views by arguing that the role of police is "fundamentally anti-Black, fundamentally White Supremacist" and "fundamentally in defense of capital." "The police oversee commodity," he said in an interview with *Mother Jones*. "One of their main historical functions is making sure that property stays property... We live in the United States where there's a history of chattel slavery, of making humans the property of other humans, and in that sense, the police, as keepers of property, are always going to be the keepers of a racial order. In that sense, the police role in making sure property stays property is fundamentally anti-Black, fundamentally White Supremacist, at the same time that it's fundamentally in defense of capital." Clover is correct only in the sense that a key function of the police is protecting private property and the rule of law—key tenets of American law and society.

Perhaps unsurprisingly, Clover is also extremely hostile to the Jewish state of Israel. He has called Zionism "eliminationist nationalism" and stated that "Israel is not a people." He has stated, apparently without irony, "I hold the simple idea, as a communist, that centralized, authoritarian states are not a very good way to organize society, and so I hope it will be uncontroversial if I say that Israel should be ended." Given that every self-declared communist country to exist in human history was ruled by an authoritarian despot, and that Israel is run by a democratically elected legislature, such musings are the height of absurdity.

In the same article, Clover defended Palestinian terrorism and violence against Israel: "We must always be on the side of rock-throwers both imagined and real. Not so as to forge a new state where there was none, but, where the state is preserved by constant and absolute violence, to instead bring it to an end."

Professor Clover's endorsement of the murder of law enforcement officers, his denigration of America and its principles, and his defense of riots over the rule of law demonstrate why he belongs among the Top Ten America-Hating Professors.

#3: Seif Da'na, University of Wisconsin-Parkside

Seif Da'na, a Palestinian-American Professor of Sociology at the University of Wisconsin-Parkside, has promoted the absurd conspiracy theory that COVID-19 may have been leaked from the U.S. Army medical command installation Fort Detrick and claims that Adolf Hitler did not do "anything out of the ordinary."

In a March 29, 2020 interview on Manar TV, a Lebanese station run by the terrorist organization Hezbollah, Da'na used the fact that we have yet to identify the exact origin of the virus in China to claim that the disease had in fact originated in an American military facility. This is the same lie being propagated by the Communist Chinese government in an effort to deflect responsibility for the worldwide spread of the virus. "As of now, there is no [coronavirus] patient zero in China," Da'na said in the interview. "Therefore, we do not talk here about a conspiracy as much as we talk about the leaking of the viruses from a laboratory at Fort Detrick in the United States."

"Perhaps this leaking was not deliberate," Da'na added. "We are not talking here about a conspiracy, even though the U.S. annihilated two whole cities in Japan during WWII, despite this being unnecessary. They were already winning the war, but they still used the nuclear bombs."

Manar TV, the station which aired Da'na's interview, is considered a "terrorist entity" by the U.S. government. In that same interview, Da'na claimed that the novel coronavirus is in fact no more dangerous to the world than Western economic policies. "[Regarding the coronavirus] – more people die every year not just from diseases that you can get vaccinated for, like malaria – from which half a million people [die] in Africa – but also from the West's economic policies – at least in the 20th century and the two decades of the 21st century," Da'na declared. "More people die every year from the consequences of these economic issues than from what is happening now."

Not content to leave it at that, Da'na went on to equate the actions of European colonialists as equivalent to those of Nazi leader Adolf Hitler. "This is exactly like what happened with Hitler," he said. "Hitler did not do anything out of the ordinary. He did not do anything that had not been done by the Europeans before... Hitler came to be viewed as Satan just because he did what he did in Europe."

Speaking at a 2015 meeting of the Northwestern University chapter of the Hamas-linked hate group, Students for Justice in Palestine, Da'na accused Israel of "conquer[ing] both land and labor" in Palestine, thus, he claims, expelling Palestinians from history and initiating ethnic cleansing.

For his spread of vicious anti-American conspiracy theories on the coronavirus and his ambivalence about the evils of Adolf Hitler, Da'na deserves to be named to the list of the Top Ten America-Hating Professors.

#4: Angela Davis, University of California-Santa Cruz

Professor Angela Davis is best known for her violent tenure in the Black Panther Party. In 1970, the radical activist provided an arsenal of weapons to the group which they then used to kill a California judge in a failed attempt to free fellow Black Panther George Jackson, who was also Davis's lover. Davis also proudly became a member of the Communist Party, expressing her support for Soviet Dictator Joseph Stalin and cheering on the Soviet invasion of Czechoslovakia in 1968, claiming that "the only path of liberation for black people is that which leads toward complete and radical overthrow of the capitalist class." She also received the Lenin "Peace Prize" from the communist police state of East Germany in 1979.

Despite this disreputable history, Davis has not only survived but thrived in the cutthroat world of academia, earning teaching positions at esteemed colleges and universities including UCLA, Rutgers, Vassar, San Francisco State, and UC-Santa Cruz where she is currently listed as a Distinguished Professor Emerita. Even through the self-destruction of the communist empire and the historical recounting of Stalin's crimes, Davis has not retracted or moderated her hate-America beliefs.

In the wake of George Floyd's death by a police officer in May 2020, and the resulting race riots and burning of large sections of Democrat-run cities across America, Davis spoke of the riots as being part of a "transformative" movement for revolution and social change. "This is a perfect example of our being able to seize this moment and turn it into something that's radical and transformative," she declared.

In other comments, she emphasized the revolutionary nature of the protests and her desire to see them bring about the abolition of the police: "The protests offered people an opportunity to join in this collective demand to bring about deep change, radical change. Defund the police; abolish policing as we know it now." *Do you see how these inane radical propaganda and myths like systemic racism; socialism is good thing; and police targeting Blacks helped brainwash students particularly on the Left-coast?*

Ever a Communist, Davis made clear that she blames America's economic system of capitalism, which has lifted millions out of poverty, for leading to the oppression of Black Americans. "This is … a racial reckoning. A reexamination of the role that racism has played in the creation of the United States of America," she said. "But I think we have to talk about capitalism. Capitalism has always been racial capitalism. Wherever we see capitalism, we see the influence and the exploitation of racism."

The radical professor made clear her further contempt for America by claiming that "the history of the United States of America is a history of racism."

Regarding statues of Christopher Columbus and America's founders, she declared that "it's natural that people would try to bring down those symbols." *Can you guess where the 'pull the statutes' movement originated?*

Professor Davis has also repeatedly directed her animosity toward the Jewish nation of Israel. She supported the terrorist Palestinian Liberation Organization (PLO) led by Yasser Arafat in the 1970s and has repeatedly aligned herself with anti-Israel, anti-Semitic organizations which are connected to terror networks. She is a supporter of the Hamas-funded Boycott, Divestment, and Sanctions (BDS) movement against Israel and has alleged that Israel is conducting "flagrant injustices" and a "massacre against the Palestinians of Gaza." *Do you wonder why the only foreign policy issue of the BLM movement is anti-Semitic Zionism?*

Davis's constant incitement of revolution in America and the overthrow of economic and law enforcement systems, abetted by her demonstrated hatred for the principles of our nation's founding, makes her one of the Top Ten America-Hating Professors.

#5: Robin DiAngelo, University of Washington-Seattle

Robin DiAngelo is an Affiliate Associate Professor of Education at the University of Washington-Seattle and a vitriolic race hustler who—despite being white herself—seeks to profit off of condemning all Whites as guilty of racism and demonizing America as built on "white supremacy."

In addition to her work as an academic, DiAngelo earns vast sums as a "workplace diversity trainer," speaking to large corporate gatherings. She is the author of the racist screed *White Fragility: Why It's So Hard for White People to Talk about Racism*, a book that has been lauded by the mainstream media and embraced as doctrine by the Left. *Do you see how this racist cancer is now spreading from malignant cells populating our universities into our businesses and down into our elementary schools?*

"My psychosocial development was inculcated in the water of white supremacy," DiAngelo states of her upbringing in California. But she is not speaking only of her own upbringing but that of every American. "The default of our society is the reproduction of racism. It's built into every system and every institution," she claims. DiAngelo makes her contempt for America clear in her speeches and writings.

"I now understand racism as a system, as a deeply imbedded system, a system that our country was founded on and that all our institutions were created out of," she states in a video of one of her addresses. "And every institution reinforces this system. And it's a system of unequal power."

In DiAngelo's world, all white people, regardless of their individual beliefs or characteristics, are racist, and should acknowledge their inherent guilt into being born into "a system of racial inequality that benefits Whites at the expense of people of color." This is her way of saying they were born in America.

"All white people are invested in and collude with racism," she claims. When white individuals attempt to deny this inherent racism, they show themselves to be guilty of "White fragility" or a lack of stamina for "enduring racial stress." By contrast, in DiAngelo's view, people of color cannot be racist because they lack institutional power in our society. These views are at odds with the founding principles of our American republic which emphasize individual action and responsibility, not collective guilt.

In a recent article in *The Atlantic*, African-American professor John McWhorter called DiAngelo's book a "racist tract," adding that "few books about race have more openly infantilized black people than this supposedly authoritative tome."

DiAngelo's malicious and hyperbolic characterization of America and its White population as racist makes her one of the Top Ten America-Hating Professors.

#6: Ibram X. Kendi, Boston University

Kendi is the Andrew W. Mellon Professor in Humanities at Boston University and also the Founding Director of the Boston University Center for Antiracist Research. He is the author of the bestselling book, *How To Be An Anti-Racist*, which has been widely embraced by the Left and the mainstream media. Kendi has made a career out of identifying "metastatic" racism in every possible aspect of American life and society and using his observations to undermine America's proud history and founding principles.

Kendi is determined to use America's original sin of slavery to discredit the entire American project. He has repeatedly used the metaphor of cancer to describe racism, calling it "literally a metastatic cancer that has been ravaging the American body from the beginning."

In a recent essay in *The Atlantic*, he writes, "From the beginning of the American project, the powerful individual has been battling for his constitutional freedom to harm, and the vulnerable community has been battling for its constitutional freedom from harm. Both freedoms are inscribed into the U.S. Constitution and into the American psyche. The history of the United States, the history of Americans, is the history of reconciling the unreconcilable: individual freedom and community freedom. There is no way to reconcile the enduring psyche of the slaveholder with the enduring psyche of the enslaved."

The radical professor goes on to wield the example of the Coronavirus as emblematic of the way African-Americans have been subjugated in all aspects of our society: "There is something about living through a deadly pandemic that cuts open the shell, removes the flesh, and finds the very core of American existence: the slaveholder clamoring for *his* freedom to infect, and the enslaved clamoring for *our* freedom from infection."

In another article, Kendi quotes Malcolm X's statement, "We don't see any American dream. We've experienced only the American nightmare"—a nightmare that in Kendi's view is still ongoing "from Minneapolis to Louisville, from Central Park to untold numbers of black coronavirus patients parked in hospitals, on unemployment lines, and in graves."

In yet another piece, unsubtly titled "We're Still Living and Dying in the Slaveholders' Republic," Kendi attempts to draw a parallel between President Trump's insistence that we open up the economy after the Coronavirus shutdowns and nineteenth century slaveholders' failure to free their slaves: "Slaveholders could have responded to apocalyptic antislavery resistance by abolishing slavery and redistributing land and rights and resources to black and White and indigenous peoples alike. Likewise, Trump could have responded to deepening economic pain from stay-at-home orders by imploring Congress to provide enough public assistance that the community could be free of economic and bodily worry." Absurdly, he slams President Trump for "want[ing] Americans to view Republicans as freeing the individual, and Democrats as confining the free individual," as if that wasn't the factual case.

Kendi believes that "All policies, ideas and people are either being racist or anti-racist. Racist policies yield racial inequity; anti-racist policies yield racial equity." Naturally, "anti-racist" policies, in his view, are the policies promoted by the radical Left.

He envisions an "anti-racist society" as "Where free, high-quality healthcare is as universal as basic incomes and fresh food? Where instead of stocking prisons with poor and mentally disabled people of color, we stock those people's communities with high-paying jobs and mental health services? Where instead of enslaving and traumatizing prisoners, we are healing and restoring them? Where guns are as controlled as police officers fearing for their lives?"

"What I mean by anti-racist policies are policies like Medicare for all, or high-quality healthcare for all that reduce racial inequities. Policies like legalizing marijuana, policies that aggressively go after climate change..." he clarified in an interview.

Ibram Kendi's castigation of America and its citizens for their purported racial sins, and his manipulative use of that accusation to promote a far-left political agenda, make him one of the Top Ten America-Hating Professors.

#7: Christine Fair, Georgetown University

Christine Fair is a Distinguished Associate Professor in the Security Studies Program at Georgetown University who prides herself on her vulgarity and offensiveness, which she wields as a weapon to upset the social order.

During the U.S. Senate hearings to confirm Judge Brett Kavanaugh to the Supreme Court, Professor Fair took to Twitter to condemn the Republican legislators who defended Kavanaugh against unproven and wholly unsubstantiated allegations that he had participated in a sexual assault decades earlier. "Look at thus [sic] chorus of entitled white men justifying a serial rapist's arrogated entitlement," Fair tweeted, referencing Senator Lindsey Graham's comments defending Kavanaugh. "All of them deserve miserable deaths while feminists laugh as they take their last gasps. Bonus: we castrate their corpses and feed them to swine? Yes." *Dr. Ford, who perpetuated this hoax, should have been jailed. Did you know she pulled down her anti-Trump website before her accusations, taught her girlfriend how to beat a polygraph test to get into the FBI, and asked that same friend to contact some high-school acquaintance of Ford's? The woman contacted was asked to lie about being at the party where the alleged rape took place. Does Ford belong in the same category as the black prostitute who made up a similar lie about the Duke Lacrosse team?*

Twitter briefly suspended Fair's account for her violent commentary, before restoring it and then suspending it again. "Fox News Failed to silence me. Thank you all for sending @Twitter messages of support. I do NOT and NEVER have condoned violence," she claimed, despite having just wished "miserable deaths" on Republican legislators. "My tweet, as I have explained, was an attempt to make YOU as UNCOMFORTABLE as I am using the language of the abuse I receive[d] by the hundreds."

"GOP doesn't care about women," Fair tweeted on another occasion. "We knew this. Fuck them."

In Fair's view, it is not only Republicans but also many feminists who allegedly don't care enough about women—or are perhaps blinded to their chains. Fair publishes a blog which is profanely titled "Tenacious Hellpussy: A Nasty Woman Posting from the Frontlines of Fuckery." In one recent essay, Fair denigrates the "White saviorism" of "American feminists" who seek to rescue women in third world countries from the evils of enforced hijab wearing, female infanticide and feticide, female genital mutilation, dowry crimes, and Sati. The professor claims that even in America, these feminists "have never been as liberated as they imagined." "While the United States has long been a terrible place to be a woman for many women, it's getting worse not better," Fair declares.

Professor Fair has also repeatedly demonstrated her complete lack of respect for divergent political views. When one of her former colleagues at Georgetown, Prof. Asra Nomani, wrote an article about why she decided to vote for Donald Trump despite her status as a "lifelong liberal" and a Muslim immigrant, Fair could not contain her rage. She instigated a monthlong tirade of insults and vitriol directed at Nomani, calling her a "wench," a "fraud," and a "fame-mongering clown show" in a series of public tweets, and adding, "FUCK YOU. GO TO HELL." Fair also resorted to using Urdu, Nomani's native language, to insult her, calling her "chutiya," or "the equivalent of a 'f**ker' in my native Urdu," Nomani alleged, as well as "bevkuf," which means "idiot." *Sounds like she should be on serious meds, do you agree?*

One tweet sent to Nomani by Fair read, "Yes, @AsraNomani, I've written you off as a human being. Your vote helped normalize Nazis in D.C. What don't you understand, you clueless [sic] dolt?" If Professor Fair is willing and able to unleash such hostility against a former professional colleague, one wonders how she reacts to students who resist her far-left views.

Fair has also voiced anti-Semitic conspiracy theories, claiming in a speech that President Trump had been influenced by Israel to "sabotage" the "Iran agreement" on nuclear weapons. *Do you wonder why democratic Israel is the main foreign relations target of the radical Left and BLM?*

For her utter contempt and harassment of those who hold different political views and her incitement of violence toward elected officials, Fair deserves her place among the Top Ten America-Hating Professors.

#8: Cornel West, Princeton University

Cornel West is a Professor of Religion and African-American Studies at Princeton University who has used his privileged status as one of academia's elite to disparage both America and Israel and to attack the foundations of American capitalism and the rule of law.

In the world of academia, West is a superstar. He has been awarded over twenty honorary degrees and a National Book Award. He has taught at Harvard, Yale, and Princeton, and has authored or edited over twenty books which are assigned for required reading in college courses across America. He is considered a revered cultural figure of the Left.

Despite his great success as an African-American man in academia, West views America as a "racist patriarchal" nation where "white supremacy" is rampant and White Americans continue "to resist fully accepting the humanity of blacks." "It goes without saying," West states, "that a profound hatred of African people ... sits at the center of American civilization."

"I think we are witnessing America as a failed social experiment," West said in a CNN interview held during the riots occurring in American cities in the aftermath of George Floyd's death. "What I mean by that," he continued his diatribe, "is that the history of black people for over 200 and some years in America has been looking at America's failure. Its capitalist economy could not generate and deliver in such a way that people could live lives of decency. The nation-state, its criminal justice system, its legal system could not generate protection of rights and liberties. And now our culture, of course, is so market-driven—everything for sale, everybody for sale—it can't deliver the kind of nourishment for the soul, for meaning, for purpose."

West has also attacked President Donald Trump as a "neo-fascist gangster in the White House" and issued not-so-subtle warnings that America must either submit to Marxism or descend into violent revolution. *Have you heard these exact words coming out of the mouths of BLM leaders? I have!*

"The system cannot reform itself," West said. He claims we must accept a "nonviolent revolution" consisting in "the democratic sharing of power, resources, wealth and respect"—in other words, socialism. "If we don't get that kind of sharing, you're going to get more violent explosions," he stated.

A longtime Marxist West is a close personal friend to notorious anti-Semite Louis Farrakhan, who has referred to Judaism as a "gutter religion" and to Adolf Hitler as "a very great man." In 2014, West wrote that the crimes of the Islamic terror group Hamas—which include suicide bombings and the kidnap and murder of Israeli citizens—"pale in the face of the U.S.-supported Israeli slaughters of innocent civilians." West supports the Hamas-funded Boycott, Divestment, and

Sanctions (BDS) movement to weaken and destroy Israel and has demonized the Jewish state by claiming that it sanctions the killing of "precious Palestinian babies" despite the Israeli military's intensive attempts to avoid civilian casualties in their defensive response to Hamas's aggression.

Professor West's numerous comments and outright falsehoods demonizing and delegitimizing both America and Israel make him one of the Top Ten America-Hating Professors.

#9: James M. Thomas, University of Mississippi

Dr. James M. Thomas is an Associate Professor of Sociology at the University of Mississippi (commonly referred to as 'Ole Miss) who was recently awarded tenure at that institution in spite of a history of extreme anti-American tweets that smear mainstream conservatives as fascists and advocate criminal action against Republican elected officials.

In a tweet from January 2019, Thomas, who tweets under the descriptive moniker @Insurgent_Prof, wrote, "MAGA teens are modern day Hitlerjugend [Hitler Youth]. Got a uniform and everything."

On Oct. 6, 2018, in response to calls from NBC's Joe Scarborough for civility, Thomas tweeted, "Don't just interrupt a senator's meal, y'all. Put your whole damn fingers in their salads. Take their apps and distribute them to the other diners. Bring boxes and take their food home with you on the way out. They don't deserve your civility."

"This is troubling and disappointing to see from one of our university professors," tweeted Mississippi Governor Phil Bryant, after Thomas's tweets urging aggression against Republicans went viral. "There is no place in a civilized society, and particularly on a college campus, for urging individuals to harass anyone."

Thomas's failure to respect others' opinions is a common theme in his writings. In a 2019 opinion piece for the *Jackson Free Press*, Thomas wrote of Confederate monuments: "There are those who believe that the men these monuments honor were just men of their time, and should be judged against the values of their era and not ours. They must also believe that the nearly four million enslaved men, women and children either had no values, or shared the values of their enslavers."

Professor Thomas has also used his Twitter account to advocate for "revolutionary change," a term which he means literally. On August 11, 2020,

Thomas tweeted: "Harris is an excellent VP pick, which of course is a point of entry for genuine criticism. But like, what thinking person sees the Presidential ticket as a legitimate path toward revolutionary change? That always come from the people (see Lenin, Fanon, Malcolm, Davis, etc)." *Are you wondering why BLM and Antifa are out today with signs reading America is finished?*

Thomas also reserves some of his harshest words for America's President, Donald Trump, and his supporters. "Supporting Trump makes you a White Supremacist, whether you think of yourself as one or not," he tweeted. "Trumpism is an authoritarian ethno-nationalist movement, whose core principle is that America is and should be a country run by and for white people..." "Any news outlet that carried that Trump rally and reported it as anything other than a fascist rally failed their ethical obligation," he tweeted on another occasion.

For his vitriolic condemnation of Americans who don't share his far-left opinions, his advocacy of revolution, and his urging of criminal action against Republican legislators, Professor Thomas deserves to be known as one of the Top Ten America-Hating Professors.

#10: Russell Rickford, Cornell University

Russell Rickford is an associate professor of history at Cornell University, as well as an America-hating, Israel-hating, enemy of capitalism.

Professor Rickford has made himself a sought-after speaker in far-left circles by denouncing America as a "White Supremacist" nation and its economic system of capitalism as inherently racist. "The architects of our security state, an incarcerous state, a warfare state, share a vision," he said at a 2017 rally in support of DACA; "a vision to increase profits and maintain the White Supremacist structures upon which capitalism depend."

Rickford further claimed that capitalist structures are drivers of inequality in America, rather than a pathway to economic mobility and societal affluence. "It is a land of barricades and checkpoints; a prison nation," he said of America. "Make no mistake, the folks who are now trying to dismantle any semblance of protection for workers and immigrants are dangerous. Their goal is the supremacy of wealth and power over human need and aspiration. They want absolute freedom from capitalism and absolute slavery for the rest of us."

The far-left professor also promotes his view that Whites are nearly universally racist. "There's a sliver, a sliver of White America that hates white supremacy and that hates capitalism," he declared at a Black Lives Matter rally in 2016.

"We've got to build grassroots, anti-racist movement to defeat capitalism altogether and it's not going to happen at the ballot box," he added, seeming to endorse violence and revolution. "There can be no human system under capitalism. Capitalism is an anti-human system."

Rickford was one of over 100 black writers and scholars to sign a letter endorsing Bernie Sanders' campaign for President. The letter claimed that *"A Sanders presidency would go a long way toward creating a safer and more just world,"* citing the candidate's support for free college education, reparations for slavery, and the cancellation of student debt. The letter also stated, *"we see Sanders' commitment to challenging the ravages of racial capitalism as connected to an ongoing and ideologically diverse Black Freedom Movement."*

Rickford is a founding member of the Cornell Coalition for Inclusive Democracy, an organization pledged to make Cornell a sanctuary campus for undocumented students, thus deliberately obstructing federal immigration law.

At one of the organization's protests in 2017, Rickford was one of hundreds who "took a knee" to protest alleged police brutality against African-Americans. But his comments on that occasion condemned not only the police but all of American society, including the very university that employs him.

"The truth is, Cornell is a bastion of white supremacy," Professor Rickford stated. "Our society is steeped in white supremacy," he said in an interview. "Why should we expect Cornell, an enterprise built on stolen land, to be any different?"

Unwilling to stop at demonizing America, Rickford turned his enmity toward the Jewish state of Israel, and led the crowd in chants of "Free Palestine."

Professor Rickford has also repeatedly pledged his support for the Hamas-funded Boycott, Divestment, and Sanctions (BDS) campaign against Israel and has signed petitions which demonize Israel as an apartheid state and compare the treatment of Palestinians in Israel to the treatment of Black Americans under Jim Crow.

In his book *Beyond Boundaries*, published in 2011, Rickford argued that America's support of Israel was responsible for the September 11 terrorist attacks. "The U.S. media and opinion makers repeatedly went out of their way to twist facts and to distort the political realities of the Middle East by insisting that Osama bin Laden group's murderous assaults had nothing to do with Israel's policies toward the Palestinians," he wrote. "Nobody else in the world, with the possible exception of Israelis, really believes that."

Professor Rickford's defamation of Israel and absurd characterization of America as a "White Supremacist" nation, coupled with his contempt for the economic system of capitalism that has made it a leader among nations, make him a clear choice for the Top Ten America-Hating Professors. *Do you finally understand how this growing cadre of venomous radicals has helped brainwash generations of Americans? Do you believe President Biden or VP Harris would ever stand up against or give tacit support to this wave of anti-American, anti-Semitic, anti-White, anti-cops, anti-fossil fuels, pro-socialist, pro illegal immigration, pro reparations, pro terrorist, pro free everything agenda?*

To keep the thread running through this book, let me summarize: The civil rights movement that welcomed Whites did a one hundred eighty degree turn and instead gave a pulpit to radical Black Power leaders to spew and practice hate against Whites, the government, and the military. In place of justified condemnation, the radicals instead received government support and legitimacy. Furthermore, when the heart of the Civil Rights Act, that there shall be no advantage due to race etc., was cut out and replaced by mandated racial quotas, the country was flooded with opportunists practicing collusion, fraud, and extortion to get rich. Moreover, we learned how the Left joined the Black revolutionaries and the devastating impact this new diversity, left-wing complex had on all levels of education as well as most sectors of society.

Chapter 6
FUNDERS AND FRIENDS OF THE RADICAL LEFT

Difference between Liberal and Conservative - Liberals think we should be equal at the finish line; Conservatives think we should be equal at the starting line.

Anonymous

It is time to identify some of the most destructive progressive organizations and highlight a case that shows the massive corruption and fraud that happens when the diversity/left-wing complex colludes with government allies. Many left-wing nongovernmental organizations (NGOs) have good social justice mission statements and have assumed the role of impartial judges and recorders of perceived human rights abuses all over the world, and receive large amounts of funding from liberals and left-wing foundations. Unfortunately, what is not out in public is their non-stated malicious agenda. These biased organizations are not the good housekeeping seal for social justice and should not be relied on to objectively report on human rights or any other issue. Let's shine some light on the stains on the very fabric clothing these groups:

Tides Foundation

Few Americans are aware of a large network of far-left philanthropists and foundations in America dedicated to destroying the American way of life, our Judeo/Christian culture, and our free enterprise system. They seek to remove America from its constitutional foundations and move it toward European-style socialism. A little known group called the Tides Foundation and its related group, the Tides Center, is coordinating much of this effort.

The Tides Foundation is a San Francisco, California-based 501(c)(3) non-profit social change corporation founded June 4, 1976. The Tides Foundation is largely credited with pioneering anonymous "dark money" transactions through advising and directing outside funds to politically liberal and progressive organizations in the areas of the environment, health care, labor issues, immigrant rights, gay rights, women's rights; and activism against gun rights, industrial development, and corporations. The Tides Foundation is the philanthropic Left's best-kept secret. From Greenpeace to the anti-Israel J Street, there's hardly a left-wing group that hasn't taken Tides money. Using a sophisticated funding model, Tides has grown into the leading platform for laundering away ties between wealthy donors and the radical causes they fund—while generating hundreds of new organizations along the way.

Tides Foundation's skill at keeping donors anonymous and grant recipient's secret became a public issue, bringing well warranted IRS attention and measures to separate its most tenuous programs from its normal grant-making operation. For all the fuss the Left makes about "getting money out of politics," their actions tell a vastly different story. When conservative donors like the Koch brothers make or facilitate anonymous donations, liberals cry "dark money" and bemoan the supposed lack of accountability. If liberals truly wanted to get money out of politics, they would need to start with their own Tides organizations, which pioneered the very practice they claim to hate.

There are several ways that Tides advances the Left's agenda. It collects money from liberal donors and gives that money to left-wing extremists making it difficult to trace the source of the funds. If a donor wants to give money to a cause for which a group does not exist, Tides will set up such an organization. It also rents office space to liberal organizations.

Taxpayer funded radical causes

It seems the liberal Tide Foundation and its offshoot Tides Center has also been given the combination to the Treasury vault. From 2002 to 2013, they together received $82.7 million in grants from the Federal Government. These grants support some of the 133 Tides Center projects. Tides Center projects include Ferguson activists and anti-Semites, but the tax data is unclear on which specific projects the government was backing. **I expect more government funding of left-wing causes going to the victimization and divisity mob. Do you?**

Cut for the radical Left Godfathers

One of the most valuable services that Tides provides is "fiscal sponsorship" for new left-leaning organizations. Sponsorship requires a fee of 9 percent or 15 percent of annual revenues depending upon the source; the fee may be adjusted after the first year of activity. In exchange for these fees, organizations can use the Tides Center's 501(c)(3) tax status and gain access to the Center's accounting, human resources, and legal services. Over the years, Tides claims to have sponsored over 1,400 "social ventures." Once a sponsored organization matures sufficiently, it can become an independent organization. Tides have spun off a number of these organizations, including People for the American Way and the Natural Resources Defense Council.

Not content with just causing problems in America, Tides has waded into Canada too. There, it funded a campaign to halt the development of the oil sands in the province of Alberta. However, the new conservative premier of Alberta, Jason Kenney, has made it clear that he is tired of the shenanigans funded by Tides and will be fighting back.

Liberal billionaire George Soros also supports the Tides Center. Hopefully one day a real journalist if one still exists, or maybe even *60 Minutes,* will follow the money trail from the Obama administration to the Tides Foundation and back to the administration's friends and favored projects. Former DOJ's Secretaries Holder and Lynch also deserve special scrutiny regarding their role in the disposition of fines and contributions in lieu of court proceedings from Wall Street firms and corporations, aka the "DOJ slush fund".

The Tides Foundation, when I wrote my book and still may be, was run by Drummond Pike, a close ally of Soros who works as a gateway for liberal donors, accepting donations from individuals or organizations and then passing them on to liberal causes. *Mother Jones*—which attacks conservative philanthropy, says: "the Tides Foundation ... gives out tens of millions of dollars each year to thousands of left-leaning groups in the U.S. and overseas." Over the years, the empire has grown, and now the Tides Network consists of the Tides Foundation, the Tides Center, Tides Inc., the Tides Two Rivers Fund, and Tides Advocacy. In 2017, Tides had revenues of over $470 million; it has nearly $400 million in assets under management.

The Tides Center, founded in 1996, is an even more nebulous organization. Instead of channeling donations from donors to nonprofits, the Tides Center sponsors liberal and progressive startups as offshoots. The organization's website states: "Fiscally sponsored projects of Tides are not separate and isolated entities; rather, they are an integral part of Tides. We receive charitable donations and grants on behalf of our fiscally sponsored projects." In short, every single one of its current 133 sponsored projects is a direct part of the Tides Center.

In July 2014, syndicated columnist Michelle Malkin, who I admire very much, wrote an exposé of liberal dark-money hypocrisy that included revealing information on Tides: "The Tides Center and its parent, the Tides Foundation, in turn have seeded some of the country's most radical activist groups of the Left, including the communist-friendly United for Peace and Justice, the jihadist-friendly National Lawyers Guild and the grievance-mongering Council on American-Islamic Relations."

Other Tides projects are just as radical: The Catalyst Project, an "anti-racist" group helped support the Ferguson riots and also trained one of the leaders of Madison, Wisconsin's white "racial justice" movement. Perhaps most alarming is Tides' anti-Semitic Arab Resource & Organization Center (AROC)—a group seeking to "empower and organize our community toward justice and self-determination." AROC's Executive Director, Lara Kiswani, was behind the October 2014 "Block the Boat" movement, which kept Israeli cargo ships from docking in California. Kiswani is also a part of the Boycott, Divestment, and Sanctions (BDS) movement, where she vehemently spews anti-Semitism. In November 2014 she stated, "Bringing down Israel really will benefit everyone in the world." The ACLU, another destructive Soros beneficiary is currently defending the hateful BDS rhetoric.

Big money doing big harm

Americans need to realize that this is how the anti-American anti-Semitic far Left in America is currently funded. Steve Baldwin of the Western Center for Journalism has done an exceptional job unmasking the financing and activities of the Tides groups and much of his findings follow:

The amount of funding the Tides Foundation and Tides Center provides the hard Left is unprecedented. Indeed, its financial disclosures show that the Tides Center has collected between $48 and $71 million each year since 1998, and the bulk of this revenue is contributed back to far-left groups. The closely aligned Tides Foundation has reported revenues of between $59 and $77 million every year since 2002. The two tax-exempt groups are supposed to be non-partisan, but they are exceptionally political and at the extreme edge regarding what non-profit groups are allowed to do politically. Altogether, both Tides groups have contributed over $500 million to the organized Left.

With the Tides Foundation and Tides Center now the largest funder of the Left in America today, Drummond Pike may be one of the most powerful men in America. This California-based, anti-war activist founded the Tides Foundation in 1976 and has been able to raise millions from America's leading foundations. What he promises them is anonymity since they are able to claim that they are simply contributing to a foundation self-described as being "committed to a society based on fairness, equal justice and equally shared economic opportunities..." That sounds fairly innocuous. The contributors, therefore, have some "deniability" about how their money is used, but Pike then directs this money to a massive network of hard-left groups. Indeed, Pike even states, "Anonymity is very important to most of the people we work with."

But this scam needs to come to an end and these donors need to be held accountable for their actions. It is extremely hypocritical for individuals and foundations whose wealth is due to America's free enterprise system to support causes that seek to destroy our way of life.

If you've ever heard the cliché "Limousine Liberal," this is a perfect description for these people. Let's shine a light on those who are paying the radicals that are looting, burning cites and destroying America's good name and values. Tides amassed its huge fortune by accepting money from virtually any source. In fact, Tides has accepted money from a Russian-supported organization, the Sea Change Foundation. In addition to the Russians, Tides has been funded by, among others, Soros' Open Society Foundations, the Rockefeller Brothers Fund, the Rockefeller Foundation, the David Rockefeller Fund, the Google Foundation, the ChevronTexaco Foundation, the Verizon Foundation, the AT&T Foundation, Ben & Jerry's Foundation, the Levi Strauss Foundation, the Buffett Early Childhood Fund, the Barbra Streisand Foundation, the Bill and Melinda Gates Foundation, the Turner Foundation, the Heinz Family Foundation, and the Service Employees International Union (SEIU).

Four of its largest supporters are as follows:

The Heinz Endowment – John Kerry's wife, Teresa Heinz Kerry, with this group has contributed at least $8.1 million to the Tides entities since 1994. This is the endowment created by the Heinz Food Empire which Teresa Heinz still has ownership interest in. Wonder why John Kerry was made Secretary of State under Obama? Follow the money trail from Tides to Obama, and government grants back to Tides.

George Soros – Soros is an eccentric billionaire agitator who has been funding anti-American groups and causes for a decade. He was convicted of insider trading in France in 2005 and is the leading force behind the effort to legalize all drugs. While he is the founder of the Open Society organization, he hides a great deal of his wealth in offshore banks that are considered to be safe havens for money laundering. He has given more than $7 million to the Tides Foundation.

Tides founder Drummond Pike serves as the treasurer for Soros' Democracy Alliance, which was a major funder of the now defunct **voter fraud** group ACORN.

Ford Foundation – This foundation consistently supports causes Henry Ford would never have supported and has become one of the largest donors to Tides, giving them millions of dollars since 1997. Moreover, the Ford Motor Company itself also gave money to Tides.

Rockefeller Foundation – They have been funding the Left in America for decades, so this is no surprise.

How ironic is it that many of these foundations originally endowed by America's first generation of great capitalists have decided to spit on that legacy. These captains of industry were on the front lines in the fight against efforts to move America toward socialism or assist terrorists who desired to destroy America. These foundations have been captured by the Left and now use the money created by free enterprise to attack the very system that enabled them to create their wealth.

The largest ($1,000,000+) Foundation Donors in 2013:

- Novo Foundation $6,395,927
- Ford Foundation $3,298,000
- The M.A.C. Global Foundation $2,683,438
- Wallace Global Fund $2,395,000
- New Field Foundation $2,340,000
- Annie E Casey Foundation $2,340,000
- Vanguard Charitable Endowment Program $2,320,000
- Fidelity Investments Charitable Gift Fund $2,128,789
- Foundation to Promote Open Society $2,014,350
- Natem Foundation Inc $1,598,356
- The Children's Investment Fund Foundation $1,500,000
- Pema Foundation $1,159,278
- Robert Wood Johnson Foundation $1,127,434
- Schwab Charitable Fund $1,070,842
- Broad Reach Foundation $1,000,000

Other large Tides donors include: the Pew Charitable Trust, the James Irvine Foundation, Citigroup Foundation, Kellogg Foundation, Hearst Foundation, Fannie Mae Foundation, JP Morgan Foundation, Bank of America Foundation, Chase Manhattan Foundation, Verizon Foundation, David & Lucile Packard Foundation, AT&T Foundation, Bell Atlantic Foundation, Citicorp Foundation, ARCO

Foundation, U.S. West Foundation, John D. MacArthur Foundation, ALCOA Foundation, Richard King Mellon Foundation, and the Carnegie Foundation.

What is really scary and threatening to America is the Tides organizations' success raising millions from fairly new foundations as well, such as foundations created by: Hewlett Packard, Verizon, ARCO, Citigroup, and AT&T. This potent combination of old and new wealth is posed to radically change America, due not only to how Tides Center and Foundation has combined this wealth to create and fund the hard-left infrastructure in America, but also due to how the media has unabashedly bought into all the myths and themes perpetrated by this network of groups.

Moreover, this is the same network used by the Obama campaign machine to manipulate public opinion. *Americans must wake up and send a strong message to the corporations linked to these foundations to stop funding these destructive radical groups.*

Over the course of its 33-year history, the Tides network has given hundreds of millions of dollars to anti-free enterprise groups, gun control groups, anti-private property groups, abortion rights groups, homosexual groups, groups engaged in voter fraud, anti-military groups, and organizations that seek to destroy America's constitutional basis. All told, over 100 leftist organizations have received funding from one of the two Tides groups. These two are currently the poster children for pushing a brainwashed generation toward America's Cultural Revolution:

The scum the Tides washed in:

Black Lives Matter

It is difficult to imagine anyone taking issue with the obvious, self-evident truth articulated by those three simple words. But when we peel away the veneer of deception, we find that Black Lives Matter (BLM) is in fact one of the most destructive, hateful, racist movements in living memory. Founded by a core group of revolutionaries who detest the United States and revere the nation's most devoted radical enemies, BLM is, at its essence, an ideological reincarnation of the Black Panther movement that flourished in the sixties.

An American Cultural Revolution is not peaceful protest!

Douglas McAdams, professor emeritus at Stanford, wrote: "It looks, for all the world, like these protests are achieving what very few do: setting in motion a period of significant, sustained, and widespread social, political change. We appear to be experiencing a social change tipping point—that is as rare in society as it is potentially consequential."

But who initiated this demand for change? After the initial protests following Floyd's death, public outrage was channeled—by trained activists working from a playbook—into manifestations that often grew riotous. The Black Lives Matter Global Network and Movement for Black Lives organizations have been the nerve center of the protests. They have been laying the groundwork for years, carefully cultivating a network that could organize protests when the moment came and amplify the message through social media.

Indeed, the leaders of the Black Lives Matter organizations fueling this summer's disturbances were trained by self-described Marxist revolutionaries who have long used the plight of Black Americans as justification for overthrowing America's constitutional order. They frankly admit that such "organizing" is the key to their goal of world revolution. Our political leaders owe it to themselves and to their fellow Americans to understand this blueprint before rhetorically embracing, let alone implementing, the radical changes that the protesters and rioters are demanding. *Are you still big supporters?*

Consider the BLM Global Network. The three women who thought up the BLM name in 2013, and then added the hashtag, later founded the global network. They remain in charge. As the *New York Times Magazine* explained, "While much of the nation's attention drifted away from Black Lives Matter, organizers and activists weren't dormant." One of the three founders, Alicia Garza, said that "the movement's first generation of organizers has been working steadily to become savvier and even more strategic over the past seven years, and have been joined by motivated younger leaders."

As the *Times* report elaborates, "One of the reasons there have been protests in so many places in the United States is the backing of organizations like Black Lives Matter. While the group isn't necessarily directing each protest, it provides materials, guidance and a framework for new activists." Deva Woodly, a professor at the New School, told *Times* reporter that, "those activists are taking to social media to quickly share protest details to a wide audience... These figures would make the recent protests the largest movement in the country's history."

Melina Abdullah, of BLM's Los Angeles chapter, told an interviewer that the demonstrations in that city had been strategically planned: "We built kind of an organizing strategy that said, build black community [to] disrupt white supremacy." Their targets, she said, were the neighborhoods where "white affluent folks" lived. "That's one of the reasons the marches and the protests were in Beverly Hills."

The goal of upending the American system is, moreover, also evident among the consultants now conducting "anti-racism training" within major corporations and foundations. These facilitators of anti-White struggle sessions disdain the capitalist system and seek its replacement—and their propaganda arm, the mainstream media, cheers them on.

If Black Lives Matter were a conservative group, its racist policies would be compared to the KKK and be labeled one of the most discredited and despised movements in American history. Can you imagine the elite Lefts reaction to a conservative movement built on a founding lie that has incited riots, inspired shootings of police, and correlated with an astounding and deadly increase in violent crime in America's major cities? But instead of being vilified, San Diego State is allowing some (this is what's wrong with American education) professor to give a course on BLM. *How screwed up is that?*

The publishing of a picture of a man that committed suicide by hanging, as a lynching, tells you all need to know about the type of low-lives that populate this organization. Indeed, the lead founder of BLM, Alicia Garza, reveres Assata Shakur the Marxist revolutionary, former Black Panther, and convicted cop-killer whose 1979 escape to Fidel Castro's Cuba was facilitated by the Weather Underground Organization and the Black Liberation Army. Other radicals Garza praised for their extraordinary accomplishments include Angela Davis (a Marxist and former Black Panther discussed earlier); Ella Baker (an avowed socialist with ties to the Communist Party USA and the Weather Underground); and Audre Lorde (a black Marxist feminist).

In recent months, you've likely heard some commentators—generally in reaction to Blacks' killings of fellow Blacks, or of police officers—tweak Garza's signature catch-phrase to suggest that All Lives Matter. But this type of ideological deviation is unacceptable to Miss Garza, who reminds us that Blacks are uniquely, systematically, and savagely targeted by the state in a way that no other people are. Stand with us in affirming Black lives, she declares. Not just all lives. Black lives. Please do not change the conversation by talking about how your life matters, too. The tired trope that we are all the same, Garza elaborates, serves only to perpetuate a level of White Supremacist domination. Black Lives Matter, but other lives? Well screw you.

In a 2015 interview, Patrice Cullors, another of the three founders, said that she and Garza were "trained Marxists." Abdullah, of the Los Angeles BLM chapter, was born a red-diaper baby—"Raised in the 70s, in the picket lines of Oakland, by activist parents," as the interviewer put it. Her paternal grandfather was Gunter Reimann, a member of the German Communist Party. Garza cut her organizing teeth as director of People Organized to Win Employment Rights (POWER), founded by Marxists Garth Ferguson, Patty Snitzler, Regina Douglas, Brian Russell, and Steve Williams. To Williams we owe the concept of "transformative organizing," which insists "that effective organizing for social change cannot simply be based on an apolitical and highly specific analysis of what is possible in the short term."

Cullors trained for a decade as a radical organizer in the Labor/Community Strategy Center, established and run by Eric Mann, a former member of the Weather Underground, the 1960s radical faction identified by the FBI as a domestic terrorist group. The "Weathermen" explained in their 1969 foundational statement that they were dedicated to "the destruction of U.S. imperialism and the achievement of classless world: world communism." The ties between the BLM Global Network and the Weathermen run deep. *National Review's* Andrew McCarthy revealed in a recent exposé that Weather Underground supporter Susan Rosenberg, whose 1984 sentence of 58 years in prison for possession "of 740 pounds of explosives, an Uzi submachine gun, an M-14 rifle, another rifle with a telescopic sight, a sawed-off shotgun, three 9-millimeter handguns in purses and boxes of ammunition" was commuted by President Bill Clinton, serves as vice chair of the board of directors of Thousand Currents—the radical, grant making institution that until July sponsored the BLM Global Network. Rosenberg was also sought on federal charges that she aided the 1979 prison escape of Joanne Chesimard, a Communist now living in Cuba, and whom Cullors quotes approvingly in her book *When They Call You a Terrorist*. (Since July, the Global Center has become "a project" of the Tides Center, another donor and supporter of the hard Left and its ideas.)

Mann, who served 18 months in prison for assault and battery and disturbing the peace, remains committed to overthrowing the American system and achieving world revolution through organizing. He calls his Strategy Center the "Harvard of Revolutionary graduate schools," or "the University of Caracas Revolutionary Graduate School." Mann says that the Center must teach people to organize strategically because "people think they can join an organization, and go out, and change the most dictatorial country in the world by just showing up. We don't think so. Organizing is a skill, is a vocation." During the Center's "six-month, intensive training program," classes offer a mix of theory—Mann's wife teaches a class on "problems of imperialism, women's studies, strategies and tactics"—with street activism, where students are held accountable. "How many people did you organize? How did it go?"

They also teach how to raise funds. "If we're going to build a revolution, you gotta ask people for money . . . the poor must pay for their own liberation, so we need to teach you to ask for money," Mann told the students. "I spend my time organizing mainly young people who want to be revolutionaries," Mann said. If you're not in organizing, "your life is meaningless," and you risk becoming a "bourgeois pig."

The challenge for students, Mann told the class, was to ask themselves, "Am I making decisions to change the system? Am I being tied to the masses?" Universities serve as vital centers of recruitment and radicalization. "The university," Mann explained, "is the place where Mao Zedong was radicalized, where Lenin and Fidel were radicalized, where Che was radicalized. The concept of the radical middle class of the colonized people, or in my case the radical middle class of the privileged people, is a model of a certain type of revolutionary." The goal for students, he told his class, was to "Take this country away from the white settler state, take this country away from imperialism and have an anti-racist, anti-imperialist and anti-fascist revolution."

In their 1969 declaration, *You Don't Need a Weatherman to Know Which Way the Wind Blows*, Bill Ayers, Bernardine Dohrn, John Jacobs, and other revolutionary leaders of the Weather Underground spoke of black people not so much as the reason for their push to destroy American society and institute world Communism, but as a means to achieve their goals. American blacks were considered a colonized subject of the United States, along with the people of Vietnam and Bolivia—another victim of U.S. imperialism. Their liberation was secondary to the general struggle; seeking Black liberation for its own sake was just a form of bourgeois nationalism. "No Black self-determination could be won which would not result in a victory for the international revolution as a whole," the document affirmed.

These are the ideological sources for what could be the largest radical movement in American history—one that could lead to real policy changes. One component is street pressure, driven by the likes of Mann and Cullors. Another takes place in plusher environments, such as Fortune 500 companies or the halls of Congress. Consultants like *White Fragility* author Robin DiAngelo told 184 Democratic legislators in a conference call in June that their policies hurt Black lives. DiAngelo told *The New York Times* that "capitalism is so bound up with racism ... [it] is dependent on inequality, on an underclass. If the model is profit over everything, you're not going to look at your policies to see what is most racially equitable."

Up to now, the American system has resisted socialism by offering prosperity and opportunity. Our politicians today need to understand what they're facing from the BLM movement and what is at stake. The "white settler state" of Eric Mann's fevered mind is in reality the American constitutional order. The imperialism that Mann, Rosenberg, DiAngelo, and others imagine is the American free-market system that has been the most successful weapon against poverty ever devised. Political leaders of either party feeling pressured to adopt BLM policies or even just mouth the rhetoric should spend some time examining the movement's intellectual sources—and its political goals.

On Fox News' "The Story" with Martha MacCallum, New York Black Lives Matter president Hawk Newsome likened the Black Lives movement to the American Revolution. "We go in and we blow up countries and we replace their leaders with leaders who we like. So for any American to accuse us of being violent is extremely hypocritical," he said. He later added, "If this country doesn't give us what we want, then we will burn down this system and replace it. All right? And I could be speaking ... figuratively. I could be speaking literally. It's a matter of interpretation." President Trump tweeted his disapproval of Newsome's remarks. Black Lives Matter leader states, "If U.S. doesn't give us what we want, and then we will burn down this system and replace it." This is Treason, Sedition, and Insurrection! *Which is correct even if you don't like Trump, agree?*

Other stated BLM radical goals are to "disrupt the Western-prescribed nuclear family structure requirement by supporting each other as extended families and 'villages' that collectively care for one another, especially our children, to the degree that mothers, parents, and children are comfortable. We foster a queer-affirming network. When we gather, we do so with the intention of freeing ourselves from the tight grip of heteronormative thinking, or rather, the belief that all in the world are heterosexual (unless s/he or they disclose otherwise)." BLM loves criminals and hates law and order. Currently they are pressuring Democrats to embrace a bill described as the 'roadmap for prison abolition.' They are also demanding their payoff for supporting Biden, including billions to be allocated to corrupt, Black run cities.

Worse still, it is not an exaggeration to say that BLM is poisoning our children and our nation. It's not just about their rallies, riots, or attempts to cancel our culture; but we now have proof of their attempts to indoctrinate our children in schools, funded by our tax dollars.

The Marxist-run Black Lives Matter organization is working in tandem with *The New York Times* and teacher unions to force every American child to take part in the 1619 Project—a revisionist and twisted version of American History.

Marxists cloaked as teachers are being paid by U.S. taxpayers to indoctrinate our own children and to teach them to hate America, especially "White America." Here are a couple of the examples of what we are seeing in public schools—I know there are more.

- A Washington, D.C. middle school teacher created a lesson plan in which students "learned" the coronavirus pandemic was caused by racism and capitalism, and in particular by the United States.
- An Illinois principal invited a BLM activist—who celebrated the execution-style killings of Chicago police—to speak at career day.

Still want to put BLM signs on your lawn?

The group recently gave the Biden and Newsom administrations an ultimatum; they must replace the Harris Senate seat with a Black. It seems they almost got their way, as our eunuch Governor, going against the Civil Rights Act again, considered candidates based on their color and national origin not merit. He chose between two black women and a Latino man; former Congresswoman Barbara Lee who, like Harris, got her start being the mistress to a black politician; Karen Bass, a deeply flawed and unqualified black woman who, like Lee, praised Cuba dictator Fidel Castro. She also attended anti-Semitic anti–American Nation of Islam events, as well as events for the Scientology cult. Newsom finally selected Alex Padilla to be the first Latino senator. Padilla, as California Secretary of State moved away from using voter ID to mass mailings of ballots in California and would support this invitation for voter fraud for the whole country. Moreover, this corrupt party hack got into hot water with his own Democratic controller for misusing 35 million from a pot of cash to hire a consulting firm with ties to the Democratic Party to conduct "voter outreach".

Marxists getting rich

Progressive and racial justice groups have seen a cascade of donations since George Floyd's death and the ensuing protests. Some estimates say they raked in billions. According to the *New York Times*, bail funds alone have received $90 million. "This is a watershed moment for all black-led organizing groups," said Kailee Scales, managing director of the Black Lives Matter Global Network, who did reveal that one of her group's online petitions alone had raised $5 million. Another person familiar with the group's fund-raising said that it had raised $10 million just on Blackout Tuesday; Ms. Scales declined to comment on that figure. What is clear is they are spending many millions to get black radical anti-American anti-Semite Reverend Warnock elected to the Senate in Georgia.

The CEO of conservative icon Brooks Brothers sent out a letter to customers expressing support of the objectives of the Black Lives Matter movement, which include a plan to "disrupt the Western-prescribed nuclear family," and "dismantle cisgender privilege." (Cisgender is a term for people whose gender identity matches their sex assigned at birth). Brooks Brothers is just the latest in a long line of "woke corporations" that have bowed to the BLM shakedown mob. Nike has been a forerunner in using its marketing to push BLM messaging, even as the anti-police propaganda incited a wave of deadly attacks on police officers. Now, Big Tech giants, including Netflix, Amazon, Apple, Google, Twitter, and Facebook are all voicing full-throated support for the radical Marxist group, as have a large number of beauty conglomerates such as Estée Lauder, Becca Cosmetics, Clinique, L'Oréal, and NYX. *If we had a responsible media, they would follow the money. Where did it go? It certainly wasn't plowed back into crime ridden Black cities or colleges.*

Antifa

Since Anti-Fascist (Antifa) is heavily composed of anarchists, its activists place little faith in the state, which they consider complicit in fascism and racism. They prefer direct action so when people they deem racists and fascists manage to assemble, Antifa's partisans try to break up their gatherings, including by force. They are a growing group of violent, hate-filled, reverse racist revolutionaries who hide their faces with masks and wear all black, as they vandalize and attack people with opposing views and even those who are rallying support of our country and our President. At least some of those associated with Antifa, punched and threw eggs at people exiting a Trump rally in San Jose, California, where the spineless mayor took the side of these thugs as his Keystone Cops watched and did nothing. The City is rightfully being sued by the victims of these hate crimes.

An article in *Its Going Down*, a media collective for anarchist and anti-fascist news and opinion, celebrated the righteous beatings. Anti-fascists call such actions defensive. Hate speech against vulnerable minorities, they argue, leads to violence against vulnerable minorities. But Trump supporters and White nationalists see Antifa's attacks as an assault on their right to assemble freely, which they in turn seek to reassert. A similar cycle has played out at UC Berkeley. February 2017, as masked anti-fascists broke store windows and hurled Molotov cocktails and rocks at police during a rally against the planned speech by Milo Yiannopoulos. This is a group that exists to suppress free speech and instigate trouble. Once again in August 2017, black-clad anarchists stormed into what had been a largely peaceful Berkeley protest against hate, and attacked at least five people, including the leader of a politically conservative group who canceled an event a day earlier in San Francisco amid fears of violence.

The group of more than 100 hooded bigots with shields cynically emblazoned with the words "no hate" and waving a flag identifying themselves as anarchists, busted through police lines, avoiding security checks by officers to take away possible weapons. Then the anarchists blended with a crowd of 2,000 largely peaceful protesters who turned up to demonstrate in a "Rally Against Hate" to oppose a much smaller gathering of right-wing protesters.

Amnesty International

It has been said that Amnesty International panders to the Left, and acts as a hit man to attack those targets identified by the Left. Their conclusions and motives, which should be carefully scrutinized, are always promoted as gospel by left-wing professors and media like the BBC, who are always looking for ammunition to unjustly attack the U.S., Israel, and other undeserving targets. Amnesty International has been exposed as having had an obvious and definite left-wing bias since the 1980s, when they were the subjects of French journalist Hughes Keraly's book.

Keraly exposed the organization's infiltration by communists and discovered that Amnesty director Derek Roebuck was an active communist himself. Keraly investigated Amnesty claims and found that, though at times they did good work exposing human rights abuses around the world, their work was severely tainted. He noted that problems arose from their agenda that magnified and, in some cases, manufactured the abuses of freedom-loving regimes, while minimizing and ignoring the abuses of regimes of the totalitarian Left.

This is instructive regarding the danger of placing monitoring responsibilities into the hands of so-called "Non-Governmental Organizations" (NGO) like Amnesty International and Human Rights Watch. Amnesty affiliates with the United Nations. This affiliation, in effect, grants this un-elected and un-accountable bureaucracy an appearance of authority and legality.

In his study of thousands of files, Keraly discovered Amnesty practices such as listing terrorists working with Ugandan dictator Idi Amin as "victims of political oppression," a title similarly used by Amnesty for Palestinian terrorists. At that time, Amnesty had done nothing to investigate the torture and concentration camps of the Soviet Union, Cambodia, or Cuba. In fact, the group had little to say at the time regarding leftist abuses.

Amnesty International still pursues a radical leftist agenda today. They support such things as the communist-inspired "UN Declaration of Human Rights," which calls for the transfer of capital from productive Western societies to Third World dictators and a guaranteed right of employment: a typical Bolshevik idea.

Now they are championing the cause of Muslims who have experienced "discrimination" in the U.S. since September 11th, and the al-Qaeda prisoners at Guantanamo Bay, Cuba. As if the most humane country in the world needs a lesson about human rights from a group that has little to say about Leftist Palestinians and their terrorist offshoots.

Once again, those willing to concede that they may be victims of years of left-wing brainwashing might begin questioning their sacred Amnesty International. Why should America, the fairest and freest country in the world, be subjected to the dirty lens of the Amnesty International microscope; while the politically oppressive Islamic world is often ignored?

Human Rights Watch (HRW)

This leading international human rights NGO has earned its stripes with its left-wing buddies (such as Amnesty International) by demonizing Israel, and stays in business by avoiding any criticism of Israel's enemies. HRW's lack of objective reporting on governments in the region is demonstrated by its inability in the past, despite an annual budget of $22 million, to produce a specific report on human rights abuses in a country like Libya, or the relative paucity of attention given to states with appalling human rights records like Syria and Saudi Arabia as compared to Israel.

So there should be no surprise when HRW wrongly describes Israel as violating international legal norms by labeling the killing of terrorist leaders like Ismail Abu Shanab and Sheikh Ahmed Yassin "liquidation" or "assassination." International law does not protect all enemy combatants from being targeted before judicial process, or grant them immunity from military operations when they use civilians as human shields.

Human Rights Watch's lack of objectivity and its complicity with left-wing buddies was highlighted during the UN's infamous racist circus called the "anti-racism" conference held in Durban, South Africa. Some noted that HRW Executive Director Ken Roth telegraphed his real convictions rather than his public face in an interview on U.S. National Public Radio (August 14, 2001), when he said, "Clearly Israeli racist practices are an appropriate topic."

So in the lead up to Durban, HRW fanned the flames of racial intolerance, notwithstanding the fact that one-quarter of Israel's citizens are actually Arab and enjoy democratic rights unlike anywhere else in the Arab world. That world has systematically forced hundreds of thousands of Jews from their countries, or killed them outright, as in the case of the Iranian Revolution.

At Durban, one role of HRW seemed to be to exclude representatives of Jewish lawyers and jurists from over 40 countries (IAJLJ), who, as members of the NGO Caucus, had a right to vote on the final NGO document. The draft included egregious statements equating Zionism with racism, and alleging that Israel was an "apartheid" state guilty of "genocide and ethnic cleansing designed to ensure a Jewish state." Having the courage to speak out against the tide of hate directed at Israel and the Jewish people by the Left and by the Arabs is not one of the strengths of Human Rights Watch, while avoiding criticizing Israel's enemies is something at which they seem to excel.

The American Civil Liberties Union (ACLU)

The joke goes, "How do you get the ACLU to stop defending enemy terrorists who vow to kill Americans? Tell the ACLU that the terrorists are really Boy Scouts." Unlike Amenity International, the ACLU was at one time an important protector of human rights. But like NATO after the Cold War, it appears to have lost its focus and direction. There is an important need for the organization to seriously re-examine and change the activities that do more harm than good, such as defending extreme people and values that undermine society. The media recently reported attempts to stop members from publicly airing their disagreements about the direction and targets of the organization. Aren't attempts to control internal and external criticism the hallmark of a totalitarian regime? But then the ACLU is big business.

They have certainly lost the forest for the trees when they fight against American institutions like the Boy Scouts and memorials to our veterans. Like the civil rights gang, the ACLU could become a serious impediment to American values and justice.

Do they go after our values because they make big money pursuing the civil rights con? Like the "people of color" extortionists discussed in Chapter 1, the ACLU profits from the disgusting abuses of the civil rights business. Indeed, they make millions of dollars in taxpayer "attorney fee awards" by turning authorization under the Civil Rights Act into a piñata of lawyer goodies. I discussed in Chapter 1 how civil rights con men and women have exploited a well-intentioned law. These diversity groups welcome the ACLU to join them in feeding at the money trough, while the taxpayers keep picking up the tab.

Elected and appointed officials at the local, state, and Federal levels have been literally terrorized about standing up to the ACLU, for fear of enormous attorney fees being imposed by un-elected judges not answerable to the taxpayers. I don't know of a single American judge who has had the guts to exercise discretion by denying attorney fees to the ACLU.

And attorney fees do seem to motivate the ACLU. The American Legion called on Congress to end judges' authority to award attorney fees in cases brought to remove or destroy religious symbols. In 1934, a private citizen strapped two pipes together to form a cross and mounted it to a rock outcrop on private land in the Mojave Desert. The purpose of the cross was to honor WWI veterans. In the year 2000, President Clinton incorporated the area into a Mojave National Preserve. The ACLU vultures swarmed in and filed a lawsuit to remove the cross, picking up some $40,000 in attorney fees. Legislation was passed to exchange the one-acre site for five acres from a private owner, placing the monument on private land. But the ACLU appealed against this legislation and picked up an additional $63,000. They ruled that the plaintiff, who later moved to Oregon, suffered a civil rights injury because he saw the cross when driving back on visits.

International ANSWER (Act Now to Stop War and End Racism)

ANSWER, one of the leading organizers of anti-war protests in the United States, has begun to openly and vociferously support Palestinian terrorists. They have played a key role in inserting anti-Israel sentiment into the anti-war movement, which has led to extreme invective against Israel during protests. ANSWER was created by the New York-based International Action Center (IAC), often attracting protestors by the tens of thousands.

Its largest and most disturbing event was the "National March for Palestine Against War and Racism," in Washington, D.C. The rally attracted nearly 200,000 demonstrators, and served as a vehicle for supporters of violence and anti-Semitic terror. The flag of the Iranian puppet Hezbollah flew from the speaker's podium. This same Hezbollah that is currently tearing Lebanon apart, bombed the U.S. Marine barracks in Lebanon in 1983, killing 241 U.S. Marines; hijacked a TWA flight in Europe in 1985; executed a U.S. Navy diver; bombed the Jewish community center in Buenos Aires in 1994, killing 85; and blew up the Khobar

Towers housing complex in Dhahran, Saudi Arabia, killing 19 American servicemen in 1996. A retired, covert U.S. intelligence officer with years of experience in the Middle East noted that Hezbollah teams have regularly done surveillance on U.S. Embassies in Europe in case they're activated to strike.

Our counter terrorism efforts against this Iran-linked group should actively pursue and prosecute the leadership of those left-wing groups and churches who support Hezbollah and other terrorist organizations. Hiding behind a curtain of free speech and the peace movement are traitors to our country, who are giving support to our enemies in the war on terrorism.

ACORN

The Tides Foundation was a key funder of the Associations for Community Organizations for Reform Now (ACORN), the federally funded 400,000 dues-paying member pressure group that engaged in numerous voter fraud and other schemes for 40 years. According to journalist Trevor Loudon writing for Capital Research Center, Tides gave grants to "ACORN ($100,000), ACORN International (three grants totaling $134,000), ACORN Institute (three grants totaling $84,793), [and] ACORN's voter mobilization arm Project Vote (11 grants totaling $845,000)."

ACORN was shuttered in 2010 with the loss of government funding after investigative journalists James O'Keefe and Hannah Giles recorded ACORN employees offering them advice on how to start up a prostitution ring. (It's worth noting that ACORN's voter fraud spinoff Project VOTE employed Barack Obama in the early 1990s.) Meanwhile, ACORN continued to aid left-wing politicians with funding from George Soros' Open Society Foundations through Obama's 2012 reelection campaign until closing in August 2017, when the group was "ultimately forced to admit that our current model had become unsustainable."

In July 2008, Dale Rathke, the brother of ACORN founder Wade Rathke, was discovered to have embezzled over $948,000 from ACORN. A month later, the *New York Times* reported that Drummond Pike—described as a friend of the Rathkes—had "agreed to buy the promissory note that required the Rathke family to repay ACORN the money." Wade Rathke was a Tides Foundation board member with ties to Big Labor, having founded the Service Employees International Union Southern Conference and served on the union's executive board.

Alliance for Global Justice (AfGJ)

Another Tides grant recipient is the AfGJ, an obscure, Arizona-based nonprofit that acts "as a conduit, keeping funds flowing to radical and anti-American groups that terrorize conservatives on campus" (*Foundation Watch,* August 2017). AfGJ is an unabashedly anti-capitalist organization and a key funder of the so-called anti-Trump "Resistance." Early last year, *the Daily Caller* exposed AfGJ for funneling $50,000 to Refuse Fascism, the group responsible for the riot that shut down conservative activist Milo Yiannopoulos's planned speech at the University of California, Berkeley, in February 2017. Since 2004, AfGJ has received over $200,000 from the Tides Foundation.

Ruckus Society

Tides have funded this group to the tune of $457,000 since 1999. The Ruckus Society comes out of the radical environmentalist movement of the 1980s; its founders, Mike Roselle and Howard "Twilly" Cannon also founded the anarchist group Earth First and the domestic terrorist entity Earth Liberation Front (ELF). Those groups rose to infamy for inflicting eco-terrorist violence and property damage on logging companies; FBI reports tally over 600 criminal acts causing $43 million in damages committed by ELF and the related Animal Liberation Front (ALF) since 1996.

National Lawyers Guild (NLG)

This is another Tides Foundation grantee. Founded in 1937 in New York City, the group was intended to act as a counterweight to the then-conservative American Bar Association; but it was later exposed by historians and the House Un-American Activities Committee as a close ally of the Soviet Union that "faithfully followed the line of the Communist Party on numerous issues ... an important bulwark in defense of that party, its members, and organizations under its control." The NLG was so extreme, in fact, that it ceased opposing the Allies in World War II as "imperialist" only when Nazi Germany broke its alliance with the Soviet Union and invaded that country on June 22, 1941. Along with the Communist Party USA, the NLG quickly lent President Roosevelt its "unlimited support to all measures necessary to the defeat of Hitlerism"—while preserving the tacit goal of aiding international communism.

MoveOn.org

MoveOn is a web-based grassroots political network of more than 2 million online activists whose general goal is to push the Democratic Party to the Left. More than a website, MoveOn is a catalyst for a new kind of grassroots involvement tailored to attract young net-savvy Democrats. They succeeded in harnessing popular entertainers to their cause in the form of rock concert fundraisers. This group does damage to the Democrats as it moves the party further to the Left and toward losers like AOC and her "Squad." Moreover, MoveOn efficiently spreads and reinforces the lies and hateful propaganda of the Left to our already brainwashed youth. During the George W. Bush administration, Tides money aided groups like the left-wing website MoveOn.org to oppose the Iraq War by financing the Iraq Peace Fund and a Peace Strategies Fund. MoveOn featured two ridiculous commercials portraying President Bush as Adolf Hitler, saying that "what were war crimes in 1945 is foreign policy in 2003."

George Floyd's death provided a windfall for divisity racketeers

The killing of George Floyd and the ensuing nationwide wave of protests are generating a record-setting flood of donations to racial justice groups, bail funds, and black-led advocacy organizations across America, remaking the financial landscape of black political activism in a matter of weeks. Money came in so fast and so unexpectedly that some groups even began to turn away and redirect donors elsewhere. Others said they still could not yet account for how much had arrived. A deluge of online donations has washed over organizations big and small—from legacy civil rights groups to self-declared abolitionists seeking to defund the police.

The huge money flow even surprised the black leaders and activists in the victimization/divisity business, which would not exist if they stopped protesting systemic racism and police brutality myths. Indeed, the fact the George Floyd had several times the amount of Fentanyl in his system to have killed him; the visual of the cop with his knee on Floyd's neck once again elicited the emotional but inaccurate charge that the cop killed him. It did further damage to America by providing life support for both the systemic racism and black target police lies debunked in earlier chapters.

ActBlue, the leading site to process online donations for Democratic causes and campaigns, has experienced its busiest period since its founding in 2004, far surpassing even the highest peaks of the 2020 presidential primary season. (ActBlue confirmed that racial justice causes and bail funds had led the way.) The site's four biggest days ever came consecutively this month as it processed more than $250 million to various progressive causes and candidates in two-plus weeks, according to a *New York Times* analysis of the site's donation ticker. And on June 2, the collective action day that was known as Blackout Tuesday, ActBlue doubled what had been, before this month, its one-day record: raising $41 million in 24 hours.

Color of Change, which already promoted itself as the largest online racial justice group in the country, quadrupled its membership from 1.7 million to 7 million people in recent days. Big corporations are making major pledges: $100 million each from Warner Music Group, Comcast, and the Sony Music Group for various social justice causes, among many companies.

Hollow-wood Looney Prunes

Hollywood has also played a major role in the brainwashing of a whole generation around the globe. There is nothing new in their thinking, as shown by the slide in ticket sales.

How about a positive movie about our great country, rather than one turning homicidal maniac terrorists into innocent victims or freedom fighters? I would buy a ticket to a movie that deals with reverse discrimination and how civil rights leaders extort money from our biggest companies; or how a drunk, black stripper with a criminal past schemed with the help of the left-wing media, Black Panther Party gangsters, and an immoral DA with political ambitions to ruin the reputation of 40 innocent white lacrosse players. How about the Dr. Ford story about how she participated in a historic smear campaign and hoax against Judge Kavanaugh? Half the country would buy a ticket to the Biden family global corruption network with insights into drug addict, pedophile Hunter. Obamagate—behind the scenes on the historical coup attempt against Trump would be also be a big hit. The Black Bagmen—How AG's Holder and Lynch misused the DOJ slush fund. Another suggestion would be a political science fiction thriller, perhaps directed by a born-again Michael Moore. In it, an evil cabal of left-wing professors, left-wing media, and Hollywood have systematically brainwashed a whole generation into thinking the good motives, actions, and dreams of the best country in the world are some kind of evil conspiracy, and the hero who uncovers the plot is a conservative family man.

In other words, how about telling the truth—something the Left has not done since the days when Ed R. Morrow dealt with the real problem of McCarthyism, and when Black civil rights needed protection, decades ago. Today, as White civil rights are being trampled by the civil rights business and government, Hollywood is stuck watching old movies and playing old roles.

I express my disdain of left-wing slander regarding America's greatness with the power of my ticket sales and by avoiding sponsors and studios supporting leftist propaganda. I cannot make the emotional swing from being upset by the hate-America speech of left-wing stars to feeling comfortable about watching them perform. The self-inflated egos of stars and their need to be in the spotlight only serve to highlight their worn-out leftist scripts. These people who have spent their lives pretending should have no credibility in the real world. Though they really have nothing new or of value to say, they stay on the stage as long as the left-wing media gives them a microphone.

Academy of frauds

Time to give them the hook and that's what's happening. According to last February's ratings, 93 percent of us are already not watching the Academy Awards. Now Oscar is wondering: How do I whittle down that last 7 percent? Answer: woke quotas.

Starting with 2024 films, your project can't even be considered for a Best Picture Oscar unless it meets a set of diversity targets of the kind you'd normally expect to see credited to a Santa Cruz/Berkeley BLM film cooperative. Kyle Smith, opinion writer for the *New York Post*, summed up this latest idiocy. "That thunk you heard coming out of La-La Land on Tuesday was the sound of the Academy grandly planting its face in the sidewalk by announcing it was formally rejecting the pursuit of artistic quality in favor of a byzantine quota system."

Like all color and sex quotas, we lose respect for those use them and it demeans the achievements of those who earned them through merit. These obnoxious continuing attempts to force respect for positions or awards with a color or sex component, whether for the Board of Directors in California, admission into a University, or job position, is repugnant to most fair–minded Americans. Do you want the athletes on your favorite team to be picked because of their skin color? Of course not!

Some of the classless mumblings from a few of those who spend worthless lives pretending to be someone else; when they are left without a script:

Robert De Niro gave a commencement address at Brown University, during which he called President Trump "an idiot" and described modern America as "a tragic, dumbass comedy." Shame on Brown!

Alec Baldwin may mimic Trump on TV but is just another anti-American great pretender who recently crapped in his pants and lost 74 million Trump viewers with his latest puerile, asinine quote. "Bury Trump in a Nazi graveyard and put a swastika on his grave."

John Cusack, back in April, claimed that those close to him have knowledge that exposure to 5G networks can weaken the immune system and, in turn, put people more at risk of contracting COVID-19 in a now-deleted tweet.

The actor faced backlash last year for a tweet critics called anti-Semitic. He later claimed a "bot" was to blame for the post.

Chelsea Handler ruffled feathers in January when she posted a tweet questioning Lindsey Graham's sexuality. Handler wrote, "Holy, f--- f---. I just [saw] the video of trumps bipartisan 'meeting' yesterday. Hey, @LindseyGrahamSC what kind of d--k sucking video do they have on you for you 2 be acting like this? Wouldn't coming out be more honorable?"

Samantha Bee commenting on the Trump administration's "zero tolerance" immigration policy that led to the separation of children from their families at the Mexico-U.S. border, Bee called the president's daughter and White House senior adviser a "feckless c---."

Brainwashed celebrities fueling the systemic racism and police targeting Blacks hoax include—Chrissy Teigen, Lady Gaga, Leonardo DiCaprio, among others— have joined and amplified the giving, too. One pop singer, Abel Tesfaye, posted receipts for $500,000 in donations. And the K-pop boy band BTS announced giving $1 million to Black Lives Matter; its fan group matched that by donating $1.3 million to a dozen advocacy groups.

Blue State Support

Interestingly, have you noted that almost all the looting, burning, destruction of small business, assault and murder happen in so-called blue states—those run by progressive Democrat Governors and Mayors? Why the current mass exodus from blue to red states? Do the blue and red states also mark the boundaries of America's ever deepening cultural divide? What differences in red state values have kept the rioting mayhem so concentrated in the blue states? Some generalizations follow:

Blue prefers a big Federal government solving problems while the red states think small local government is more productive, less expensive, more transparent, and responsive to the public they serve. A corollary would be the high percentage of blue citizens preferring socialism to the red choosing free market capitalism. Socialist policies in blue states increase regulations and limit worker choice on joining unions. Big government of course requires high taxes that also chase people to low tax red states.

167

Law and order issues are another major reason why millions have been moving to red states. Red states are tough on crime while blue state policies favor criminals. Ignoring crimes, reducing sentences, emptying jails, and defunding the police are popular on the Left but are abhorrent to red state Americans. *Which values are you most comfortable with?*

Chapter 7
ANTI-SEMITIC ZIONISM

Anti-Semitism is a noxious weed that should be cut out. It has no place in America.

- William Howard Taft

I've always been supportive of the right of Israel as a state, and I've always fought against anti-Semitism, even in my own community.

- Harry Belafonte

OK, in the past six chapters we learned that radicals hijacked the civil rights movement and act for revolution and personal greed. We learned how the Divisity/Left coalition and our government colluded to supply funds, legitimacy, and pseudo intellectual cover to support a vast array of radical groups, media actions, and causes. In this chapter I try to comprehend how my religion and Israel became an easy target for Blacks, the Left, and the Alt-Right, and how our own government and non-government organizations' bias supplies the ammunition for these escalating horrific attacks.

Black anti-Semitism

Martin Luther King Jr. said in 1965, "How could there be anti-Semitism among Negroes when our Jewish friends have demonstrated their commitment to the principle of tolerance and brotherhood not only in the form of sizable contributions, but in many other tangible ways, and often at great personal sacrifice. Can we ever express our appreciation to the rabbis who chose to give moral witness with us in St. Augustine during our recent protest against segregation in that unhappy city? Need I remind anyone of the awful beating suffered by Rabbi Arthur Lelyveld of Cleveland when he joined the civil rights workers there in Hattiesburg, Mississippi? And who can ever forget the sacrifice of two Jewish lives, Andrew Goodman and Michael Schwerner, in the swamps of

Mississippi? It would be impossible to record the contribution that the Jewish people have made toward the Negro's struggle for freedom—it has been so great."

When Rabbi Abraham Joshua Heschel and the Rev. Martin Luther King Jr. marched side by side from Selma to Birmingham in 1965, the image symbolized the powerful "Black-Jewish" alliance. Certainly, a shared commitment to equality and concerted joint action between Blacks and Jews had helped produce substantial civil rights advances. By the late 1960s, however, this potent coalition seemed to unravel as the two groups split over both style and policy. Having been part of this golden age, I bemoan the decline of this era of Black-Jewish cooperation when we worked together toward a vision of the just society, marked by a shared defense against bigotry and discrimination, and a liberal vision of the post-civil rights-struggle world. The alliance produced dramatic victories in court, in state legislatures, in Congress, business, and public opinion, but buckled in the late 1960s, under constant reverse racist attacks by militant Black Nationalist separatists who expelled white people, allied with third-world anti-Zionism, and spouted anti-Semitic rhetoric. Jews often "stood in" for Whites in Black people's minds, and absorbed the full force of their racial resentment and anti-Semitism promoted by a new breed of loud crude black revolutionaries.

As James Baldwin observed, "Just as a society must have a scapegoat, so hatred must have a symbol. Georgia has the Negro and Harlem has the Jew." Jews served this "stand-in" function because Jews showed greater willingness than other Whites to do business in black neighborhoods, often as landlords, shopkeepers, and middlemen. It seems Jews have been the scapegoats throughout history and it is time to stand up strongly against those, whether Blacks, Whites, Left, or Right who want to continue to type cast us in that role. Just because a minority foolishly may have been given some kind of protected class status, it does not give them the right to make racist remarks and take racists actions.

Alt–Right anti-Semitism

It was confusing and horrific to see the KKK and other alt-Right groups spouting anti-Semitic slogans as they protested the taking down of confederate statues in Charlottesville, but not chanting their traditional anti-Black rhetoric. Indeed, they immediately went after the Jews at their rally at the University of Virginia. These White nationalists brandished torches and chanted anti-Semitic and Nazi slogans.

Why the Jews?

It is hard to understand the behavior of these lunatics but here are two scenarios that have some traction. First, racist remarks' prohibition, real or perceived, against Blacks has become so ingrained in popular culture that it immediately sets off a six-alarm response from the media, law enforcement, government, black militants, progressives, and professional diversity agitators. On the other hand, there is little coverage, concern, or protests because American Jews are still the victims of a majority of religious hate crimes in the U.S., despite making up less than 2 percent of the population. (Even after adjusting for population, Jews are still more targeted than Muslims.)

While Blacks have the forces to strongly protect, attack and counterattack, Jews have allowed themselves to become easy targets from all sides; Left, Right, Black and White. We expect attacks from the far-right since there is such a long history of such outrages but it is particularly discouraging to see Jewish leaders pandering to support Islamic, Black, and Left causes while these same groups are abandoning us and currently commit more anti-Semitic and anti-Israel acts then the far-right.

Another scenario to why the alt-Right are again attacking Jews is perhaps because they are seeking answers as to why the White race is suffering and being discriminated against so much lately. There must be someone who is manipulating the social order behind the curtain. Who controls business, media, banking, entertainment, education, and even Washington, D.C.? It is, of course, the Jews. Jews function for today's White nationalists as they often have for anti-Semites through the centuries, as the demons responsible for anything not going as the "great unwashed" would like.

Jews, therefore, are the only "white people" obsessively targeted by White Supremacists. So are we really White, not at all, or something in between? What would I mark as my color on those government's race quota forms? I refuse to answer those questions, because to me it is another form of racism to collect and use that information. Racism after all, is essentially the result of socially constructed categories imposed by bigots to separate out groups: white from nonwhites, Germans from Jews, and so on.

Any anti-racists worthy of the name must be there to defend us. Otherwise, once again they are simply ceding Jews to their assailants and effectively abetting their persecution. Where are the Left, Black, and Muslim voices supporting the Jews as real anti-Semitic racism again plows through the streets all over the world?

Left-wing anti–Semitic anti-Zionism

Allan Johnson, a Brit, coined the term 'anti-Semitic anti-Zionism' for the attempt by the Left to morph the hateful old racist stereotype of what the Jew-devil was into what Israel is now: uniquely malevolent, full of blood lust, all-controlling, the hidden hand, tricky, always acting in bad faith, the obstacle to a better, purer, more spiritual world, uniquely deserving of punishment, and so on.

Johnsons' 'anti-Semitic anti-Zionism' has three components: a program, a discourse, and a movement. First, 'anti-Semitic anti-Zionism' has a political program: not two states for two peoples, but the abolition of the Jewish homeland; not Palestine alongside Israel, but Palestine instead of Israel.

Second, 'anti-Semitic anti-Zionism' is a demonizing, intellectual discourse as seen through academic boycotts of Israel. The Left is imprisoning itself within a distorting system of such claptrap crap as: 'Zionism is racism'; Israel is a 'settler-colonialist state' which 'ethnically cleansed' the 'indigenous' people, went on to build an 'apartheid state' and is now engaged in an 'incremental genocide' against the Palestinians. And most disgusting is the ugly phenomenon of Holocaust Inversion—the deliberate and systematic Nazification of Israel in street placards depicting Netanyahu as Hitler, in posters equating the Israel Defense Forces (IDF) as the SS, in cartoons portraying Israelis as Nazis, and even in the language of intellectuals.

Finally, 'anti-Semitic anti-Zionism' is a presence within the global social movement, the "Boycott, Divestment, and Sanctions," (the BDS movement) to exclude one state—and only one state—from the economic, cultural, and educational life of humanity: the little Jewish democracy. BLM pressures Democrats to embrace a bill described as 'roadmap for prison abolition.'

What Does BDS Really Want?

Media often report that the Boycott, Divestment, and Sanctions (BDS) movement is a "protest against Israeli occupation of the West Bank"—but facts prove otherwise.

What are the facts?

The U.S. Senate recently passed a landmark bill to punish companies that discriminate commercially against Israel. While the ACLU, a few media, and several presidential candidates opposed this Act saying it violates speech rights, this rationale has nothing to do with political speech and everything to do with commercial discrimination against a religious and ethnic group—Jews. Imagine the ACLU, media, and politicians objecting to an act of Congress meant to protect the existence of a religiously Muslim or Black country. While the U.S. constitution protects free speech, it also prohibits discrimination against ethnic, religious, and racial groups.

BDS doesn't just criticize Israeli policy, it opposes its entire agenda; it is dedicated to turning the world's only Jewish state into the 51st Muslim-majority nation. BDS website, literature, and public speeches make clear that is precisely the intention of the movement. BDS opposes Israel's occupation of the entire Holy Land. The BDS slogan says "Palestine shall be free from the (Jordan) river to the (Mediterranean) sea"—**meaning the entire state of Israel.** Indeed, BDS founder, Omar Barghouti admits, "If the canard that the Combating BDS Act is a violation of occupation ends, would that end support for BDS? No." Why do the media neglect this damning fact?

While BDS attacks Israel it doesn't criticize any other nation for its discrimination based on ethnic, religious, and racial identity. It ignores the slaughter in Syria and Turkey of the Kurds or brutal discrimination against Palestinians in Arab Lebanon and throughout the Muslim world. Indeed, BDS opposition to the Israeli policies in the territories and Gaza appears no more than an excuse invented by Israel haters to justify their, anti-Semitic/Zionist movement.

Myth: No criticism of Israel can be anti-Semitic

Philip Klein, in a 2016 *Washington Examiner* piece, expounded on the former Obama administration's use of rhetoric to deceive and to further fracture the anti-Semitic anti-Zionism conundrum facing Jews and Israel. Former Secretary of State John Kerry, in one of his overblown harangues about Israel, said that if Israel doesn't cut a deal with the Palestinians soon, it will either cease to be a Jewish state or it will become "an apartheid state," and lamented that "too often ... anyone who disagrees with Israel policy is cast as anti-Israel or even anti-Semitic." Klein notes "that Kerry, a non-Jewish former Senator and presidential candidate in a powerful cabinet post, used his position to casually downplay claims of prejudice against a religious minority that makes up less than one-fifth of one-percent of the world's population, yet has been persecuted for thousands of years, slaughtered by the millions, whose adherents are regularly targeted around the world, and are the most under attack in the United States."

What Kerry was trying to say was that not all criticism of Israeli policy is anti-Semitic. The Left has repeated this argument so often that it now serves a pernicious purpose. True, one can criticize current policies of the Israeli government and not be anti-Semitic. But it's also true that much of the criticism of Israel is anti-Semitic. The problem is that through constant repetition, the "not all criticism of Israel is anti-Semitic" polemic now translates into "no criticism of Israel can be anti-Semitic." Sadly, this has helped anti-Semites launder their hatred of Jews by disguising it as just a criticism of Israel. This can be widely seen by the wave of attacks against Jews on college campuses, where reports of anti-Semitic incidents have been rising, and where it's hard to distinguish between attacks on Jews and attacks on Israel.

Obama attempts to polarize and politesse Israel. Israel enjoyed strong bipartisan support in the congress, and public opinion before Barack Obama came on the scene. That support has been weakened by his administration and has helped the Left, Blacks, and Islamists to inflict damage to the country and its reputation.

Klein notes that when Hamas joined the Palestinian government, the Obama administration still pledged to work with the government and acted as though it was a legitimate peace partner and that Israel was really to blame for the lack of progress in negotiations. Indeed, throughout his administration, Obama and his subordinates used rhetoric that fed into such arguments, creating space for liberal authors and advocates to take them further, which in turn have added fuel to spreading anti-Semitism. They reinforced conspiratorial narratives about the influence of Jewish lobbyists throwing money at lawmakers in order to exert a powerful and negative influence on U.S. foreign policy at the behest of another government. They criticized Israel relentlessly and obsessively, even when there has been no clear policy objective, and in the process diverted attention from a global humanitarian crisis.

During the fight over the Iran deal which gave billions in cash to the world's leading sponsor of terrorism, made Iran a more powerful conventional threat, and left the door open to it developing a future nuclear bomb, Obama couldn't accept that anybody would have actual objections to this uniquely naïve and stupid policy on the merits. Instead, he smeared his opponents with rhetoric that played into anti-Semitic stereotypes.

In a tense meeting with Democratic senators critical of the deal, Obama said, "He understood the pressures that senators face from donors and others." He said at a press conference that he hoped Congress evaluated the deal, "not based on lobbying but based on what's in the national interest of the United States of America"; on the *Daily Show*, he attacked money and lobbyists working against the deal, obviously referring to the pro-Israel lobbying group AIPAC. This promotes the narrative of wealthy Jewish donors corrupting lawmakers to advance the interests of a foreign power.

It's clear that in past controversies his administration drew zero distinction between the pro-Israel lobby and Jews, giving liberal writers and websites greater leeway to amplify Obama's thinly veiled charges of disloyalty and influence peddling among wealthy Jews. *Politico* ran a cartoon that portrayed Netanyahu building a settlement on top of the U.S. Capitol, planted with the Israeli flag bearing the Jewish Star of David, and with a cement truck stamped with the word AIPAC. *The Huffington Post* published a piece by Yale Professor David Bromwich titled, "Netanyahu and his Marionettes," actually portraying lawmakers who opposed the deal as puppets of the Israeli government and Jewish donors. It also attacked Sen. Chuck Schumer for putting the interest of Israel ahead of America. The liberal website *Daily Kos* ran a cartoon describing Schumer as a "traitor," featuring him in the form of an animal standing in front of an Israeli flag.

The Obama administration has focused obsessively and myopically on criticisms of Israel to the exclusion of other foreign policy issues. Okay if Kerry has a problem with Jewish communities in East Jerusalem and the West Bank. But what was the point, after allowing the United Nations to gang up on Israel on the matter, of speaking for over an hour, disproportionately lashing out at Israeli settlements while skimming over Palestinian terrorism? And why was it so important to give such a negative speech against Israel as likely his last major speech in government?

Even if we give Kerry, Obama, and liberal critics of Israel the benefit of the doubt that their criticisms of Israel are not rooted in any animus toward Jews, which Joe Klein and I do not, it doesn't mean that their words and actions aren't helping to legitimize anti-Semitism. Expect the Biden administration to resurrect the Obama era anti-Semitic/Zionism polices already being pushed by radical "squad" members like Rashida Tlaib. The squad and the Left are committed to reversing Trump's historical accomplishments in the Middle East. *Moreover, did you know BLM has only one foreign affairs policy—that being supporting anti-Israel activities? Seems anti-Semitism is the one thing that the KKK and BLM (the Black KKK) have in common.*

Left-Wing Fascism

The Left is looking more and more like the Right. The Left has always had a fascist totalitarian side that does not tolerate multiplicity of ideas, yet the fractionalized Left is so diverse no one can find its claim to legitimacy. There are areas of common interest. The Left is anti-fascist but not necessarily anti-war. The radical Left requires taking up arms to overcome oppression. Therefore, they have had no problem supporting the Russian or Cuban revolution.

They compare President Trump to "Hitler" as they praise Latin America's dangerous left-wing radicals, while labeling the conservatives and libertarians fascists. In fact, the opposite is true. The American Right stands for limited government, individual rights, morality, personal responsibility, and capitalism. While like fascism, the left-wing is anti-capitalistic, anti-Semitic, and promotes national programs to control education, healthcare, and welfare.

A 2003 Anti-Defamation League survey of university faculty in the U.S., which traditionally identify as left-wing, found that 5% are strong anti-Semites and 65% are against current Israeli policies. Moreover, across the country, Jewish students who want to study in Israel face unfair barriers and restrictions. In some cases, students must forego college credit and financial aid to discover their Jewish homeland. This is because college and university administrators have suspended or placed significant restrictions on study abroad programs in Israel. Yet students are free to study in other Middle East countries, even though Israel is the only democratic nation in the region.

As expected, two of the largest state university systems in the country—the University of California and California State University—are among the worst offenders. These systems have been the dark stars of left-wing culture for so long that it will require a sustained public outroar to dismantle their sick culture that brainwashes students to hate America and Israel, while promoting the agenda of terrorists, minority racists, and left-wing radicals.

The brainwashing by the left-wing and Islamists begins early.

Did you know during this new school year children within our American public school system grades 5 through 12 are:

- Required to learn about the Five Pillars of Islam and asked to create posters about them?
- Asked to read and provide life lessons from scripture from the Quran and how it is implemented into Muslim life?
- In Virginia, students are required in this program to copy the Shahada, the Muslim profession of faith that declares, "There is no god but Allah, and Muhammad is the messenger of Allah."

- In New York, students are shown videos of Islamic terrorists justifying their attacks against Israel—these in classrooms within the state and some within the shadow of where the Twin Towers once stood.
- In Massachusetts, reading materials for the course funded by Arab states are required course reading for our children—materials as PJTN has long trumpeted—that are filled with pro-Palestinian/anti-Israel content. Parents should not be shocked when their Christian kids arrive on the college campuses of America steeped in anti-Semitism and carrying signs to march for the BDS Movement.
- In California, middle school students study Islam for several weeks as part of world history. Their textbooks devote 55 pages to Islam—far more than to any other religion. Islam is presented in a wholly positive way, with Muslim religious beliefs as factual and Muhammed as a hero. By contrast, Judaism and Christianity are given little space, and nothing positive is said about Christianity.
- Furthermore, the schools use handouts supplied by Saudi Arabia to give teachers ideas for activities. At one school, the teacher asked students to fast; at another to dress like Muslims, learn the Five Pillars of Islam, and memorize an Islamic prayer that extols the greatness of Allah. At another school, the front grounds of the school featured a banner for the day that read, "There is one God, Allah, and Muhammed is his prophet." Within the course study across the board, children are presented visual aids such as videos of Christians converting to Islam and giving encouragement on the virtues of Allah. Students are virtually being taught how to be a good Muslim.

Parents requesting that their child receive an alternative assignment are denied. They are told that their child will have a failing grade if they do not complete the Access Islam course studies. Recently a mother expressed her deep concern when her third grader came home with a spelling list that contained the word "shahada" as part of the words to learn and know. A former high school teacher expressed her concern in saying: "There is a major difference between requiring teachers to implement a curriculum with lessons intended to make students 'culturally awake and informed' and a curriculum intended in its entirety that favors any particular religion over another. It is shocking that this mandatory curriculum is being administered in U.S. public schools where no other religions are promoted or taught to this magnitude. This is unconstitutional."

Yes, it is unconstitutional on both the national and state level.

The Clarion Project recently noted: "The U.S. Department of Education's presentation of the 'Access Islam' program completely contradicts America's stance on the Israel-Palestinian conflict. The U.S. has shown our ally support of Israel and does not recognize a country called 'Palestine.'"

The question to be posed: How can America publicly support Israel and yet allow anti-Israel, pro-Islamic propaganda to be a mandatory course in any American classroom? And this in a nation with a public school system where no other religion is openly promoted and the Bible is not welcomed to be openly read? Prayers at football games, as you'll recall, are considered dangerous expressions of faith. Was Christianity being taught as a mandatory subject in America's schools, we all know that the left-wing ACLU would be battering down doors to get to the Supreme Court!

Growing anti-Semitism

Members of which of these groups were most likely to be a victim of a hate crime in 2018: **Muslims, Blacks, or Jews?** Based on media coverage, you would probably say Muslims or Blacks. According to a Google news search for the term "hate crimes" along with the name of each of those three groups, there are **1.85 million results** for "hate crimes + black" (or 165,000 results for "hate crimes + Black American"), **80,800 results** for "hate crimes + Muslim", and only **65,400 results** for "hate crimes + Jew". Based on news reports, you might think that Blacks were far more likely than Jews to be the victim of a hate crime and that Muslims were somewhat more likely to be a hate crime victim compared to Jews. *This is another example of the biased left-wing Google search engine covering for Blacks and Muslims.*

Hate crime data released today by the FBI for 2018 reveals that there were 2,426 Black/African-American victims of hate crimes last year, 920 Jewish victims, and 236 Muslim victims. Adjusting for the population size of each group (43.84 million Blacks in 2018 according to the Census Bureau and 6.2 million Jews and 3.6 million Muslims based on Pew Research Center data), the **hate crime victimization rates** last year per 100,000 population of each group were **14.8 for Jews, 6.6 for Muslims** and **5.5 for Blacks** (see chart above). Therefore, adjusted for population by group, American Jews were 2.7 times more likely than Blacks to be a victim of a hate crime last year and more than twice as likely as a Muslim to be a hate crime victim.

The FBI data for 2018 on **anti-religion hate crimes** also reveal that of the 1,617 victims of anti-religious hate crimes last year in the U.S., 920 were Jews (56.9% of the total) and 236 victims were Muslims (14.6% of the total). Obviously, since more than half of the anti-religious hate crime incidents in 2018 were against Jews, there were more hate crime incidents last year of anti-religious hate crimes against Jews (920) than incidents of hate crimes against *all other religious groups combined* (397). The FBI data also show that there were more Jewish hate crime victims last year than gay men who were victims of hate crimes (863).

Without any adjustments for population, there were nearly four times as many Jewish hate crime victims (920) last year as Muslim victims (236). And yet there are 23.5% more media reports on hate crimes against Muslims than news reports on hate crimes against Jews. The Jewish community in the United States experienced near-historic levels of anti-Semitism last year, with attacks against Jews and Jewish institutions doubling in number, according to new data from the Anti-Defamation League.

The ADL recorded a total of 1,879 anti-Semitic incidents across the country in 2018, the third-highest year on record since the New York-based Jewish organization began tracking such data in the 1970s. Those incidents included cases of assaults, harassment, and vandalism. The report found that college campuses in America are becoming "increasingly hostile for Jewish students who support Israel." It cites a 2018 survey that revealed 238 incidents of harassment, vandalism, and assault targeting Jewish students on 118 campuses across the U.S. In New York, city police noted a 22% rise in violent anti-Semitic attacks, according to the report.

Based on hate crime victimization rates and the fact that Jews are so disproportionately targeted in hate crimes compared to Blacks and Muslims, is it fair to say that hate crimes against Jews are routinely under-reported by the media relative to the reporting of hate crimes against Blacks and Muslims?

Indeed, Is America experiencing Europe's growing anti-Semitism? That was at the center of a conference by the Hudson Institute's Center for Religious Freedom, featuring experts on anti-Semitism in Europe and results from a May 2019 poll of Americans.

For example, the poll found that instead of anti-Semitism becoming normalized, most Americans think anti-Semitism is increasing in the U.S. (and see it as a problem in society). But 20% don't believe 6 million Jews died in the Holocaust, and those respondents are more likely to be young.

"America is facing a shocking spike in anti-Semitism and, in addition to traditional sources on the extreme right, this time it includes left-wing progressives and Islamists," the Hudson Institute said in its press release about the event.

An Anti-Defamation League's (ADL) poll measuring anti-Semitism in the country discovered that more than half of U.S. citizens surveyed agree with at least one anti-Semitic stereotypical statement. The poll, which studied Americans' perceptions of Jews showed **11 percent of respondents "intensely harbor" anti-Semitic views** by agreeing to six or more anti-Jewish statements. **That percentage would translate to about 28 million people.** ADL polls over the last 25 years have consistently shown between 11 and 14 percent of citizens have extreme anti-Semitic mindsets, prompting the group to conclude that the increase in anti-Semitic attacks is caused by a growing willingness to act on these beliefs instead of a rise in people who hold these beliefs.

"In recent times, we've been horrified by an uptick in anti-Semitic violence," ADL CEO Jonathan Greenblatt said in the poll's release. "Our research finds that this uptick is being caused not by a change in attitudes among most Americans. Rather, more of the millions of Americans holding anti-Semitic views are feeling emboldened to act on their hate."

The poll tested 11 stereotypical anti-Semitic statements, including "Jews still talk too much about what happened to them in the Holocaust," which 19 percent of respondents agreed with. Participants were also asked if "Jews want to weaken our national culture by supporting more immigrants coming to our country," which received 10 percent support. The sample was also questioned on other stereotypes, including Jews being "more loyal to Israel than to America" which received 24 percent support, and others including Jews having too much power in the business world, with 15 percent agreeing. Fourteen percent of individuals also said they agree that Israel sometimes "behaves as badly as the Nazis." *Where are these horrific views formed? It is not the Right that controls the media, Big Tech, academia, or the anti-Semitic Black churches or the radical Dems.*

But the poll still showed positive statements associated with the Jewish community, with 79 percent saying Jews "place a strong emphasis on the importance of family life" and 66 percent saying "Jews have contributed much to the cultural life of America."

In a just-released survey by the American Jewish Committee, more than 80 percent of Jewish respondents say they have witnessed an increase in anti-Semitic incidents in the United States over the past five years, with 43 percent indicating that the increase has been significant. That anti-Semitism is spiking is not only a matter of perception, however. The Anti-Defamation League reported a 150 percent increase in recorded incidents comparing 2013 with 2018.

At the Hudson Institute conference Hon. Elan Carr, the U.S. Department of State's Special Envoy to Monitor and Combat Anti-Semitism, spoke eloquently about the rather deceptive idea that there is a "new" anti-Semitism. He shook his head. "It's just the same old thing," he explained. Ancient accusations against Jews, such as the infamous "blood libel," are newly packaged in such twisted guises as "Israelis are child murderers," and "Jews have infected Palestinian children with the AIDS virus."

The best-selling author of *Hate: The Rising Tide of Anti-Semitism in France (and What it Means for Us),* Marc Weitzmann, traced the beginnings of today's virulent strain of French anti-Semitism to the 1990s, when dozens of Algerian terrorists relocated in France and began to multiply their ranks exponentially. This was soon followed by the 2000 demise of Israel's "Peace Process," marked by the deadly Second Intifada in Israel. *Do you know that one of the first actions the Biden administration promised to do is to reverse Trump's ban on immigration from Muslim countries that harbor terrorism, anti-Semitism, and hate America? Do you think that will increase anti-Semitic hate crimes?*

The following (thanks to Hudson Institute) are some of McLaughlin's major findings:

- Contrary to fears that anti-Semitism has become normalized in the U.S., most voters are familiar with anti-Semitism and believe it is increasing. In an open-ended question, 62% of participants described anti-Semitism as a hatred of Jews or bigotry.
- Religious intolerance is seen as the leading cause of anti-Semitism (25%), followed by Muslim extremism (19%).
- Attempts by college campuses to shut down pro-Israel speakers are viewed by a majority (54%) of likely voters as anti-Semitic.
- The Boycott, Divestment, and Sanctions (BDS) movement is seen as anti-Semitic by a majority of likely voters by a nearly 3-to-1 ratio. A plurality of respondents thinks the U.S. should oppose BDS campaigns.
- It is not Islamophobic to criticize Congresswoman Ilhan Omar for her views on Israel, noted 63% of respondents; and 40% of likely voters have an unfavorable opinion of Congresswoman Omar, while 21% have a favorable opinion.
- The Democratic Party is not doing enough to combat anti-Semitism within its own party, respondents noted by a 2-to-1 ratio (48% to 22%).

- A solid majority (57%) of respondents want Israel to be the United States' closest ally in the Middle East.
- An overwhelming majority (80%) believe it is true that in the Holocaust, 6 million Jews were targeted and exterminated. Respondents under 40 years of age were 31% less likely to believe that the Holocaust occurred.
- By a 2-to-1 ratio, likely voters have a favorable opinion of Israel. A majority believes that U.S. support of Israel is "about right" or "too little."

The McLaughlin national survey was conducted in May among 1,000 random, registered and likely voters in the 2020 election.

Left-wing Trope

Like so many areas of censorship, the Left, with the help of their media and Big Tech propaganda arms, have been trying to downplay the rise in Black and Muslim anti-Semitism including the ugly statements made by BLM and radical Muslims such as Tlaib in the Democratic party. These radicals continue to be supported by associates of the corrupt billionaire George Soros. American Jews believe that the hike in white supremacy goes hand in hand with the hike in anti-Semitic incidents across our country: 89 percent of AJC respondents believe the extreme political right presents a threat to Jews. They ignore the fact that most recent hate crimes against the Jews are committed by Blacks and Muslims.

Like those unwashed losers who try to make the Jews scapegoats for everything going wrong in their lives; the do-nothing Left tries to pin all of America's and their own failings on Donald Trump. Even with respect to generations of overt far-right anti-Semitism, they have found the source: the start of the presidency of Donald Trump. To those not brainwashed, this is as disgusting as the 14% of American bigots that compare Israel to the Nazis or the 20% that are Holocaust deniers.

Moreover, it is the complete opposite of the facts. ***The truth is no President in history has done more for Israel or had grandchildren that are being brought up Jewish.***

Myth: President Trump is OK with White Supremacists

Like the "Hands up don't shoot" and "No justice, no peace" harmful but baseless slogans, the Left uses "There are good people on both sides"—a statement they attributed to Trump after Charlottesville. That is the place where the BLM and Antifa terrorists found their match with other low-lives in the KKK. At that event, the KKK was not chanting anti-Black but rather anti-Semitic slogans that many of the radical Blacks there believe or have said in one form or the other. Indeed, with four decades of anti-Semitism and bigotry by Louis Farrakhan along with scores of black leaders including the current Democratic candidate for the Senate from Georgia; Jessie Jackson, Al Sharpton, Reverend Wright, Minister Rodney Muhammad, Ice Cube, DeSean Jackson, and Nick Cannon, all of whom have been criticized for posting or making anti-Semitic comments. *Do you remember Obama posed with Farrakhan and Wright was his minister?*

Like so much the Left made up about Trump to undermine his Presidency, from Russia collusion to the impeachment circus, Trump saying "There are good people on both sides" is another despicable, dangerous hoax. The recent bigotry and anti-Semitism erupting is in no way emboldened by President Trump, by his saying that "There were very fine people on both sides" in the Charlottesville riots. In the transcript of his remarks on FactCheck.org, Trump condemned white supremacy several times and was referring to the pulling down of a statue of Robert E. Lee when he spoke of "very fine people." People do disagree with the destruction of statues, and that is their right to do so. On the day of Heather Heyer's savage killing, he unequivocally issued a statement condemning hatred and violence by anyone. You can fault President Trump for many things, but distorting what he said at Charlottesville and thereafter is not good journalism; it's grasping at some political advantage.

Another hoax is that proud Americans, who support Trump and counter the BLM Antifa's rioting and destruction of their cites, are White Supremacists. The "Proud Boy" hoax is a good example of the on-going smear tactics used to reinforce left-wing brainwashing.

Enrique Tarrio insists that the Proud Boys aren't White Supremacists, and he would be in a position to know. For one, he's the international chairman. For another, **he's Black.**

"I denounce white supremacy," Mr. Tarrio said in a Thursday interview with WSVN-TV In Miami. "I denounce anti-Semitism. I denounce racism. I denounce fascism. I denounce communism and any other -ism that is prejudiced toward people because of their race, religion, culture, and tone of skin."

Mr. Tarrio headed the rising tide of those defending the Proud Boys against accusations of racism after President Trump came under fire for refusing to denounce the right-wing activist group at Tuesday's debate. Like so much of these myths perpetuated by the Left, its fake news and Big Tech propaganda affiliates; these had legs and hurt Republicans with Jews.

Forty-one percent of respondents to AJC's survey believe that the Republican Party bears all or close to all responsibility for the current levels of anti-Semitism. And 58 percent naively stated that the Democratic Party bears no, or close to no, responsibility for it. It's therefore hardly surprising that American Jews continue to show strong support for the Democratic Party; in the 2018 midterm elections, exit polls showed that three-quarters of Jewish Americans voted for Democrats.

Despite the facts of Trump's historic pro-Israel achievements that earned him five Nobel Prize nominations, somehow Jews blindly backed Democrats who support groups like BLM and scores of other progressive organizations that are blatantly anti-Semitic/Zionists. *Isn't this another good example of the Left's on-going successful brainwashing campaign?*

Chapter 8
MESS MIGRATION

"We have the most generous immigration policy, but what is a concern is when illegal immigrants come and undermine a variety of the systems that work in order to make our society function."

-Madeleine Albright

Emma Lazarus' quote, "Give me your tired, your poor, your huddled masses yearning to breathe free," still chokes me up. I'm proud of America's immigration record, and grateful that my Russian grandparents were allowed to pass under Lady Liberty's torch into this blessed land. Emotionally, I am pro-immigration, and value my many immigrant friends, and am saddened by images of their plight. But as an objective reviewer of immigration facts, particularly the impact of historically high levels of illegal and legal immigration, I am deeply disturbed.

In this chapter, I will dispel the myths related to the premise that mass and illegal immigration is good for America. Illegal immigration is good for Agribusinesses and others looking for cheap labor, for politicians always ready to sell out the American public for votes, left-wing open border radicals, and for the Catholic Church when they are looking for a source of new members. But the reality is that America's immigration policies have launched us into a risky experiment unlike any experienced by another country.

Despite the naïve, incredibly dangerous open border policy mutterings of the Biden administration, this country simply does not have the capacity, treasury, or will to accommodate and assimilate an unending wave of mass migration. We are already seeing many signs of a Balkanized, fragmented, strife-torn, and dysfunctional America. The politicians just don't get it; they will destroy our country and culture with their open border/amnesty programs. *Do you believe taxpayer expenses will increase if the Left succeeds in blocking serious border security reforms, allowing more illegal aliens to gain access to public services? Do you have a country without borders? Is this what you want?*

According to the Federation for American Immigration Reform (FAIR), illegal aliens living in the U.S. now number 14.3 million; that's up from 12.5 in 2017. And illegal immigration is costing taxpayers a whopping $131.9 billion annually. While President Trump has taken meaningful steps to curb illegal immigration and build the border wall, many left-leaning lawmakers in Congress, spurred on by the powerful anti-borders lobby, have put up fierce resistance to fully securing our southern border and reinforcing immigration law. These open border forces keep the country vulnerable to invasion by illegal aliens, human traffickers, drug smugglers, disease, and terrorists.

For too long the politicians in Washington have been hearing from the powerful radical, and well-funded no-borders, new world order lobby groups, even those representing foreign governments. These groups continue to funnel massive amounts of money into efforts to preserve former President Obama's unilateral action on amnesty and other pro-illegal alien policies that promote and reward illegal aliens breaking our law.

Center for Immigration Studies (CIS) Director of Research Steven Camarotta divulged some staggering statistics about the extent to which illegal immigrants have infiltrated America to give birth to U.S.-born children as a reason to stay in the country. A report reveals that there are 297,000 births per year to illegal immigrants in L.A. That means that there are more anchor babies born to illegal aliens in the metropolitan area of Los Angeles, California, than there are United States total births in 14 states—plus the District of Columbia. I don't remember voting to turn the U.S. into a Third World country, to change our culture by allowing millions to cross our borders illegally.

At the same time, current levels of <u>legal</u> immigration are also simply unsustainable. That is why it is essential to modernize our legal immigration system and ensure that those selected to enter our country can stand on their own two feet without government assistance.

Critical Tipping Point

If our government, under Biden, will use its power to continue to bring in over a million immigrants a year and reward illegal immigrants with official job status, and benefits within our country, what will American citizenship even mean? What about the sanctity of borders and the rule of law? What about our security, traditions, and freedoms? The radical Left wants to decriminalize illegal border crossings, which will incentivize more illegal immigration. *Is that what you want?*

The sad truth is, America is rapidly becoming a nation of illegal immigrants, many of whom have no respect for our borders, laws, values, or the English language. By failing to support lawful immigration, we've undermined the rule of law and sanctity of our borders, thus encouraging even more illegal immigration. On the other hand, cutting immigration levels, both legal and illegal, would go a long way to protect U.S. jobs for American workers, improve wages, and reduce the number of immigrants receiving taxpayer-funded benefits.

Before You Read the Myths, Know the Facts

Police commanders may not want to discuss, much less respond to, the illegal alien crisis, but its magnitude for law enforcement is startling. Moreover, the brainwashed Google monoculture monopoly pawns believe the myth that the social warriors are doing good covering up the many negative impacts of illegal aliens. The sad truth is they have become a biased, censored search engine that has been degraded into a propaganda arm for the Left and the victimization and divisity extortionist's destroying America. For example, Google, the fake news media, and the anti-borders lobby make it very difficult to get facts about rampant illegal alien crime.

Previous administrations have also deliberately kept Americans in the dark about illegal immigrant crimes. They go as far as making the outrageous claim that illegal aliens commit crimes at a lower rate than native born Americans. *This myth is another example of Google left-wing monoculture perpetuating biased dangerous propaganda. How sick it was to watch their CEO on TV lie to congress about Google being an objective, unbiased search engine. He appeared incompetent even as a liar.*

Moreover, most states like our federal government keep information and statistics about illegal immigration, crimes committed by illegals and the costs borne by you the U.S. payer out of public view. It is in fact difficult, but not impossible to locate accurate crime statistics involving illegal immigrants. The statistics are buried both to suit a political agenda and to avoid public outcry. Once you read below you will quickly understand why:

According to a report conducted by FAIR, *illegal aliens are incarcerated up to five and a half times as frequently as citizens and legal immigrants. In fact, today there are an estimated 2 million criminal aliens in the U.S.*

The pro-illegal immigrant lobby misrepresentation of comparisons in who commits crimes between illegal immigrants and American citizens is part of the Lefts on-going conspiracy to whitewash over a growing crime wave threatening progressive-run cities.

This assertion is false in most cases. Here are the vetted statistics:

Opponents of federal efforts to enforce the immigration laws enacted by Congress repeatedly claim that illegal immigrants are "less likely" to commit crimes than U.S. citizens—and thus represent no threat to public safety. But that's not true. In California, there are just over 92 illegal immigrants imprisoned for every 100,000 illegals; as compared to 74 citizens and legal non-citizen immigrants. In Arizona, the rate is nearly 69 illegals imprisoned for every 100,000, as compared to 54 citizens and legal non-citizen immigrants. In New York, over three times as many illegal immigrants or 169, are imprisoned for crimes per 100,000, as compared to only 48 citizens and legal non-citizen immigrants. Only in the states of Texas and Florida do illegal immigrants commit less crimes than their legal immigrant counterparts (Texas with 54.5 illegals imprisoned per 100,000, compared to 65 legal immigrants; and Florida with 55 illegals imprisoned, compared to 68 legal immigrants.)

Illegals account for most federal crimes.

Non-citizens constitute only about 7 percent of the U.S. population. Yet the latest data from the Justice Department's Bureau of Justice Statistics reveals that *non-citizens accounted for nearly two-thirds (64 percent) of all federal arrests in 2018.* Just two decades earlier, only 37 percent of all federal arrests were non-citizens.

These arrests aren't just for immigration crimes. Non-citizens accounted for 24 percent of all federal drug arrests, 25 percent of all federal property arrests, and 28 percent of all federal fraud arrests.

We need the border wall

Research conducted by the federal government oversight organization Judicial Watch in 2014 documents that *50 percent of all federal crimes were committed near our border with Mexico.* Of the 61,529 criminal cases filed by federal prosecutors, 40 percent, or 24,746, were in court districts along the southern borders of California, Arizona, and Texas.

Texas is an epicenter for illegal immigrant crimes

The Western District of Texas had the nation's most significant crime rate with over 6,300 cases filed; followed by the Southern District of Texas with slightly over 6,000 cases. The Southern California District with nearly 4,900 cases; New Mexico with nearly 4,000 cases; and Arizona with over 3,500 criminal cases ranked 3rd, 4th, and 5th. *In fact, in 2018, a quarter of all federal drug arrests took place in the five judicial districts along the U.S.-Mexico border*. Crime analysis by both the Department of Homeland Security (DHS) and Texas law enforcement authorities indicate that between June 2011 and March 2017, over 217,000 criminal immigrants were arrested and booked into Texas jails.

In researching the criminal careers of these defendants, it was revealed that they had jointly committed over nearly 600,000 criminal offenses. Their arrests included nearly 1,200 homicides; almost 69,000 assaults; 16,854 burglaries; 700 kidnappings; nearly 6,200 sexual assaults; 69,000 drug offenses; 8,700 weapons violations; over 3,800 robberies; and over 45,000 obstructing police charges. In determining the status of these offenders in the U.S., it was confirmed by DHS that over 173,000 or 66 percent of these immigrant criminal defendants were in our country illegally at the times of their arrests.

Nearly 3 percent of illegal immigrants in Arizona end up in state prison or jail during the course of a year, four times the rate of U.S. citizens and legal residents, according to a study that uses federal reimbursements for prisons and jails to try to calculate one of the most important yet elusive statistics in the immigration debate. In New Jersey, illegal immigrants are incarcerated five times more often, and rates on the West Coast are triple that of legal residents and citizens, according to the study by the Federation for American Immigration Reform.

In 2018, a quarter of all federal drug arrests took place in the five judicial districts along the U.S.-Mexico border. This reflects the ongoing activities of Mexican drug cartels. *Last year, Mexican citizens accounted for 40 percent of all federal arrests. In fact, more Mexicans than U.S. citizens were arrested on charges of committing federal crimes in 2018.* Migrants from Central American countries are also accounting for a larger share of federal arrests, going from a negligible 1 percent of such arrests in 1998 to 20 percent today.

The relationship between illegal immigrants and violent crime

The U.S. Department of Justice and the U.S. Sentencing Commission reported that as of 2014, illegal immigrants were convicted and sentenced for over 13 percent of all crimes committed in the U.S. According to the FBI, 67,642 murders were committed in the U.S. from 2005 through 2008, and 115,717 from 2003 through 2009. The General Accounting Office documents that *criminal immigrants committed 25,064 of these murders.* Indeed, illegal immigrants clearly commit a level of violent and drug related crimes disproportionate to their population. In California alone, over 2,400 illegal immigrants out of a total prison population of 130,000 are imprisoned in the state's prison system for the crime of homicide.

The U.S. Department of Justice documents that in 2014, 19 percent or over 12,000 criminal cases filed by prosecutors were for violent crimes; and over 22 percent or 13,300 cases were for drug related felonies. That same year, the U.S. Sentencing Commission found that 75 percent of all criminal defendants who were convicted and sentenced for federal drug offenses were illegal immigrants. Illegal immigrants were also involved in 17 percent of all drug trafficking sentences and one third of all federal prison sentences. Non-citizens accounted for 24 percent of all federal drug arrests, 25 percent of all federal property arrests, and 28 percent of all federal fraud arrests.

FAIR based its calculations on federal government reimbursements to states and localities under the State Criminal Alien Assistance Program, which pays some of the costs of holding illegal immigrants in prisons and jails. To make the payments, the federal government must determine whether an inmate is definitely or possibly in the country illegally. FAIR used the number to then calculate overall incarceration rates.

The extreme costs of keeping illegal immigrant criminals in this country

According to research and statistics by the U.S. Departments of Justice and Homeland Security, U.S. taxpayers are footing an annual bill of nearly **$19 million a day to house and care for an estimated 300,000 to 450,000 convicted criminal immigrants who are eligible for deportation and are currently residing in local jails and state and federal prisons across the country.** These figures include not only those immigrants who are in the U.S. illegally, but all immigrants here who commit and have been convicted of crimes. The institutional burden of illegal immigration also includes a federal crime rate higher than that of citizens. Considering it costs the federal government $32,000 annually for each prisoner, the approximately 25,000 noncitizens in our prison system amounts to nearly $1 billion in expenses annually, not to mention the expenses of state correctional facilities and immigration enforcement.

The overall figures for border enforcement have skyrocketed as well. The number of border patrol agents has increased by almost five times over the last 25 years, and nearly doubled in the last 15 years. Meanwhile, the costs of protecting the southern border with Mexico have increased by nearly tenfold in the same period of 25 years to almost $4 billion annually. This does not even factor in the 43 percent of illegal immigrants who fail to show up to their scheduled court hearings following their detentions.

Other accounting estimates indicate that the total cost for all corrections, medical, and support services for adults and juvenile immigrant criminals nationally to be over $1.8 billion dollars. So the next time you hear some Open Borders politician or pro illegal immigrant surrogates advocate on their behalf, ask yourself why we as American citizens need to bear the increasing costs of violence, victimization, and burdensome taxes in subsidizing illegal immigrant criminals who shouldn't be in our country in the first place.

"Sanctuary state" "Sanctuary cities"

California politicians fight deporting criminal illegal immigrants. Politicians who declare their jurisdictions to be sanctuaries for illegal immigrants who commit crimes are needlessly endangering their law-abiding citizens.

Illegal immigrants released by local police in California after their arrests for minor offenses go on to be charged with more serious crimes such as murder, rape, and assault, according to a new government report. Those crimes could have been prevented if these sanctuary jurisdictions had turned over those accused to federal immigration officials for deportation.

The decision by a California appeals court overturning the conviction of an illegal immigrant who shot and killed Kate Steinle in San Francisco in 2015 put the national spotlight on the serious problem of crimes committed by people in the U.S. illegally. The appeals court in San Francisco overturned the conviction of Jose Inez Garcia-Zarate on a charge of being a felon in possession of a firearm. Garcia-Zarate was earlier found not guilty of first- and second-degree murder, involuntary manslaughter, and assault with a semi-automatic weapon. Garcia-Zarate said he unwittingly picked up a gun, which he said was wrapped in a T-shirt, and it fired accidentally.

Critics will try to downplay the importance of a Justice Department's report by pointing out that the majority of crimes in the United States are handled by prosecutors in state and local courts. In one case, police in San Francisco arrested an illegal immigrant from Honduras again and again over nine months as he repeatedly was released and then booked again for more offenses rather than turned over to federal officials. Had San Francisco turned over the illegal immigrant to ICE after his first arrest in February 2018, the report suggests, it's likely the government would have deported him and the San Francisco Police Department would not have had to charge him in the course of <u>nine arrests between April 2018 and January 2019.</u> The San Francisco Police Department does not enforce immigration laws and department policy prohibits SFPD members from placing administrative immigration holds or ICE detainers on arrestees, making it a popular destination for criminal aliens to operate. *What happened to once great cities all run by Democrats that are all experiencing record high crime rates? Do you think Biden will be strong on law and order, or will he support the BLM backed BREATHE Act, described as a "roadmap for prison abolition?"*

When ICE determines an illegal immigrant accused of a criminal offense is in police custody, the agency issues a detainer. The paperwork is supposed to ensure the alleged offender will be transferred to federal authorities at the conclusion of his or her time in the local jail, instead of being released. But sanctuary jurisdictions—as a matter of policy—ignore the detainer, which in some cases means the criminal illegal immigrants are released and able to commit new crimes rather than be deported. Additionally, some jurisdictions willfully decline to honor ICE detainers and refuse to timely notify ICE of an alien's release, and may do so even when an alien has a criminal record. Unfortunately, a number of aliens who have been released under these circumstances have gone on to commit additional crimes, including violent felonies. ICE maintains that most of these crimes could have been prevented if ICE had been able to assume custody of these aliens and remove them from the country in accordance with federal immigration laws. ICE released the report as the agency seeks to deport illegal immigrants whose cases were adjudicated and who received final deportation orders.

Numerous mayors have vowed not to cooperate with ICE enforcement actions. Los Angeles Mayor Eric Garcetti, with Police Chief Michel Moore at his side, told illegal immigrants over the weekend: "Your city is on your side." The new report notes an irony to the outcome of sanctuary policies. "Ultimately, a jurisdiction's decision to ignore ICE detainers increases the need for ICE's presence in communities and requires additional resources to locate and arrest removable aliens," the report says. *LALA land is ground zero for illegal alien crime. Homicides are up by one-fifth since last year; shame on a Mayor and District Attorney who side with criminals over residents. Are you visiting there soon?*

Revolving jail door

A recent report from the Texas Department of Public Safety revealed that 297,000 non-citizens had been "booked into local Texas jails between June 1, 2011 and July 31, 2019." So these are non-citizens who allegedly committed local crimes, not immigration violations. The report noted that a little more than two-thirds (202,000) of those booked in Texas jails were later confirmed as illegal immigrants by the federal government. According to the Texas report, *over the course of their criminal careers those illegal immigrants were charged with committing 494,000 criminal offenses.*

Some of these cases are still being prosecuted, but the report states that there have already been over 225,000 convictions. *Those convictions represent: 500 homicides; 23,954 assaults; 8,070 burglaries; 297 kidnappings; 14,178 thefts; 2,026 robberies; 3,122 sexual assaults; 3,840 sexual offenses; 3,158 weapon charges; and tens of thousands of drug and obstruction charges.*

These statistics reveal the very real danger created by sanctuary policies. In nine self-declared sanctuary states and numerous sanctuary cities and counties, officials refuse to hand over criminals who are known to be in this country illegally after they have served their state or local sentences. **You do know Biden will not stop this lunacy but rather support even more of it?**

This refusal to cooperate with federal immigration officials suggests that state and local officials supporting the sanctuary movement believe it's better to let these criminals return to their communities rather than being removed from this country. Not all of their constituents would agree. *I don't, do you?*

What is highly relevant to the current debate about immigration policy are reports that identify thousands of crimes that should not have occurred and thousands of victims that should not have been victimized because the perpetrators should not be here. *Are you hearing a lot about criminal reform but not the staggering increase in victims in states run by so-called progressives? Do you prefer Trump's strong law and order stance to the Left's calls to defund the police or BLM's call to empty our jails?*

We know all around the country some individuals would be alive today—and their families would not be mourning their loss—if we had a secure border and an effective interior enforcement system. Instead of trying to obstruct enforcement of our immigration laws, state and local officials should do everything they can to help the feds reduce the very real—and all too often fatal—dangers posed by criminal illegal immigrants. *Do you agree?*

One of the worst recent examples of a state official who refuses to help federal immigration authorities carry out their duties is North Carolina Gov. Roy Cooper. The Democratic governor recently vetoed a bill that would require local law enforcement to cooperate with federal immigration authorities. Cooper did so just days after Immigration and Customs Enforcement (ICE) agents captured an illegal immigrant charged with first-degree rape and indecent liberties against a child. The man arrested in that crime was on the loose because he had been released from custody by county officials, despite the existence of a federal detainer warrant for him.

Politicians who declare their jurisdictions to be sanctuaries for illegal immigrants who commit crimes are needlessly endangering their law-abiding citizens. That is shameful.

Did you know that Mexico regularly intercedes on the side of the defense in criminal cases involving Mexican nationals? Mexico has **NEVER** extradited a Mexican national accused of murder in the U.S., despite agreements to do so. I thank the Federation for American Immigration Reform (FAIR) for their help in debunking some of the following immigration myths.

Myth: Illegals pay in more than they cost

Breaking the Piggy Bank

With states straining under gaping budget shortfalls, public schools are facing some of the most significant decreases in state funding in decades. While these massive budget deficits cannot be attributed to any single source, the enormous impact of large-scale illegal immigration is dramatic. Setting aside the legal and moral questions that shape immigration policy, there is a significant tax burden imposed on citizens and legal immigrants tied to a leaky border. President Trump made headlines last year for questioning the costs of illegal immigration. Our dutiful firefighters in the mainstream press fact checked each word and called his $250 billion figure an exaggeration. However, looking at the substance of his argument shows that he was likely on the mark.

A FAIR report, "The fiscal burden of illegal immigration on United States Taxpayers," found the costs of illegal immigration are mind-blowing. This report *estimates* **the annual costs of illegal immigration at the federal, state, and local level to be about $113 billion**; nearly $29 billion at the federal level and $84 billion at the state and local level. This is even after deducting the $19 billion in taxes paid by illegal immigrants living in the country, including those in the above-ground economy and those in the underground economy. Those receipts do not come close to the level of expenditures paid out by economy and taxpayers each year.

About two-thirds of this amount is absorbed by local and state taxpayers, who are often the least unable to share the costs. The bulk of the costs—some $84 billion—are absorbed by state and local governments. The annual outlay that illegal aliens cost U.S. taxpayers is an annual amount per native-headed household of nearly $1,000 after accounting for estimated tax collections. The fiscal impact per household varies considerably because the greatest share of the burden falls on state and local taxpayers whose burden depends on the size of the illegal alien population in that locality.

As the debate on illegal immigration rages in Washington and state capitals, it's troubling to see both sides rely on emotional rhetoric to the detriment of facts. The impact of illegal immigration on public education is a case in point. No one can deny that increasing numbers of children of illegal immigrants attend public schools in the United States and that U.S. taxpayers pay the costs. Those sympathetic to illegal immigration tend to remain silent about these costs, while illegal-immigration opponents often fall short on specifics. In the interest of more informed discourse, here are the numbers:

Education for the children of illegal aliens constitutes the single largest cost to taxpayers, at an annual price tag of nearly $52 billion. Nearly all of those costs are absorbed by state and local governments. At the federal level, about one-third of outlays are matched by tax collections from illegal aliens. At the state and local level, an average of less than 5 percent of the public costs associated with illegal immigration is recouped through taxes collected from illegal aliens.

Myth: The Cost of Not Educating Undocumented Children is Higher than Educating Them

Fact: This kind of statement is absurd. It assumes that disallowing illegal alien children from entering our schools and/or deporting them are not options. The idea that undocumented children are being punished for their parents' bad deeds is ludicrous. Undocumented children already have citizenship and the right to an education in another country. California's schools have a "don't ask, don't tell" policy regarding who gets to go to school. This policy is a powerful magnet that attracts illegals to California. The costs are enormous. Undocumented children are being rewarded, often with special grants and privileged programs. *We do not want to punish children for illegal status, but why should we reward them?*

Few disagree that if the current rate of illegal immigration continues, one school will have to be built each day to accommodate the undocumented children and citizen children of undocumented parents. *Nearly all the increase in public school enrollment over the past 20 years is due, not to the Baby Boom generation having children, but rather to lax federal immigration policies and practices.*

One of the major drivers of the increasing costs is the 4.2 million children of migrants, who automatically become American citizens. Taxpayers are indeed on the hook for over $45 billion in state and federal education spending annually. The taxpayers' hard-earned contribution toward school expenditures does not represent the total costs.

The threat to send illegal immigrants to sanctuary cities and states becomes clearer when looking at the local costs of poor border policy. The proposal underlines states like California, which has the highest burden related to its large noncitizen population. Home to 2.2 million illegal immigrants as of 2016, a full 15 percent of students are undocumented or have parents who are. The total costs of education due to immigration will nearly double in the state over the next 50 years.

The special programs for non-English speakers incur not only an additional fiscal burden, but also present a hindrance to the learning environment. A study found that dual language programs represent an additional $279 to $879 per pupil, depending on the class size.

Myth: The U.S. is Hostile to Immigration

Fact: The number of foreign-born people in the United States grew last year to its highest share in over a century, according to Census Bureau data published on Thursday. The increase took the number of foreign-born residents to 44.5 million in 2017, up 1.8 percent from a year earlier. The administration has said it wants to restrict legal immigration, and has stepped up efforts as well to detain and deport immigrants in the country illegally since President Donald Trump took office in January 2017.

But so far, said Randy Capps, a demographer at the Migration Policy Institute, the government hasn't restricted legal immigration much and America's strong job market likely fueled part of last year's increase in the foreign-born population. "The economy's definitely a factor in this, not just in more people coming but in more people staying," Capps said.

Foreign-born residents made up 13.7 percent of the U.S. population in 2017, up from 13.5 percent in 2016, according to the Census Bureau's estimates. That put the proportion of immigrants in the United States last year at the highest since 1910, when they made up 14.7 percent of the population.

The data also showed that an increasing number of immigrants were Asian or had advanced university degrees, extending a trend that has been in place for over a decade during which immigration from Mexico slowed. The share of immigrants from Mexico fell to 25.3 percent last year from 26.5 percent in 2016, while the share from China rose to 6.4 percent from 6.2 percent.

Myth: Illegal Aliens Pay Taxes That Benefit the Economy

Fact: Most illegal aliens do not receive a typical paycheck with tax deductions. They are typically paid in cash, and therefore do not pay taxes. Even when they do pay taxes (it is possible, if they use fraudulent social security numbers or government-assigned tax ID numbers), their income does not allow enough in taxes to cover medical expenses for all the children.

The Federation for American Immigration Reform (FAIR) is one of the few groups devoted to highlighting the myths regarding legal and illegal immigration and making sensible suggestions for reform. Like so many views that do not support the brainwashed narratives of the Left; Google also hides FAIR and other sites presenting facts about the negative impact of illegal immigration.

FAIR's report, "The Fiscal Burden of Illegal Immigration on United States Taxpayers (2017)," by Matthew O'Brien, Spencer Raley, and Jack Martin, estimates that the net fiscal costs of illegal immigration to U.S. taxpayers is $116 billion. In the last few years, how many times have you heard a media talking head or a liberal politician say that the illegal immigrants are primarily "hardworking people who pay their taxes"? Yes, most immigrants I've met are hardworking people. But the truth of the matter is that illegal immigrants pay less than 0.1% of all Federal income taxes, even though they represent over 4.0% of the population.

Just look at the statistics or visit the maternal ward at the LA County hospital. The illegal immigrant women have thousands of children per year, free of charge, and then can't afford to support them. Most of us, including immigrants, like Bernie Sanders's promises of free everything and learn quickly how to get cash assistance and food stamps, based on these children. In fact, some states like CA, OR, and WA are handing out free cash and other benefits to illegal aliens! These states are handing out China virus relief money to thousands of people who have no right to be in our country in the first place.

Indeed, modern America is already a welfare state, and waves of low-skilled immigrants and their political lackeys are continually using that welfare to unravel our social safety net—one that is already torn. According to TREA Senior Citizens League, under the proposed "totalization" plan known as the U.S./Mexico Social Security Treaty, if all Mexican citizens who worked in the U.S. could start

197

collecting Social Security benefits, even if they are here illegally it **would cost more than $110 billion by 2040.**

Myth: It's about Cheap Labor

Fact: From the socialists who are so anxious to blame business, we hear that it is all about cheap labor. Isn't that what the whole immigration issue is about? Businesses don't want to pay a decent wage. Consumers don't want expensive produce. But the phrase "cheap labor" is a myth, a farce, and a lie. There is no such thing as "cheap labor."

Take, for example, an illegal Mexican who sneaks into the country with his wife and five children. He takes a job for $5 or $6 an hour. **At that wage, with six dependents, he pays no income tax, yet at the end of the year, if he files income tax, he gets "earned income credit" of up to $3,200, for free.** He qualifies for Section 8 housing and subsidized rent. He qualifies for food stamps. He qualifies for free (no deductible, no co-pay) health care. **His children get free breakfasts and lunches at school**, and bilingual teachers and books are provided. **He qualifies for relief from high energy bills. The aged, blind, or disabled qualify for SSI, and once qualified, they receive Medicare.** All of this is at that taxpayer's expense.

Myth: America Has Room for Immigrants

Fact: The open spaces one sees from an airplane are not where the multitude of new immigrants and their families will settle. They continue to settle in the already-overcrowded urban area of the country, just like immigrants always have. Much of America's open spaces are occupied by food production, national parks, wilderness, and uninhabitable land. All of our open space is threatened by population encroachment, as well as resource grabbing by business. Both of these threats are made worse by the sudden influx of illegal immigrants. *Do you think the environmentalists on the Left should encourage mass migration? Population growth is depleting resources and increasing pollution in many of the countries these immigrants are coming from. What will their impact be on our limited natural resources?*

Ripping the social safety net

Much of the almost $30 billion in medical and assistance funding is due to **the fact that noncitizen families in the United States are twice as likely to receive welfare payments** than **native born families.** A full half of noncitizens receive Medicaid, compared to 23 percent of native-born citizens, while almost half of noncitizens are on food stamps. Of particular concern is that noncitizens that stay in the long term are more likely to use these programs than those who just arrived. Half of new noncitizens receive welfare, but the figure jumps to a stunning 70 percent among those who have been in the United States for more than 10 years.

Californians are saddled with $23 billion in tax dollars for services relating to the illegal population, which makes up more than 10 percent of the state budget. Californians pay 11 percent of their incomes in state and local taxes already. The additional burden imposed by illegal immigrants is $600 in costs to each citizen annually.

This is a financial crisis, and one that we allowed to happen. For all of the debate over wall funding, Americans should keep in mind that recurring costs due to illegal immigration well exceed the amount to build such a wall. When you notice your paycheck deductions or see our unsustainable government debt, consider how we allowed ourselves to get to this point.

Is Education Important to You?

Here are the words of a teacher who spent over 20 years in the Los Angeles school system: "Imagine teachers in classes containing 30 to 40 students of widely varying attention spans and motivation; many of whom aren't fluent in English. Educators seek learning materials likely to reach the majority of students, and that means fewer words and math problems and more pictures and multicultural references."

This year, there will be almost 37,000 "unaccompanied" alien minors who will be enrolling in public school in the United States. These kids will require special Limited English Proficient (LEP) classes conducted in Spanish, or in other languages indigenous to Central America, as well as other taxpayer-funded services, such as free and reduced school meals. Once again the costs of federal government's failed immigration policies are borne at the local level, and the nation's public school system is where the costs are most visible.

We have heard often enough that we are a nation of immigrants. True enough, but the immigrants that came through Ellis Island wanted to learn English and to become Americans in every way. Now, too many immigrants come here demanding that lessons be taught in their own language, special privileges called affirmative action, and ethnic studies that glorify their cultures. The government uses taxpayer money to provide signs, bulletins, printed material, and automated recordings in immigrant languages.

Myth: Illegal Aliens Don't Affect Politics Because They Can't Vote

Fact: In the 2020 election the public missed another politically driven power grab by the Left, including radical lobby groups like La Raza and others supported by George Soros to corruptly influence the outcome of American elections by enabling ineligible non-citizens to vote. *Do you believe non-U.S. citizens should be allowed to vote in American elections? Do you believe states should be allowed to require potential voters to produce an official form of citizen verification prior to be allowed to vote?*

The main reason politicians support amnesty for illegal aliens is to include these voting blocks in their political parties. When illegal aliens ultimately become voting citizens, most vote in blocks—not for the good of America, but for economic gain and benefits for their crowd. Their gains usually come at the expense of another group. One such example is promoting policies of amnesty for their illegal countrymen in the U.S. *Do you believe amnesty of any kind will make it easier for non-U.S. citizens in California to vote in U.S. elections?*

As these minorities become a majority in many congressional districts, the legislators with Hispanic and Asian surnames set agendas that continually take more from the system than they give back. They exert political pressure on business and government to supply money and jobs to help solve the problems of their needy districts. This demographic shift continues to exert what Robert Dahl called "minority rule," in which public policy is arrived at by neither a majority nor a minority, but rather through the compromises of various organized and vocal minorities. The old squeaky wheel syndrome is the oil that moves our politicians to cater to the needs of a vocal and growing minority.

Myth: Chain Migration is good for America

Fact: In 2015, the United States granted 1,051,031 immigrants lawful permanent resident status. That's nearly enough people to populate a major city the size of Dallas, Texas. Why are so many immigrants accepted each year?

Under the United States' current immigration system, most migrants receive a green card simply because they are the relative of an earlier migrant, not because of what they can contribute to American society. This creates a "chain" of immigrants who can then sponsor other immigrants in the same manner. These, in turn, may sponsor more immigrants, and so on. Indeed, as more and more immigrants are admitted to the United States, the population eligible to sponsor their relatives for green cards increases exponentially. This means that every time one immigrant is admitted, the door is opened to many more.

While an annual cap on the admissions of immediate relatives of U.S. citizens was eliminated, most other immigrant categories remain subject to annual limits. As a result, there is a backlog of immigrant visa applications for those categories in countries like India and the Philippines. The wait can often be decades long. There is evidence that these long lines encourage many intending immigrants with marketable skills to seek admission to countries with merit-based immigration systems. Additionally, some argue that the long waits caused by chain migration encourage people to cut the line by immigrating illegally.

The Future of Chain Migration Policy

President Trump was calling for an end to chain migration in favor of a system that admits new migrants based on merit—what they are able to contribute to American society. He has endorsed the RAISE Act, introduced by Senators Tom Cotton (R-Arkansas) and David Perdue (R-Georgia). If passed, the current, overly-broad "family reunification" policies will have been replaced with a system designed to attract immigrants with job skills needed in the U.S. economy, as well as the education and language ability required to succeed. It would also eliminate immigration pathways for extended family members, allowing only the spouses and unmarried minor children of the primary applicant to qualify as derivative beneficiaries.

Simply put, chain migration doesn't place the interests of American citizens first. As a result, many well-deserving immigrants with skills and values that could potentially enhance the cultural and economic goals of the United States are passed over in favor of the relatives of previous migrants, no matter what they bring to the table. This is unfair to both American workers and those who have worked hard to form skills that could benefit this nation.

Replacing chain migration with a merit-based system would both lower the overall number of aliens accepted into the country each year, and ensure that those accepted are able to further the United States' cultural and economic priorities. Immigration based on merit: another sensible Trump policy that will be reversed by an idiotic, destructive, unworkable, Biden open-border and increased immigration policy.

Myth: Issuing California Drivers Licenses to Illegal Aliens will make Our Roads Safer

Fact: Many Illegal aliens currently drive without licenses. Society must assume that anyone who would break the law and drive without a license would continue to break driving and other laws even if they were licensed. It is absurd to think that illegal aliens are going to run out and buy car insurance, just because they are given a license. Indeed, one of the most profitable documents now being sold to illegals is fraudulent proof of insurance documents.

Myth: The Immigrants/Illegals Will Assimilate Into Society

Melting pot vs. Patch work quilt

Assimilation is generally defined as adopting the ways of another culture and fully becoming part of a different society. Whereas integration is typically defined as incorporating individuals from different groups into a society as equals. The difference is subtle but significant.

When immigrants assimilate, they accept the ways of their host and become a full part of the community. Assimilation implies that immigrants, through education and experience, can earn their way into the host culture and be seamlessly accepted as full members of their new community.

By contrast, integration suggests boundaries. It is defined in terms of equality. But in this context, equality indicates that a host is obligated to embrace foreign cultures as equal, even when they conflict with the values and traditions of the host. Integration may sound wonderful, but this isn't always the case. Imagine the chaos that would result if a mass migration of Britons insisted the United States integrate their tradition of driving on the left side of the road, rather than assimilating to the American preference for the right side. That's an amusing example. But the situation becomes dire if one considers the wider implications of integration over assimilation—especially when mass migration is from countries where free speech, women's rights, religious choice, honor killings, female genital mutilation, polygamy, child labor, or slavery is considered acceptable.

A major fear today among the American people is another Muslim terror attack. It is our government's chief responsibility to enact whatever public policies are necessary to reduce that fear and eliminate the threat. This is a significant data point in the public debate over Muslim immigration. Donald Trump, of course, has famously proposed a suspension of Islamic immigration until we can figure out a way to screen out jihadists. Indeed, the primary role of government is to keep us safe.

To be sure, a majority of Muslims and their children are well integrated into American society, and we should welcome and encourage their continued assimilation. However, the attacks in Europe and the United States are and will be stark reminders that mass immigration sometimes sows the seeds of violent conflict.

What lessons can we learn from other countries with no jihadi attacks and those with many?

This means there is much we can learn from Japan, which has been virtually free from Islamic unrest. Simple demographics tell the story. There is a simple reason we never read about jihadi attacks in Japan. There are no Muslims there. No Muslims, no terrorists are a fact; not Islamaphobia in Japan. Sometime stating facts and dealing with reality sucks but it is time to put on big boy pants and stop inviting unnecessary trouble to cross the pond.

It was not long ago, Europe's leaders had a pipe-dream of a multicultural continent, its aging cities saved by millions of new migrants eager to join a stable, prosperous society. That dream has faded, with Europeans now opposing new migration by wide margins. Once-peaceful German and Swedish cities have seen a spike in crime, a resurgence of anti-Semitism, and growing political unrest—all associated with the migrant influx.

In 2016, Pew Research found that 59 percent of Europeans thought that immigrants imposed a burden on their countries. In addition, less than a third believe immigration has improved their countries, with 63 percent of Greeks and 53 percent of Italians, respectively, stating that immigrants have made things worse in their economically challenged countries. As the British political thinker Kenan Malik acknowledged in a 2015 *Foreign Affairs* essay, "multiculturalism" has devolved from "an answer to Europe's social problems" to a fraught reality of "fragmented societies, alienated minorities, and resentful citizenries."

In most places, the welcome wagon has lost its wheels. Even most progressive European countries; like the Netherlands, France, Denmark, Norway, and Germany have imposed stricter immigration controls over the last two years.

Unlike the United States, Canada, Australia, or New Zealand, modern Europe never produced melting pot societies. Though French Protestants and Jews, for example, played important roles over the centuries in the development of contemporary merchant and trading centers; immigrants were relatively marginal in much of the continent's economic advancement.

What migration did occur, though, proved mostly successful. France, for instance, benefited as far back as Charlemagne from Jewish merchants, who served as intermediaries with Islamic civilizations of that age. Later, Armenians, eastern

European Jews, Spaniards, Italians, and Vietnamese settled in the country, each group largely integrating into the mainstream culture and economy.

In the 1950s and 1960s, the mass migration of Turks into Germany, and North Africans into France in the 1990s and 2000s, brought in a new workforce. **But this one didn't integrate.**

Today, vast slums blight parts of the urban and suburban landscape in French and German cities. As a recent Organization for Economic Co-operation and Development (OECD) study notes, immigrants in Europe are having a hard time with socioeconomic assimilation. This is a particularly sad truth for Muslim immigrants, employed at lower rates in Europe than in America, according to R Street and the Cato Institute. The absence of social cohesion has created cultural tension—**discrimination against nonwhite applicants is far worse in France or Sweden than in the "systemic racist" U.S.**

Part of the problem lies with economic change. In Europe's reindustrializing economy, new immigrants have more difficulty finding higher-wage, entry-level work than in the past. *Many countries favored by immigrants, notably Germany, have among Europe's lowest economic-growth rates, while the fastest-growing countries—like Hungary and Poland—are also ones with strict immigration restrictions. Have you had enough of the let's make America like Europe babble? Reality sucks as do facts, for the do and know nothings; whose free everything, socialist utopian dreams, and experiments, have in reality turned into Frankenstein nightmares and gulags for the masses.*

Most mainstream European politicians, regardless of their constituents' views, believed the arrival of refugees as an economic opportunity; even if it wasn't popular. Popular it is not, particularly among working- and lower middle-class voters who are more likely to compete with newcomers for jobs, benefits, and social services.

The shift in opinion has even occurred in Sweden, long proud of its tolerance but now coping with a social enmity unfamiliar to a historically homogeneous country. As in America, their academic, media, and corporate establishments hope to crush these movements, whose growing adherents are opposed to the elite's multicultural vision.

Cultural differences mainly drive the conflict between native Europeans and the new arrivals. Unlike earlier waves of immigrants, who arrived when secularism was broadly ascendant, even in the Middle East, the recent Muslim refugees in Europe and America typically come from countries with much more conservative views on homosexuality, women's rights, and even female genital mutilation.

Throughout Europe, clerics who minister to the growing Muslim population continue to indoctrinate poorly educated workers against Western values. Already in the United Kingdom, after 25 years of intense Muslim immigration, Islam features 3,000 mosques, 130 Sharia courts, 50 Muslim Sharia Councils and dozens of 'no go zones' where Moslem 'Sharia' patrols ensure no one disobeys Sharia Law. Main rules of Sharia Law: Islamic law opposes free speech, women's rights, and religious choice. It advocates honor killings, female genital mutilation, four wives per husband, and women as property of men, arranged marriages, wife beating, decapitation, and Islam supreme over all other religions. *Do you agree with Biden to immediately let more people with these medieval beliefs into our country; because Trump kept them out?*

Cultural conflict is not primarily the result of the migrants themselves. Earlier migrant waves arrived in Europe when the continent felt confident about its culture. Today's newcomers enter European societies where many people—notably in the intellectual Left—reject core values, rooted in Christianity and democracy, that shaped their culture. Filling this void is the naïve, doomed to fail left-wing campaign to replace the current colorblind republic with a multicultural race-based republic; one that values diversity and gives advantage based on one's color or sex rather than colorblind individuality and merit.

Ironically, the progressives most committed to multiculturalism and migrations are also responsible for bringing in new residents who reject secular Europe's liberal values. Rather than confront this societal threat, some European politicians and figures like the Archbishop of Canterbury have even suggested that Muslim Sharia law—at least as it applies to banning blasphemy—could supersede national law.

Rise of Anti-Semitism in Europe

Another distressing development tied to the new migration is the resurgence of anti-Semitism. Ever since the Holocaust, Europe's Jewish communities have struggled to remain viable; today, nearly 75 years after the defeat of Nazi Germany, the continent's Jewish population is less than half of what it was at war's end in 1945.

Despite the much smaller Jewish footprint, anti-Semitism in Europe is intensifying. *Some 90 percent of European Jews, according to recent surveys, have experienced anti-Semitic incidents.* Like in America, Europe's naïve liberal intelligentsia and even some Jewish organizations would like to blame the usual suspect villains as the primary culprits behind the anti-Semitic resurgence, but *a detailed survey from the University of Oslo found that in Scandinavia, Germany,*

Britain, and France, most anti-Semitic violence comes from Muslims, including recent immigrants. Similarly, a poll of European Jews found that the majority of anti-Semitic incidents came from either Muslims or from the Left, where the motivation is tied to anti-Semitic/Zionism; barely 13 percent traced it to right-wingers.

Violence against Jews, moreover, is worst not in right-wing hotbeds but in places like the migrant-dominated suburbs of Paris and Sweden's Malmo. It's the centers of European progressivism—Paris and Berlin, for example—where Jews are urged not to wear kippah or a Star of David. And in Great Britain, its figures like Labour Party leader Jeremy Corbyn who have links with jihadi groups. Corbyn's political rise constitutes for Britain's Jews what former Chief Rabbi Jonathan Sacks calls "an existential crisis."

By contrast, in authoritarian and anti-migrant Hungary, Jews appear much safer from persecution. Even Jews who detest Viktor Orbán—scorned as a fascist in the West—credit him for making Budapest one of the safest and most welcoming cities for European Jews. The Hungarian government maintains close ties to Israel—a rarity in Europe. Orbán's regime has also made Holocaust denial illegal, established an official Holocaust Remembrance Day, and refused to cooperate with the anti-Semitic, far-right Jobbik party.

Europeans are reconsidering, with good reason, the multicultural future being thrust on them. Their dilemma: how to handle the developing world's inevitable migration pressures while dealing with their own continent's dismal demographic picture, the result of decades of low birthrates.

America will hopefully, as my Father hoping to save his young son the pain of cuts on his face used to say to me, "learn to shave on my beard"; in other words learn lessons from my painful mistakes and avoid repeating them.

The U.S. must escape the assimilation problems experienced in Europe before they arrive on our shores. We have learned in France, as Paris burned, that millions of Muslim immigrants allowed into France to do low-end jobs, while the economy was healthy, never assimilated into the French society.

Can we risk that non-merit immigration won't fail here?

Alien values and culture

Although the United States currently has a much smaller (and generally more secular) Muslim population than Western Europe, a non-trivial share of Muslim

Americans do seem to hold troubling views about terrorism. For example, a 2013 Pew poll found that 8 percent of U.S. Muslims consider suicide bombings and other violence against civilian targets often or sometimes justified. **A 2015 poll found that nearly a quarter of U.S. Muslims believes it is justifiable to use violence against those who give offense to Islam.**

Sometimes those attitudes have translated to actual violence. Syed Farook and Tashfeen Malik that went on a rampage in San Bernardino had the potential connection to radical Islam. Farook, who was reportedly born in the United States, is another egregious case of failure to assimilate. And this wouldn't be the first example. Nidal Hassan, who infamously killed 13 people in a mass shooting at Fort Hood in 2009, was born and raised in Virginia. Muhammad Youssef Abdulazeez, who killed five soldiers at military installations in Chattanooga, Tenn., came to the United States as a young child. David Headley, a U.S. national formerly named Daood Sayed Gilani, helped plot the 2008 Mumbai attacks and other terrorist operations. One of the shooters at the Curtis Culwell Center (where images of Muhammad were being displayed) was Texas-born Nadir Soofi. Soofi's two accomplices were American converts to Islam.

Unfortunately, Islamic law diametrically contradicts Constitutional democratic-republican law in every way. Today in Canada, America, and Europe—Muslims dictate the rules with millions of followers creating parallel societies inside of Western countries. According to **Infiltration** author Paul Sperry, there are now 1,209 officially recognized mosques in this country, with an estimated 80% of them controlled by Saudi Arabia. Saudi money and the Saudi brand of Wahhabi Islam gave rise to al-Qaeda. This ideology, fueled by immigration, is now finding a well-financed home on these shores.

Once they arrive, no one understands why they fail to leave their barbaric rituals and become modernized. Many do but as Britain, France, Germany, and most of Europe have found, the dream of Muslim assimilation is quickly fading; and with Biden promising more immigration from Islamic countries, it could become a nightmare here. Just today a CIA agent was killed today in Somalia fighting Islamic terrorism, a major problem in that country. Yet because of chain migration, the most immigrants to Wisconsin are Somalis. Indeed, most of these Third World immigrants come to the U.S. for personal economic reasons, not to cherish our democratic system.

Research journalist Peter Goodchild, on his understanding of to how and why Muslims cannot and do not assimilate into Western countries, says, "The Muslim world-view differs greatly from that of the Westerner, largely because Muslims are tribalist. There are many forms of Islamic culture, and tribalism is very much an Arabic characteristic, but it is common throughout the Muslim world. Muslim tribalism is also similar to that of native people in the Americas, or in Africa. Allegiance is to the tribe, not to a 'country.' Arabic countries did not even exist until such political entities were forced upon them in the 20th century by the British and the Americans. The essence of tribalism is that a man's (and secondarily a woman's) loyalty is to the tribe. (Even in my Omani classrooms in 2008-11, if there was a student in a class who was not in the same tribe as the other students, then there could be trouble.) Muslims have two names, just as Westerners do, but the big difference is that a Westerner's last name is a family name, whereas a Muslim's last name is that of a tribe.

"Because a Muslim belongs to a tribe, he is raised from birth to regard people outside his own tribe as enemies. Because other people are enemies, it is senseless to speak of a 'crime' against them. For example, killing someone from another tribe is not 'murder.' 'Lawrence of Arabia' fell into this problem when he was trying to unite the Arabs and get them to side with the British against the Turks in WWI.

"The issue of tribalism came up—with apparently little awareness on the part of Westerners—in the last few years, when large numbers of Muslim migrants poured into Europe. Westerners were appalled by the 'crimes' being committed. But from a Muslim perspective these were not crimes at all. And from a Muslim perspective, Westerners are basically subhuman because they have no tribes. Because they have no tribes it is senseless to say that a Muslim is committing a 'crime' against such people."

With worldwide Muslim terror events becoming regular front-page news, leaders of Western countries might ask themselves why they promote Muslim immigration. Where Islam gains a foothold in any host country, conflict ensues at the local level until it boils over onto the national stage. While Muslims lay low in the beginning stages of their "hijrah" ('seeding' as advocated by the Quran to spread Islam) of host countries, as their numbers grow, they push for Sharia Law.

Many so-called immigration rights groups are left-wing radicals that fan the fire with their rhetoric, encouraging immigrants to preserve their culture and language at taxpayers' expense. Among these groups, the word assimilation is considered xenophobic. Most Americans did not give politicians permission to exchange our country's high moral values into an "I hate America" gang culture. I don't remember voting to allow massive illegal immigration into the country, or to allow our way of life to be turned upside down in order to make lawbreakers feel more at home.

The United States is the only nation that accepts hundreds of thousands of immigrants each year. We continually absorb more immigrants than all other industrialized nations combined. Despite recent restrictions, liberal U.S. immigration policies are a time bomb that will change American society even more dramatically in the future.

"Immigrants devoted to their own cultures and religions are not influenced by the secular politically correct façade that dominates academia, news-media, entertainment, education, religious and political thinking today," said James Walsh, former Associate General Counsel of the United States Immigration and Naturalization Service. "They claim the right not to assimilate, and the day is coming when the question will be how can the United States regulate the defiantly unassimilated cultures, religions and mores of foreign lands? Such immigrants say their traditions trump the U.S. legal system. Balkanization of the United States has begun." In America, Congress and our presidents betray the USA with continued Muslim immigration. **It's a matter of time and numbers**.

Myth: Americans Support Illegal Immigration

With hundreds of thousands of demonstrators shouting in the streets, demanding rights for illegal aliens, and the U.S. Congress and President supporting their efforts, one might believe the myth that Americans support illegal immigrants.

Fact: The general public overwhelmingly favors immigration reform. Poll after poll shows that Americans want well-enforced, sensible, and sustainable immigration laws. A Rasmussen Reports national telephone and online survey finds that two-out-of-three voters think illegal immigration is a serious issue, but nearly half of voters think the government isn't working hard enough to stop it.

Americans think that illegals have a lot of gall coming here and demanding rights that aren't theirs to have. A USA Today/Gallup poll revealed that 61% of Americans say that the U.S. should make illegal immigration a crime, while 81% say illegal immigration to the United States is out of control. Almost 80% believe that controlling our borders to halt illegal immigration is extremely important.

The American public, it appears, is most likely in favor of a mixed approach to immigrants living in the country illegally. That would include some effort to deport illegal immigrants (presumably in particular those who break laws and commit crimes), with a bigger effort to develop a pathway to citizenship for those living here illegally.

Myth: America Wins in our Immigration "Lottery"

What is the Visa Lottery?

The diversity visa lottery issues 55,000 visas each year by lottery, to nationals of countries considered underrepresented in the immigrant flow. Until 1965, our immigration system favored immigrants who reflected the ethnic characteristics of our society. Heightened concerns about racism brought about by the civil rights movement led to the scrapping of the system. Ironically, the current visa lottery system is a throwback to the earlier race-conscious system. It structures the immigrant admission system to discriminate among immigrant-sending countries in order to increase the number of immigrants from "underrepresented" countries.

The year 1995 marked the beginning of the permanent "diversity" lottery for 55,000 visas per year. Unlike the transitional system, it is supposed to discriminate against countries that have large flows of immigrants already, like Mexico and the Philippines. The Act was cleverly worded, however, so that the lottery would remain open to the Irish. That is one of the major faults with the lottery system: because it is "designer immigration," it invites tinkering for or against nationals of a given foreign country.

In November 1994, by executive agreement, President Clinton accepted to set up a one-country immigrant visa lottery for Cubans. In November 1997, Congress adopted an amnesty for Nicaraguans and Cubans and special screening provisions for other Central Americans who had come illegally to the United States during the revolutionary fighting in their homelands. To offset this adjustment process, the ceiling of 55,000 on lottery immigrants was lowered to 50,000 until the amnesty process was completed.

What is Wrong with the Visa Lottery?

Anyone who is not a national of one of the overrepresented countries is eligible if they otherwise meet the admission criteria and have at least the equivalent of a high school education. Unlike the normal visa criteria, the visa applicants do not need to have a sponsoring family member or employer. They don't even have to apply from their home country. They can be already in the United States in legal or illegal status. How then can they show that they are not likely to become a public charge in the United States? That is taken care of for many of the applicants by the fact that they are already working illegally in the United States.

That is a second major flaw with the lottery system. It acts as a system to legalize the status of persons who are illegal aliens already here. They don't have to go back home to file their lottery application, they can do it from their local post office here. The message to the illegal alien community here is that we are not serious in saying that they should not be here.

As noted above, the visa lottery is an inappropriate form of tailoring our admissions policy to the social objectives of one group of politicians or political activists or another. The system meets no national need, since there are no specific skills or ability required. In addition, as also noted above, the visa lottery acts to reward illegal aliens already in the United States and thereby to communicate the message that we are not serious in our efforts to combat illegal immigration. Other undesirable effects of the visa lottery are as follows:

Unwanted Competition for America's Minorities

The visa lottery is bad public policy in that it disadvantages American-born minorities. In effect, the post 1994 visa lottery is a form of affirmative action program for foreigners. Our domestic affirmative action programs do not distinguish between foreign-born minorities and native-born minorities. As a result, new African immigrants, for example, are thrown into competition with African Americans. Many American blacks consider this undesirable competition.

Reinventing Our Nation

The visa lottery was crafted to satisfy narrowly focused ethnic interests. The designers knew that today's immigrants become tomorrow's sponsors for other immigrant family members under the chain migration system that characterizes our overall system. They apparently were not satisfied with the dramatic demographic change the nation has undergone over the past 25 years and is expected to undergo over the next 25 years. In both the past and the future, the major vehicle for ethnic change is immigration; but rather than a fairly gradual, passive process of change as in the past, the lottery designers increased the pace of change in our society. If this direction for our immigration policy represented a national consensus of what we as a nation wanted, the policy would be unexceptionable. However, there has never been any effort to explain to the public the nature of this program.

Rather than being based on public consensus, it is a program that was adopted behind the public's back.

Absence of Public Support

Americans have clearly expressed a strong majority view that immigration is too high and should be lowered. That view was expressed by 83% of respondents in a large national Roper poll. Clearly, the 55,000 immigrant lottery visas would be a prime candidate for elimination in any reductions. The Commission on Immigration Reform tacitly adopted that position by eliminating the lottery from its recommended immigration framework. In hearings before the Commission, representatives of various immigration groups were asked what programs should be considered most expendable. The visa lottery was the most often cited candidate for elimination. It has very little support.

Fueling Illegal Entry

Not only does the visa lottery reward aliens illegally residing in the United States, it seems likely to promote additional illegal immigration. Millions of applications are received for the annual 55,000 visas. Millions, therefore, are encouraged to take the first step toward trying to gain residence in our country. For the vast majority who do not win, the thought may have been planted to take their chances in the next year's lottery from inside the United States.

The Issue of Equity to Other Visa Applicants

There is also a question of equity. Our immigration preference system has led to visa waiting lists of family-sponsored immigrants that may require a wait of years to get a visa. Is it appropriate to admit ahead of them—without any wait—persons who win the lottery drawing? And, doesn't it seem obvious that the presence of lottery winners who were illegally here would reinforce the message to those in the visa waiting list, that they too might as well take their chances on immigrating illegally and hope to become legal immigrants through the lottery?

The Population Growth Message

The visa lottery also sends the message to the world that we think that we need more immigrants. Why else would we be issuing lottery visas? Do we want to promote the view internationally that we still have unlimited space for new settlers? Do we want foreigners to think that the United States is immune from the population pressures being experienced by most of the world and that it is still a refuge from the crowding and environmental degradation that is being experienced elsewhere? In fact, the United States already has a population that may be too large for long-term sustainability, especially in terms of our damage to the environment, and we need to be adopting policies to stabilize our population, not fuel further growth.

The message that we should be sending to the world is that the United States is fully populated, but we will keep the immigration door open to immigrants who meet narrowly defined national interests. Others who try to come illegally will be apprehended and sent back home. In other words, we will still accept applications to join our society, but we will no longer encourage them.

Exploiting the Aspirations of the Gullible

Another reason that the visa lottery should be abolished is that it is an easy target for exploitation by unscrupulous persons who take advantage of the aspirations of foreigners to immigrate to the United States. Numerous firms are advertising abroad that they can facilitate the lottery entry requirements for a fee. In fact the entry procedure is simple and costs nothing other than postage. The problem is that many people around the world are not well informed about the lottery and are easy prey for these unscrupulous agents. Unfortunately, they are not breaking any U.S. law by their activities, and the only thing that would shut down their operations would be to abolish the lottery.

Security Concerns

Congress held an eye-opening hearing on the problems with the visa lottery program, revealing that many specific terrorism-related offenses in the U.S. have occurred at the hands of those who have benefited from the visa lottery. One such case was that of Hesham Mohamed Ali Hedayet, the Egyptian national who killed two and wounded three during a shooting spree at L.A. International Airport in July of 2002. He was allowed to apply for lawful permanent resident status because his wife was a visa lottery winner, and despite his own admission to the INS that he had been accused of being a member of a known terrorist organization.

If that wasn't bad enough, the visa lottery program is also wrought with fraud. The State Department confirms that the lottery is "subject to widespread abuse," and more specifically that 364,000 duplicate applications were detected in one year alone. Furthermore, the lottery is unfair to immigrants who comply with our laws, because it does not prohibit illegal aliens from applying for visas through the program. Thereby, foreign nationals that comply with our laws are treated the same as those blatantly violating them.

As Congressman Bob Goodlatte noted, the visa lottery is a flawed policy and is foolish in the age we live. Those in the world who wish us harm can easily engage in this statistical gamble with nothing to lose. Our immigration policy should be based primarily on our national security and economic needs, not on arbitrary systems lacking basic safeguards.

Chapter 9
JUSTICE IS JUST

It's not the voting that's democracy; it's the counting.

Tom Stoppard

A blindfolded woman holding a pair of scales is symbolic of America's justice system. The system is indeed blind, not necessarily to guilt or innocence, but rather to the damage the legal system itself is causing our country. Indeed, judges and lawyers are most often the problem rather than the solution. In this chapter, lawyers and their politician cousins become easy targets.

Here Comes the Judge, There Goes the Constitution

In the last few years, Federal courts have ignored the separation of power and begun to interfere with laws enacted by the Legislative branch of government. The courts now impose their own rulings as laws on communities that never voted for them. In 1994, voters in California passed by a substantial margin the ballot measure known as Proposition 187, denying most public benefits such as welfare to illegal aliens. Within a year, a Federal judge ruled the law unconstitutional. Similarly, in 1996 the voters of California passed Proposition 209, a ballot measure that effectively abolished Affirmative Action programs and prohibited racial discrimination by state government. Again, a Federal judge ruled the new law unconstitutional—this time in just three weeks.

Furthermore, the U.S. Ninth Circuit Court struck down as unconstitutional the official English language amendment to the Arizona state constitution. Likewise, a U.S. district judge ordered the Kansas City School District to spend $740 million to meet education standards set by his dictate.

A California judge contributed to the "civil wrongs" that continues to allow the race victim card to be used. This time, it was to trump the minimal standards required to graduate high school. Judge Freedman, just weeks before graduation, said he intends to block the state's exit exam. This would allow students to receive diplomas even if they couldn't pass basic English and math tests. The judge said that he found merit in the argument that the exam was unfair, since all California students do not have access to the same quality of education. So by dropping the bar, this activist judge presented our businesses and colleges with more dead-enders and devalued the diplomas of students from the same schools, who had worked hard to master basic survival skills. The only bar these "students" will raise will be the corner bar.

This Judicial Revolution

The Federal courts have appointed themselves as virtual dictators to determine which laws are valid or not, without regard for the wishes of voters, legislators, or even the text of the Constitution. Judges since the 1920s have used a variety of pseudo-constitutional doctrines and devices to override laws they have disliked.

One such device is the misinterpretation of the Constitution's Commerce Clause empowering Congress to regulate commerce among the several states, with foreign nations, and with Indian tribes. They purposely misinterpret this clause to justify Federal regulation of virtually any activity that remotely affects interstate commerce. This includes upholding the 1964 Civil Rights Act and its prohibition against racial discrimination by private enterprises in hotels restaurants and theaters. The courts used this Clause in ways having nothing to do with the intent of the language or of the principles of those who originally drafted and adopted it. **This alteration of the Commerce Clause's original intent is an example of how one subtle change is negatively impacting our future.**

Original intent is an important concept worth understanding when selecting judges at every level. Simply stated, original intent is the only legitimate means of interpreting any law. We should look to the intentions of those who drafted and enacted law as essential reliable guides to the law's application. In recent history, there has been a judicial revolution in the United States, intent on overthrowing the doctrine of original intent.

Even some Supreme Court justices think it is their job to "evolve" our laws to meet their own subjective view of reality. Retired Supreme Court Justice William Brennan was one of the architects of this judicial revolution. In a *New York Times* editorial, he acknowledged his own abandonment of the original intent principle. "I approached my responsibility of interpreting it (the constitution) as a 20th-century American," Brennan recalled, "for the genius of the Constitution rests not in any static meaning it may have had in a world dead and gone, but in its evolving character."

Wrong—the whole point of a written Constitution lies precisely in its "static meaning"! By fixing its meaning in writing, the framers tried to make it impossible for people to change the meaning of the laws to suit their own purposes. If we employ Brennan's evolving document, courts could simply impose on the written laws whatever meaning they wish, without regard to the original meaning in the language.

Our Judicial system can no longer be considered just, when it's judicial revolution seriously compromises the American values won in our own revolution. Since most of us are not directly impacted, we have not begun to consider seriously the ways to halt the judicial revolution and restore the Constitution. Who will be our next Paul Revere and sound the alarm? If not reversed, expect to feel more anger as you continually learn of more arrogant judges using the Constitution as notepaper to compose agendas for their buddies and themselves.

Prejudging Judges

Experienced law professors and litigates, as well as the general public, are reporting that too often judges are simply unwilling to listen to facts and reason. They start instead with predilections heavily favoring one view. If asked, of course, they deny ever having made such predilections. They then prove impervious to facts and viewpoints contrary to their bias, and are steadfast in their opinion even when there is evidence supporting different facts, or when those facts are not denied by opposing council. In many cases, judges literally make up counter facts.

An on-going example is the three-ring circus surrounding the case of General Flynn. The clown running this circus is a Judge Sullivan who, though he has no standing, has filed a petition for rehearing; has ignored the "massive" amount of information in the Justice Department's motion to dismiss; and can't even get basic facts right, such as the date of Flynn's mandamus petition, as well as other key aspects about the petition and the facts supporting it. Sullivan even wrongly asserts that Flynn already had "two separate judgments of conviction," when in fact no convictions were ever finalized or entered into the record.

Judge Sullivan's extraordinary actions arise solely from his partisan disagreement with the Government's decision to dismiss the case against General Flynn. Not only did he wrongfully libel this decorated General with an idiotic and baseless assertion of treason, but he has been vocal that General Flynn should be punished severely. Flynn's attorney noted, "The district court has hijacked and extended a criminal prosecution for almost three months for its own purposes." It's time for this rogue judge to follow the lead of Ringling Bros. and Barnum & Bailey—and shut down this circus.

An analogy to the typical judges' resistance to facts is the O.J. Simpson jury, who were not going to let facts get in the way of prejudices. Another is Justice O'Connor's support of Affirmative Action for the simple reason that she had negative experiences as one of a few female law students.

When judges act on the basis of their prior predilections, ignore facts, and even make up supposed counter facts, they destroy a central tenet of the judicial system: decisions of cases are to be based on facts rather than prejudice. They injure persons by such decisions, and in the case of the Simpson jury, destroy faith in the judicial system, leading to bitterness toward a system that reneges on its promise to be fair.

This bad situation is made worse when the disregard for facts is combined with other acts that compound the bias. For example, a judge may ensure that facts contrary to the side he favors are kept to a minimum by denying discovery of those facts. Discovery is the legal process occurring before trial, where each party receives documents from the opposing side and questions the persons involved. Judges sometimes, almost unbelievably, hold secret hearings barring one party from examining witnesses and learning facts.

There are also examples of judges disqualifying knowledgeable and experienced counsel who would be best qualified to uncover and present those facts. Judges have refused to be excused from hearing a case, even when they have ignored or buried facts and have then been accused of bias.

I was involved in a vote recount that involved an entrenched New York Democratic Congressional incumbent, a former judge himself, who was running against an idealistic reformer who I worked for. The vote was very close, with the incumbent winning by about 300 votes, so a recount was ordered. The recount, after taking out scores of invalid votes from dead people and double counting, showed my boss, the reformer, as the winner by a few votes, say 15. The incumbent challenged the recount in court. The sitting judge, a known associate of the incumbent, refused to disqualify himself saying, "though he was a friend of the Congressman for 30 years, he could be impartial." He then reviewed the recount and gave the reformer all but 18 of the challenged votes—just enough to assure another victory for the incumbent.

Who Is Judging Judges?

Political conservatives continually charge that judges are overriding the will of the people, as expressed in statutes relating to abortions, gay rights, Affirmative Action, religion, and so forth. The Left, on the other hand, makes charges of bias by businesses against women, minorities, handicapped, Spanish speakers, and so on. In the meantime, the lawyers charge trial judges with tyrannical and arbitrary misuse of their position, and even bribery.

However, conservatives, liberals, and lawyers all agree that the commissions and boards dealing with judicial misconduct are not effective. Due to this lack of power, few judges are taken to task by commissions, which are largely comprised of judges themselves, and staffed by defenders who are predisposed to protect wayward judges rather than punish them for misusing their position.

Packing the court

As soon as President Trump announced he would fill the Supreme Court vacancy created by the death of Justice Ruth Bader Ginsburg, progressives warned that they would retaliate by enlarging the size of the Court.

With the Democrats possibly about to seize control of the Senate, these threats linger in the air as a warning: "If the Court doesn't rule as we say, eventually we will fill it with justices who will." Of course, federal courts are not supposed to bend to the will of politicians, nor should they follow public opinion. Quite the contrary, our founders created an independent judiciary by design.

Judicial independence isn't an abstract concept. It's a rule that protects federal judges from outside interference so they can render decisions fairly and objectively on the basis of the law and the facts before them. Judicial independence is so important that Article III of the Constitution gives federal judges lifetime appointments to insulate them from political and social pressures.

To be sure, the Constitution does not dictate the number of Supreme Court justices. But since 1869, the Court has consisted of nine members (eight associate justices and one chief justice). And, while there might be non-political reasons to alter the size of the judiciary, our founders certainly did not intend for politicians to tamper with the structure of a co-equal branch of government for political gain. Current efforts to pack the Court attempt to do just that.

They are a brazen attempt to turn our independent judiciary into a dependent and subordinate instrument of left-wing politicians—one that is impossible to square with the Constitution's separation of powers principles.

Packing the Court would be truly revolutionary. It would change the fundamental structure of our government, depriving the judiciary of the ability to check unconstitutional government overreach.

After destroying our independent judiciary, what's next? Will proponents of Court-packing seek to dismantle the Senate, claiming its "unfair" to the majority of Americans who live in larger states? Adding two more states and eliminating the Electoral College that would assure one party rule and destroy America's democracy is being openly considered by the Democrats. Perhaps not surprisingly, adding additional Supreme Court justices is a popular tool of authoritarian rulers. In 2004, for example, Venezuelan dictator Hugo Chavez added 12 new seats to his country's Supreme Court to ensure that the Venezuelan judiciary would not stand in the way of his attempts to consolidate power and confiscate thousands of private businesses. The expanded Venezuelan court then stood by as Chavez and his successor, Nicolas Maduro, imposed socialism and deprived citizens of fundamental rights. In 2017, the Venezuelan high court declared the legislature illegitimate and transferred all lawmaking power to itself. When riots ensued, the packed court backed down. But it has continued to allow Maduro to rule without consulting the legislature. *Is that what you voted for?*

There was a time when Americans of both parties opposed Court-packing schemes. When President Franklin D. Roosevelt attempted to pack the Court in 1937, the Democratic-controlled Senate Judiciary Committee called his plan a "dangerous abandonment of constitutional principle" and an "invasion of judicial power." Opposition was so fierce that Roosevelt had to back down.

Although some far-left Democrats like Alexandria Ocasio-Cortez have favored Court-packing for several years, as recently as 2019, Justice Ginsburg herself expressed grave reservations about changing the number of justices on the Court. In an interview with NPR, Ginsburg warned that changing the number of justices would politicize the Court, threaten its independence, and undermine its legitimacy. "Nine seems to be a good number. It's been that way for a long time," she said, adding, "I think it was a bad idea when President Franklin Roosevelt tried to pack the court."

But Justice Ginsburg has died, and so too has most of the Democratic opposition to Court-packing. When asked about enlarging the size of the Court in the aftermath of Ginsburg's death, Senator Minority Leader Chuck Schumer said, "Everything is on the table." And a number of Democrats in Congress have explicitly said they would expand the Court as payback for the confirmation of Justice Barrett.

For his part, Joe Biden in his usual opaque manner says that he will convene a "commission" to study the issue. The purpose of such a commission is obvious: to make clear to the current justices that they are on thin ice—that if they dare rule against the wishes of the political branches, retribution awaits them. If that isn't a threat to the rule of law, I don't know what is. I suspect that if proponents of this scheme understood more about the 1937 attempt at court packing, as well as the effects of court packing in various banana republics, they would reject this terrible idea. It is such a bad idea that in 1937, the Democratic-controlled Senate Judiciary Committee called Roosevelt a plan a "dangerous abandonment of constitutional principle" and an "invasion of judicial power." Opposition was so fierce that Roosevelt had to back down. *Do you agree one must be either brainwashed or an extreme radical to support a position that upsets the balance of powers that separates a democracy from a banana republic dictatorship? Does it surprise you that in a Google search most of the upfront pages are populated almost exclusively by fake news and other Left-leaning sites that support court packing idiocy?*

Radical Prosecutors

"We got trouble in River City."

Appearing again on top of my "most dangerous and unwanted by any civil society list" is corrupt billionaire Democratic donor George Soros. His latest is a well-timed coup attempt to undermine our democracy by bankrolling the successful campaigns of a new crop (crap) of district attorneys who now preside over big cities with skyrocketing crime and frayed relationships with police departments.

> "Soros-backed DAs in Philadelphia, St. Louis, Los Angeles, San Francisco and other cities have fired scores of experienced prosecutors and, as promised, stopped prosecuting low-level quality-of-life crimes such as disorderly conduct, vagrancy and loitering. Their laissez-faire criminal justice philosophy bucks the get-tough 'broken windows' approach, made famous by then-New York Mayor Rudolph W. Giuliani, which targets minor offenses to cut off the criminal element in the bud."

> "There is nothing progressive about the rogue prosecutor movement. Elected rogue district attorneys have not worked within the law to enhance

221

public safety, protect victims' rights, lower crime, and serve their community. They usurp the constitutional role of the legislative branch by refusing to prosecute entire categories of crime, abuse the role of the county prosecutor, fail to protect victims of crime, and ignore rising crime rates caused by their radical policies. They exist because George Soros and a handful of other billionaires have invested heavily in the election of district attorneys who are working to reverse engineer and dismantle a criminal justice system that, while not perfect, has resulted in the lowest crime and incarceration rates in decades. When an extreme leftist won election to be the chief prosecutor for San Francisco, most right-minded people might have dismissed the outcome as par for the course in liberal 'Bagdad by the Bay.'"

"But that would have been a mistake. When San Franciscans elected Chesa Boudin, they didn't vote in a run-of-the-mill progressive out to decriminalize property violations and spout 'soft-on-crime' slogans. They elected the former advisor to Venezuela's leftist dictator Hugo Chavez. Boudin is the tip of the spear in a revolutionary effort to upend the American system of justice—from within."

Consider this background.

"In 1981, Boudin's parents, Kathy Boudin and David Gilbert, left their infant son with a babysitter before they helped orchestrate the robbery of a Brinks truck – in which its security guard and two police officers were murdered. Kathy Boudin actively distracted Nyack police, who had stopped the get-a-away truck, and convinced them to put away their drawn weapons. Seconds later, her accomplices jumped out of the truck and executed two of the officers and wounded others."

"Legally adopted by domestic terrorists Bill Ayers and Bernardine Dorhn, Chesa Boudin has repeatedly downplayed the crimes of his parents and the terrorist group Weather Underground – including numerous bombings, violent prison breaks, and other robberies. His parents' heinous crimes were committed on behalf of an extremist break-away faction of the terrorist group, which is dedicated to the violent overthrow [of] the US government. They did face justice and were sent to prison for their violent acts. However, now District Attorney-elect Boudin considers imprisonment 'an act of violence in and of itself.'"

"He offers non-specified interventions to eradicate the conditions that cause criminal behavior. At the same time, he specifically plans to end enforcement against public urination, prostitution, and public drug use – and further decriminalize theft. This is just the opposite tack that turned New York City around under former Mayor Rudy Giuliani and Police Commissioner Bill Bratton. Broadly, Boudin has pledged to simply flout the laws he disagrees with saying, a 'district attorney can challenge the legitimacy of laws by declining to bring charges in certain cases.'"

"This is the same approach the bigoted prosecutors, judges, and juries of the Deep South took toward crimes against African Americans for decades. It does not only undermine the rule of law – it erases it. So, why does the radical son of terrorists in the Leftist capital of America matter to you? Because his comrades are coming to your prosecutor's office, if they aren't already there."

"Extreme leftist candidates have won dozens of local district attorney elections (from liberal big cities such as, Boston and Philadelphia, to moderate suburban counties such as Fairfax, Virginia, and Harris County, Texas). Billionaire progressive activist George Soros and his myriad organizations pour millions into these normally low-spending, local elections."

As rioters destroy small businesses and private property, some prosecutors are deliberately refusing to hold these perpetrators accountable. In Portland, a local prosecutor dismissed charges on 59 individuals connected to the riots, including nine cases involving felony charges such as arson and theft. Unfortunately, this isn't a surprise given that left-wing groups fund political campaigns for district attorneys in order to advance their radical agendas.

"The progressive Left has ousted longtime prosecutors in places such as St. Louis, and its members are not finished – they are only getting started. The leftwing is even targeting Democrats. Jackie Lacey, the first African American and first woman to lead the Los Angeles County District Attorney's Office, which covers more than 10 million people, faces a carpet bagging competitor in George Gascon. Gascon resigned as the elected district attorney in San Francisco just to run against Lacey in the Democratic primary – funded, of course, by Soros and his allies. (Meanwhile, Gascon's former colleagues in San Francisco have endorsed Lacey.)"

"The consequences of this radical leftwing effort are dire for residents. In Philadelphia, where leftist Larry Krasner took office as the city's district attorney in 2018, violent crime has risen in city. This year alone, gun assaults are up by 11 percent, murders jumped 6 percent, and robberies increased by 7 percent. And there's a direct link between the spike in crime and the district attorney's approach to prosecuting offenders. Krasner has dismissed charges against violent criminals at an eye-popping rate: 57 percent higher dismissal rate than his predecessor for homicide and 15 percent for all violent crimes – while obtaining 7 percent fewer violent crime convictions. Among so-called nonviolent offenders, 45 percent of suspected drug dealers have had their cases dismissed."

"The same story is playing out across the country. Serious offenses and quality of life crimes go unchecked by these progressive prosecutors, who put ideology above public safety. In Dallas, newly sworn in District Attorney John Creuzot announced he would not prosecute drug offenses or theft under $750. A massive violent crime spike followed, especially in South Dallas. With an ineffectual police chief and deluded district attorney blaming poverty for crime, Texas Governor Greg Abbott acted to stop the bloodshed and sent in state troopers to police the area. Violent crime tumbled 24 percent within a few months."

"Meanwhile, in St. Louis, a left-wing district attorney has driven 65 of her own career prosecutors out of public service – more than 100 percent turnover. A similar exodus of veteran and accomplished prosecutors is occurring in Philadelphia, Houston, and Denver. The crime-fighting professionals who have devoted their lives to public safety would be right to feel under siege as their supposed colleagues and superiors denigrate, distrust, and desert them. Progressive district attorneys seem to disdain their prosecutors and the front-line police officers with whom they are supposed to work. Boston's district attorney declined to prosecute Antifa rioters who threw bottles of urine at police."

"Meanwhile, some of these officials have publicly declared law enforcement to be inherently racist. Others, such as Baltimore District Attorney Marilyn Mosby – who presides over the highest murder rate in the country – suggests with no evidence that 'hundreds' in the city's police force are corrupt liars."

This summer, six Philadelphia police officers were shot by a career violent felon in a stand-off. Bystanders taunted the officers and threw objects at them. Philly's federal prosecutor, William McSwain, laid the incident and rising crime at Krasner's feet, saying "the crisis was precipitated by a stunning disrespect for law enforcement."

"Krasner, who made his career suing the police 75 times, had previously called law enforcement racist and 'war criminals,' but his election victory party two years ago further clarified his approach as supporters chanted 'F— the Police.'"

"A familiar chant went up at the victory party of Boudin: 'F—the POA [Police Officers Association].' Boudin and others' disdain for public safety, the rule of law, and the brave men and women who police our streets and put away violent criminals is dangerous and disturbing. It is a fundamental violation of their oath to 'well and faithfully discharge the duties [they are] about to enter.'"

Much of the above section comes from an article by James Varney of The Washington Times that accurately sums up another of the latest radical Left strategies to destroy America. Do you want radical pro-criminal prosecutors who hate America in your area?

Here comes the Calvary

There's a dire need to counteract the influence of pro-rioter, Soros funded, far-left radical prosecutors; with unbiased training on how to properly prosecute those who commit crimes during a protest. U.S. Senators Kelly Loeffler (R-Ga.) and Tom Cotton (R-Ark.) introduced legislation to help prosecutors successfully charge those who commit violent crimes during protests. The *Training Our Prosecutors (TOP) Act* will reauthorize a U.S. Department of Justice (DOJ) grant program to increase training for district attorneys to address recent rioting in America. The legislation also updates the DOJ grant program that covers basic training for prosecutors to include training on prosecuting violent crime and property destruction that occurs during protests.

"Local prosecutors are on the front lines of justice, ensuring that criminals are kept off the streets," Cotton said. "Now more than ever—as roving bands of insurrectionists loot and murder in cities across the country—we need our prosecutors properly trained and equipped to put these criminals behind bars. Our legislation will provide funding for desperately needed training so that prosecutors can help keep us safe."

"Prosecutors throughout the country need increased funding to support training to ensure their offices continue to serve their communities in an ethical and professional manner," said Nancy Parr, National Defense Attorneys Association President and Commonwealth's Attorney for the City of Chesapeake, Virginia. "Senator Loeffler's legislation takes important steps to increase funding for organizations that regularly provide training and technical assistance to State and local prosecutors which will improve the effective administration of justice nationwide."

Myth: There is no Significant Voter Fraud

I'm ignoring the many serious voter fraud allegations currently being litigated from the 2020 election. For example, the USPS contract driver who delivered a truck load of ballots from Bethpage, NY, to Lancaster, PA, where no one was willing to sign for the shipment; or the ease of changing voter tabulations with a simple thumb drive on Dominion voting machines as was alleged in Venezuela and elsewhere. Other proof of current voter fraud being buried and covered up by Google includes a video of poll workers in Georgia. This surveillance video shows suitcases of ballots being pulled from underneath a table, covered by a tablecloth, after the poll workers were told to go home for the night. The poll workers say they assumed everyone was leaving the building and the counting was done, but four people stayed behind. Once everybody left, these four people began counting the ballots that were hidden in the suitcases underneath the table.

Let's instead look at *The Heritage Foundation's Election Fraud Database* which presents a sampling of proven instances of election fraud from across the country. Each and every one of the cases in this database represents an instance in which a public official, usually a prosecutor, thought it serious enough to act upon it. And each and every one ended in a finding that the individual had engaged in wrongdoing in connection with an election hoping to affect its outcome—or that the results of an election were sufficiently in question and had to be overturned. It is important to remember that every fraudulent vote that is cast invalidates the vote of an eligible voter, effectively disenfranchising that voter. In addition to diluting the votes of legitimate voters, fraud can have an impact in close elections, and we have many close elections in this country. This database is not an exhaustive or comprehensive list. It does not capture all cases and certainly does not capture reported instances or allegations of election fraud, some of which may be meritorious, that are not investigated or prosecuted. Because of vulnerabilities in the system, election fraud is relatively easy to commit and difficult to detect after-the-fact.

Moreover, some public officials appear to be unconcerned with election fraud and fail to pursue cases that are reported to them. It is a general truism that you don't find what you don't look for. This database is intended to demonstrate the vulnerabilities in the election system and the many ways in which fraud is committed.

Preventing, deterring, and prosecuting election fraud is essential to protecting the integrity of our voting process. Reforms intended to ensure election integrity do not disenfranchise voters and, in fact, protect their right to vote. Winning elections leads to political power and the incentives to take advantage of security vulnerabilities are great, so it is important that we take reasonable steps to make it hard to cheat, while making it easy for legitimate voters to vote.

Americans deserve to have an electoral process that they can trust and that protects their most sacred right, and they have the right to know when the integrity of that process is imperiled. Voter fraud isn't found—except when it's looked for and then it turns out to be everywhere. Troy, NY, City Councilman Anthony DeFiglio, who forged signatures on applications for absentee ballots, spoke some truth describing it as a "normal political tactic"; American voters get that. In spite of the "nothing to see here, folks" message they receive regularly, 64 percent believed voting fraud was "serious" according to a Rasmussen poll.

Overwhelming evidence backs them up. In the 2008 Minnesota Senate race, Al Franken won by 312 votes. After a watchdog group identified 1099 votes cast by ineligible voters, prosecutors were forced by Minnesota law to investigate. So far, 177 people have been convicted of voting fraudulently and more are awaiting trial. A close gubernatorial race in Washington State in 2002 spurred investigations that also found thousands of illegal votes cast.

This year, Maryland congressional candidate Wendy Rosen dropped out after she was found to be voting in two states. Albany mayoral candidate Paul Etheridge was indicted last year on three felony counts of fraudulent absentee voting. NAACP official Lessadolla Sowers is in prison for perpetrating a massive vote fraud scheme in Mississippi.

It goes on and on. The undisputed champion of voter fraud is ACORN, supposedly disbanded in 2010, but actually still doing business under multiple names. Their operational model is to hire unqualified workers and incentivize them to "register" as many voters as possible at the last minute, thus overwhelming local election officials. When registrations are challenged, voter suppression is alleged, even though duplicates and obvious errors are common.

It's more than an anecdote here and there. A study this year by the Pew Trust estimated that 24 million defective voter registrations are currently on file. Nearly two million dead people are still listed as voters, 2.75 million voters are registered in two places, 70,000 in three and 12 million contain incorrect addresses. One of eight registrations authorizes voters to vote in elections for which they're not eligible.

With all this going on, it's frankly suspicious that the Biden and before that the Obama administration used all the tools at its disposal to try to prevent states from implementing photo ID laws. Americans understand that, especially in an age of heightened security, a photo ID is a part of everyday life. It's inherently reasonable to protect voter integrity with the same process needed to board a plane, buy a beer, or cash a check. Several surveys have shown that about 1 percent of eligible voters lack photo ID and the rest can easily obtain one for free. Yet corrupt Attorney General Eric Holder, who misused the DOJ slush fund enriched by settlements with business, played the race card. He likened photo ID laws to a "poll tax" and congressional Democrats had a bill in play that would void photo ID laws in 17 states, including those that have them.

Photo ID laws by themselves wouldn't come close to eliminating voter fraud. If anything, it's more important to clean up registration files. Unbelievably, the federal Motor Voter Act, for no good reason, actually prohibits doing this.

If we care about ballot integrity, we should also abolish early voting, except in true cases of need, and avoid Internet voting like the plague. It may be convenient to vote at home, but the only way to assure that voters are who they say they are is for them to appear in person. Anything else is just catnip for those hoping to cheat. Although no fair-minded person supports voter suppression, November's election might have been decided by illegal votes and Trump and the rest of us should only want legal votes counted. The saying goes "voting isn't democracy but counting votes is." *Don't we all want transparency?*

The insightful commentary from the Heritage Foundation by Hans A. von Spakovsky provides solid, objective insights on voter fraud. Hans served as a member of the Federal Election Commission for two years. Before that, he was Counsel to the Assistant Attorney General for Civil Rights at the U.S. Department of Justice, where he specialized in voting and election issues. He also served as a county election official in Georgia for five years, as a member of the Fulton County Board of Registration and Elections.

President Trump's concerns about illegals voting was derided as a witch hunt by the Democrats and the media, and his commission to investigate was stonewalled and eventually shut down because several states refused to cooperate. There is, however, good reason to be concerned. **The evidence is indisputable that aliens,** both legal and illegal, are registering and voting in federal, state, and local elections.

Let's look at some facts:

In 1998 the California Secretary of State reported that 2,000 to 3,000 of the individuals summoned for jury duty each month in Orange County claimed an exemption from jury service because they were not U.S. citizens. Of these individuals, 85 to 90 percent were summoned from the voter registration list, rather than from the Department of Motor Vehicles (DMV) records. These numbers are even more concerning when one considers that only a very small percentage of registered voters are called for jury duty in most jurisdictions. While some of those individuals may have simply committed perjury to avoid jury service, this represents a significant number of potentially illegal voters: 20,400 to 30,600 non-citizens summoned from the voter registration list over a one-year period.

In 2005, the U.S. Government Accountability Office found that up to 3 percent of the 30,000 individuals called for jury duty from voter registration rolls over a two-year period in just one U.S. district court were not U.S. citizens. While that may not seem like many, just 3 percent of registered voters would have been more than enough to provide the winning presidential vote margin in Florida in 2000 and for Trump in 2020. Indeed, the Census Bureau estimates that there are over a million illegal aliens in Florida, and the U.S. Department of Justice (DOJ) has prosecuted more non-citizen voting cases in Florida than in any other state.

Moreover, following a mayor's race in Compton, California, aliens testified under oath in court that they voted in the election. In that case, a candidate who was elected to the Compton City Council was permanently disqualified from holding public office in California for soliciting non-citizens to register and vote. The fact that non-citizens registered and voted in the election would never have been discovered except for the fact that it was a very close election and the incumbent mayor, who lost by less than 300 votes, contested it.

Stop talking about Russian interference which all sides agree did not change one vote in the 2016 Presidential election, and think about the actual number of illegal alien voter fraud that continues to help elect Democrats, and which the Left and the media in 2020 would like to keep as another dirty secret.

As a matter of fact, non-citizen voting in a 1996 congressional race in California may have stolen the election. Republican incumbent Bob Dornan was defending himself against a spirited challenger, Democrat Loretta Sanchez. Sanchez won the election by just 979 votes, and Dornan contested the election in the U.S. House of Representatives. His challenge was dismissed when the House Committee on Oversight and Government Reform turned up only 624 invalid votes by non-citizens who were present in the U.S. Immigration and Naturalization Service (INS) database because they had applied for citizenship, as well as another 124 improper absentee ballots. The investigation, however, could not detect illegal aliens, who were not in the INS records.

The Oversight Committee recognized the elephant in the room: "If there are a significant number of documented aliens in INS records, on the Orange County voter registration rolls, how many illegal or undocumented aliens may be registered to vote in Orange County?" There is a strong possibility that, with only about 200 votes determining the winner, enough undetected aliens registered and voted to change the outcome of the election. This is particularly true since the California Secretary of State complained that the INS refused his request to check the entire Orange County voter registration file, and no complete check of all of the individuals who voted in the congressional race was ever made.

Because of deficiency in state law and the failure of federal agencies to comply with federal law, there are very few procedures in place that allow election officials to detect, deter, and prevent non-citizens from registering and voting. Instead, officials largely depend on an "honor system" that expects aliens to obey the law, but there are many cases showing the failures of this honor system.

Many aliens believe that the potential benefit of registering far outweighs the chances of being caught and prosecuted, since many district attorneys will not prosecute what they see as a "victimless and non-violent" crime. On the other hand, aliens acquiring a voter registration card that then can be used for many different purposes, including obtaining a driver's license, qualifying for a job, and even voting, is a great benefit; particularly since it is an easily obtainable document, routinely issued without checking of identification, or verification of eligibility.

The importance of this benefit was illustrated by a federal grand jury in 1984 that concluded that large numbers of aliens registered to vote in Chicago. The grand jury reported that many aliens "register to vote so that they can obtain documents identifying them as U.S. citizens" and have "used their voters' cards to obtain a myriad of benefits, from social security to jobs with the Defense Department." **The U.S. Attorney at that time estimated that there were at least 80,000 illegal aliens registered to vote in Chicago, and dozens were eventually indicted and convicted for fraudulently registering and voting.**

The grand jury's report resulted in a partial cleanup of voter registration rolls in Chicago, but just one year later, **INS District Director A. D. Moyer testified before a state legislative task force that 25,000 illegal, and 40,000 legal, aliens still remained on the Chicago rolls.** Moyer told the Illinois Senate that non-citizens registered so that they could get a voter registration card for identification, adding that the card was "a quick ticket into the unemployment compensation system." ***Do you get it my friends; voter fraud exists and is rampant?***

Lawsuit Abuse

The number of lawsuits in the U.S. has tripled in the last 30 years. The business community must pick its battles carefully, to survive the risks of fighting this abuse. Staggering legal costs, extensive delays, and huge judgments can severely affect a company's bottom line.

The U.S. has gone overboard in protecting individual liberties at the cost of endangering the economy. Indeed, polling corporate executives revealed that 83% say that their decisions are increasingly affected by the fear of lawsuits. Small wonder, with law firms grossing well over $100 billion, according to Department of Commerce estimates.

The legal system is rigged in favor of big business—lawsuits are a devastating competitive weapon for those like Google, Facebook, and Microsoft, who can afford them. Indeed, tort reform, including ending class action suits and preventing people from suing a company if they misuse a product, would spark an explosion of productivity in America.

Not just business, but all society as well, suffers as left-wing professors and diversity exploiters use lawsuits and tenure to protect their dangerous, irrational ideas and lies. They put a chill on those who want to expose their lies, by silencing the critics trying to tell the truth. Lawyers and judges act like the secret police of totalitarian regimes around the globe. By killing dissent and controlling the thinking of the masses, they keep evil dictators in power.

Legal Vultures

Looking for a growing business opportunity? Go on TV and find anybody who claims to have an asbestos-related injury.

A RAND report states that over 600,000 people in the U.S. filed claims for asbestos-related injuries, costing businesses more than $54 billion by the end of 2000. Indeed, three decades after Manville Corporation collapsed under an avalanche of asbestos litigation, personal-injury claims continue to pile up at a rate of 85 per day. The Manville Trust has already paid out $4.3 billion.

The RAND study found that 65% of compensation over the past decade was paid to people with non-cancerous conditions. Increasing claims by those with no cancer and little functional impairment explain the recent growth in the asbestos caseload. There are too many lawyers in America already, and in 2019, 33,954 students graduated from law school in the United States. Too many lawyers mean too many more frivolous lawsuits. *Of course a Google search will find scores of sites by fraudulent lawyers looking for an asbestos claim but barely a word about the massive fraud attempts. You do know liability lawyers are big supporters of Democrats where the businesses these leaches sue are usually Republican?*

International Criminal Court (ICC)

Whatever the motives behind the creation of the International Criminal Court, let's not be blind to the fact that the preservation of a decent world order depends chiefly on the exercise of American leadership. For both geo-political and constitutional reasons, we should not be in the business of delegating leadership or compounding difficult exercises by creating unaccountable, supra-national bodies.

Like most attempts at building international convention, the ICC created a Frankenstein similar to the UN, which is now its partner in crime. The ICC is based on an emotional attachment to the abstract ideal of an international justice system, and runs contrary to American standards of constitutional order as well as the principles of international crisis resolution. The concerns expressed by John R. Bolton (our former U.S. Ambassador to the United Nations), before the Senate Foreign Relations Committee about the 1988 creation of the International Criminal Court (ICC) in Rome, are as valid today as they were then, since no major, substantive change has been made to the treaty.

Bolton stated that the conference created "not only a court with sweeping and poorly defined jurisdiction, but also a powerful and unaccountable prosecutor." Bolton saw through the obvious but concealed agenda of those states looking to create more international organizations to bind nations in general and the United States in particular.

Unfortunately, President Clinton signed the ICC treaty—one that he himself admitted was flawed—having no intention of submitting it to the Senate for ratification. His purpose was to put the U.S. in a position to help correct the flaws. But as others have noted, the treaty was not only flawed, but actually dead on arrival. Without the U.S., the ICC would have hopefully rested in peace, but the naïve support for the ICC left the U.S. in a weaker position than if we had simply declared the treaty a non-starter in the first place. The ICC was created as an organization outside the UN system; a decision I would normally say was wise. Unfortunately, by excluding the UN, the Security Council and the veto power of the U.S. as one of the Council's five permanent members, was also eliminated.

The American concept of separation of power reflects our belief that the various authorities legitimately exercised in government are placed in separate branches, as a necessary system of checks and balances. Europeans, however, may feel comfortable with a system that vests the ICC Prosecutor with enormous law enforcement powers accountable to no one. Bolton concluded that the ICC is in fact a "stealth approach to eroding constitutionalism. Americans should find this unacceptable."

Be aware of liberal Democrats under pressure from left-wing Europeans to pump life back into the ICC Frankenstein. The Left would love to have such a weapon to use against U.S. troops and their leaders; a type of Nuremberg trial to denigrate our courageous war heroes. Uninformed, biased, left-wing Euro-trash prefer to support terrorist regimes in Palestine, and the cowardly toads that run Iran would love to target our troops in their kangaroo courts. These are the kinds of things we can expect from an overly powerful ICC.

Criminals Rights Injustice for Victims

This year, according to the Bureau of Justice Statistics' National Crime Victimization Survey (NCVS), 3.3 million U.S. residents age 12 or older were victims of violent crime in 2018. Based on the soaring crime rates in progressive run cities, do you think crime will increase or decrease with left-wing radical pro-criminal prosecutors and defund the police efforts being pushed by BLM and other Biden supporters?

When it happens, the victims will be in for a number of surprises. Somewhere along the way, the criminal justice system began to serve lawyers, judges, and defendants. Victims are now treated with institutionalized disinterest. The neglect of crime victims is a national disgrace. They may suffer untold emotional grief, financial hardship, and public humiliation, only to watch the offender become the center of attention in a legal system that tips the scales ever more heavily in favor of the criminal. Criminals are the bottom feeders of society, and do not deserve the attention and rights they are currently receiving.

Plea Bargains

According to a recent study from the Pew Research Center, of the roughly 80,000 federal prosecutions initiated in 2018, just two percent went to trial. More than 97 percent of federal criminal convictions are obtained through plea bargains, and the states are not far behind at 94 percent.

Why are people so eager to confess their guilt instead of challenging the government to prove their guilt beyond a reasonable doubt to the satisfaction of a unanimous jury? Albert Alschler, professor at the University of Chicago, thinks, like many others, that there is nothing good about plea-bargaining. Alschler starts with what the sentences lead to. "You have two people who've committed the same crime. They have the same background, and one is going to get twice as severe a sentence as the other because he's exercised the right to trial."

The argument in favor of plea-bargaining asserts that by pleading guilty instead of going to trial, the uncertainty of trial outcome is reduced. For the state, it also saves time and money. The bottom line is that almost all felons serve less time and are out on the street earlier to become repeat offenders as a result of this revolving door justice. I do, however, agree that the system would collapse if every case went to trial; we squander too much money on the judicial system as is.

Sentencing Guidelines

To check plea-bargaining abuses, we must have sentencing guidelines like the Three Strikes Rules that take away discretion from liberal judges, who allow repeat felons to prey on society by continuing the plea bargain game. In response to rising crime rates, California instituted these strikeout laws. Under these laws, the second or third felony offense is met with more severe punishment than the first. Opponents and those who care more about these losers than protecting society claim that the laws are expensive and do not deter crime, but as usual, convict coddlers are wrong.

A three strikes law requires a person who is convicted of a severe or violent felony, along with two additional qualifying felonies, to serve a mandatory life sentence in prison. More than half of the states in the U.S. currently have some form of a habitual offender law. In California, even misdemeanor offenses have been qualifiers as a "strike" under these laws.

The benefit of a three strikes law is that it can remove potentially violent offenders from the general population. This keeps a community safer. The disadvantage is the cost of housing an offender for the rest of their natural life. In the United States, the average cost of incarceration can be as high as $75,000 per year.

What Are some of the Pros of a Three Strikes Law?

1. It is a deterrent against crime.

Strong laws typically help to reduce the rate of crime that a community experiences. Those who would be at-risk for offending have a value proposition that must be considered. Is the benefit of the crime worth the risk of what happens to them should they get caught? With the threat of a lifetime in prison on a third felony, the value proposition often swings toward not committing the crime.

2. They can reduce felony arrests.

In California, felony arrests have declined by up to 20% in some years with the implementation of three strikes laws. This is an additional point of emphasis to show how such a mandatory sentence can act as a deterrent to crime.

3. It keeps habitual offenders in prison.

45% of federal inmates are arrested again within 5 years of their release. According to the Bureau of Justice Statistics, 77% of all inmates are arrested again within 5 years. A 2014 Swedish study, reported by PolitiFact, found that 1% of the population accounted for 63% of all violent crime convictions. The three strikes law is designed to keep these habitual offenders in prison so that the rest of the society can experience greater safety.

4. It provides justice for victims.

One of the biggest fears that most victims have is that the offender who committed a crime against them will one day return to do the same thing once again. This is especially true when considering violent crime. Although any system of justice implemented by humans is going to be imperfect at some level, the three strikes law helps to protect victims and give them the peace of mind that they need.

5. The three strikes law applies to convictions only.

Because convictions are the emphasis of the law, people are still treated as being innocent until proven guilty. No matter how many arrests may occur for an individual, if they are not convicted of a crime, then they don't have any strikes count against them on their record.

6. It works!

Data from the FBI Uniform Crime Reports and the Bureau of Justice estimates that during the first two years after the legislation's enactment, approximately eight murders, 3,982 aggravated assaults, 10,672 robberies, and 384,488 burglaries were deterred in California using the three strikes legislation.

The law resulted in an increase of 17,700 further larcenies, as criminals substituted strike able offenses with non-strike able offenses. The deterrence of these crimes saved victims approximately $889 million. Since some criminals substitute other crimes not on the list of strike able offenses, the study suggested that the list be expanded to include the most common substitutes for strike able offenses as well. *Of course, as hopefully you will have learned by now, a Google search will lead with pages of biased left-wing reasons three strikes is a failed policy and almost no support for this effective deterrent.*

Getting Away with Murder

What do Lefty, "never-met-a-killer I didn't like" journalists and political activists, naïve "all criminals are innocent" student lawyers, and their media-savvy, "watch me again twist DNA evidence to free the guilty" experts have in common? They all use shoddy statistics!

Jaime Sneider in the *Columbia Daily Spector* reviews a Columbia University study that claimed there was an amazing 68% "error rate" in capital punishment. The study concluded that capital punishment is "collapsing under the weight of its own mistakes." The widely circulated study immediately set off my right brain bullshit meter when I first heard it. Instinctively, I know that more O.J.'s were getting away with murder, and every con claims to be innocent, but 99.9 % are as guilty as hell.

Sneider points out, and **the media failed to mention, that Columbia Law Professor James Lieberman's meaning of "error rate" was not that 68% of people on death row were found to be innocent. On the contrary, Lieberman and his co-authors were unable to find a single case in the 23 years they reviewed cases in which an innocent man was executed.** *This was another case of a big lie told long enough to become truth.* In the *Wall Street Journal*, professor of law Paul Cassell revealed that the 68% error rate "turns out to include any reversal of a capital sentence at any stage by appellate courts – even if those courts ultimately upheld the capital sentence."

Likewise, the one in seven ratios, commonly purported to expose the egregious level of errors made in death penalty cases, are misleading. Disseminators of the statistic say that for every seven people executed, one has his sentence overturned. MIT professor Arnold Barnett called the ratio "meaningless," because it does not constitute an error rate as many people ignorantly assumed.

An error rate is computed by dividing the number of innocent persons executed by the total number executed. (Remember not a single innocent person was executed in the 23-year Columbia study.) Reporting how many people were not executed "yields no insight," according to Barnett, simply because it does not necessarily represent a flaw in the system. It instead shows that the system corrected itself, not that any execution was or has been incorrectly performed.

Ah, the Criminal Version of the Racism Song Again. Another lie perpetrated to help murderers and rapists supports the misconception that those sitting on death row are victims of racism. Unfortunately, the ranting, anti-death penalty, diversity crowd and their professors at left-wing law schools have just one more lie to use in their propaganda mill. *The Bureau of Justice Statistics shows that convicted White murderers are more likely to be sentenced to death than their Black counterparts.*

In looking for another means to push their agenda, capital punishment opponents argued that black murderers with white victims are more likely to get the death penalty than white murderers with black victims. The numbers are easily distorted because 80% of the United States is White, and only 13% is Black. If murderers selected their victims at random, for every ten murders committed by Whites, only one victim would be Black, whereas for every ten murders committed by Blacks, eight victims would be White.

Justice Delayed Is Justice Denied

Many activists also argue that the death penalty is too expensive, saying it costs more than simply giving convicts life sentences. But of course, the reason for the added expense of executing people is not the result of added due process, but the unnecessary delays in Federal courts. Between 1977 and 2017, the average time a condemned prisoner sat on death row increased five times more from just over four years to over twenty years in 2017.

Society overcompensates for the risk of sentencing an innocent person to jail by going to the other extreme and freeing many guilty people, who are then allowed to elude punishment in this life. As the O.J. trial clarified, society must lower the ridiculously high burden of proof, the DNA game, and the "if it doesn't fit we must acquit" circus games. We are innocent victims suffering as "innocent" criminals slip though the growing flaws in our justice system.

A major contributor to the brainwashing of America and the reversal of society's moral compass is the manipulation by the dangerously biased, unprofessional media, as I will expose in the next chapter.

Chapter 10
MEDIA MALICE

There is no such thing as objective reporting ... I've become craftier about finding the voices to say the things I think are true.

– Boston Globe reporter Dianne Dumanoski

The major responsibly for disseminating and reinforcing the misguided beliefs and lies that have brainwashed a generation and will terribly damage Western civilization can be directly attributed to today's media. Through the power of selecting what topics to cover, which commentators to interview regarding certain stories, what polling data to use, what part of a story to highlight, and whom to favor and whom to attack, the media continually uses smear and malicious propaganda techniques to promote their agenda.

Forty-seven percent of Americans rely on broadcast television for their news. They form their opinions based on what they hear and see, and to a lesser extent, read. Citizens cannot cast informed votes or make knowledgeable decisions on matters of public policy if their information is distorted as it was so severely in the last election. Western Democracy depends on fair and unbiased television, social and other news media. Sadly, the press in America promulgates lies and spreads deadly cancer of propaganda throughout America and other countries. To prevent the continued spread of lies, the media must be sanitized and studied using the clean and well-lit microscope of truth to detect and eradicate their pathogens.

Is There A Liberal Bias In The Media?

Of course there is! But you would never know it if you searched Google, which either censors proof of the bias, as shown below, or floods its site with left-wing propaganda to drown out anyone willing to tell the obvious truth. Indeed chest-pounding left-wing activism professing to be journalism defines the Trump era, and yet shameless journalists and Google sites still claim media bias is a myth. This is a little like arguing that "research" shows there's virtually no evidence of

BLM assaulting Trump supporters or looting. Everyone's seen it. No one is fooled. The only fool is the one who thinks denying the obvious just might work. *Do you think Google will eventually get that?*

Many of you were brainwashed to hate Trump by listening to liberal propaganda being played every single night for years on MSNBC and CNN. **With over 95% negative Trump coverage, of course the media is biased!** It seems the "professional norms" for these fake news broadcasts have included demeaning Trump and the Republicans nightly as a dangerously ignorant gang shredding democracy. You would have to ignore almost every story written or broadcast over the last four years about President Donald Trump and his allegedly racist, sexist, homophobic, Islamophobic voters.

Moreover, so much of the coverage was just factually wrong! Remember how for the four past years, Rachel Maddow on MSNBC carried and spilled the anti-Trump polluted water nightly for the Left. After years of baseless accusations reinforced by sociopathic liars like Adam Schiff and other swamp creatures that hiss with forked tongues, Trump-Russian collusion proved, like the impeachment circus, to be nothing but another costly left-wing hoax. *Do you think an apology will be coming soon for so much waste of time and money for such Trump libel? Can you name one Democrat accomplishment in the past 12 years? I'm serious.*

A Double-Standard on Diversity

For years, enhancing the diversity of newsroom staffs has been a central priority for reformers both outside and inside the news media, particular within the rarified media elite. Of course, when they talk about more "diversity," media chiefs almost always mean increasing the percentages of women reporters, African-American reporters, Asian-American reporters, Hispanic reporters, or representatives of other demographic minorities.

Their argument: a newspaper or television station cannot be fair and balanced if its staff does not reflect the community they serve. It seems like a good idea in the classroom but hiring based on color, national origin, or sex rather than merit is doomed to fail along with the reputations of once great news organizations. Indeed, we all experience daily what studies confirm; all forms of media have experienced a dramatic lowering of journalistic standards, trust, integrity, and sales. Great newspapers that once earned awards are now as credible as the tabloid next to them on the news stand with headlines of a coming Martian invasion. It seems you must take a course in "yellow journalism" along with the required worthless ethnic–studies for social activist courses to get a job for the failing *New York Times* these days.

But when it comes to the political and ideological make-up of newsrooms, the media's pro-diversity logic breaks down. On the one hand, those who wish for more demographic diversity say reporters are not interchangeable—a white male reporter and a Hispanic female reporter, for example, would make different decisions about how to cover a news story as a consequence of their different backgrounds and experiences. Thus, a diverse news staff theoretically helps a news organization remain sensitive to all sides, resulting in better and fairer news coverage. Again, it's a shame such academic theories fail so miserably in the real world.

But few in the media acknowledge the corresponding requirement for ideological diversity. While it seems obvious that audiences would benefit if the news, especially political news, was reported and edited by a diverse mixture of liberals, conservatives, and moderates, most influential media figures deny what we all know; that today's journalists' political views affect the news. Either journalists are so lacking in ideology, or they would like us to cover our ears and eyes and believe the utter nonsense, that professional standards are so strictly enforced that it makes absolutely no difference whether newsrooms include more liberals and far fewer conservatives than the communities they cover.

All studies show the news media are far more liberal than the public and the most elite news organizations—the networks, big newspapers and newsmagazines— are the most liberal of all. Moreover, the Media Research Center's documentation of media content over the past two decades shows this liberalism does skew the news.

Journalists, after all, are not robots—their profession requires them to make choices. Liberal journalists often choose story topics that represent a liberal agenda, they choose to interview liberal-leaning policy experts, and they question officials from a mainly liberal perspective. At the same time, they rarely choose to focus on issues representing the conservative agenda, they choose to minimize the number of conservative policy experts they interview and instead prefer to bring in Left-leaning academics or some angry Black who either teaches or preaches an anti-American, anti-White, systemic racist agenda. They rarely challenge public officials with questions representing a conservative point of view or in Biden's case nothing more challenging than his preferred ice cream flavor.

Individually, such decisions may be entirely defensible, but collectively they push news content to the Left. And while conservative journalists may make entirely different choices, introducing a rightward bias, **it is an indisputable <u>fact</u> that liberals in the media vastly outnumber the conservatives.**

It may not be a vast left-wing conspiracy, but the effect is the same. The media elite would like us to believe that their news is impartial, objective and non-partisan. But the public knows the news they produce is slanted—tilted in favor of liberal policies and liberal politicians and against conservative policies and conservative politicians.

If news reporters were as ideologically diverse as their readers and viewers, it follows that much of the bias that tarnishes the media elite would disappear. If executives, editors and producers insisted on equal treatment of conservatives and liberals, much of the public's confidence in the news media ability to be fair and objective could be restored.

If the media elite were the pragmatic non-ideologues, then one would expect to find occasional support for at least a few conservative policy positions, even if their overall bent was still left of center. But none of the surveys found that the national media are populated by independent thinkers mixing liberal and conservative positions. Instead, most of the journalistic elite offer reflexively liberal answers to practically every question a pollster can imagine. *The public clearly sees the media's bias; when will the media finally acknowledge it?*

Liberal bias in the news media is not the result of a vast left-wing conspiracy, but rather an unconscious groupthink mentality that allows only one side of a debate to get a fair hearing. When that happens, the truth suffers. This makes it so important that news media reports be politically balanced, and not biased. *When was the last time you heard a positive report about Trump's peace efforts in the Middle East that got him nominated for five Nobel Prizes? You didn't if you only watched the channels most popular with Democrats.*

A Harris poll confirms what the public already knows; the media is biased and uses their bias to try to move the public toward their distorted view of reality. The results of the poll are as follows.

- Most Americans think the media is biased, and almost 49% think the media usually doesn't "get the facts straight."
- Some two-thirds believe the media doesn't "deal fairly with all sides" in social and political reporting.
- Almost three-fourths of Americans see a "fair amount" or "great deal" of political bias in the news. And by a more then 2-to-1 ratio, poll respondents said the bias is liberal rather than conservative.
- More than 60% surveyed prefer media to "simply report the facts," not "weigh the facts" or offer suggestions about how to solve problems.
- Nearly 60% believe the news media has "too much influence." Some 47%

believe journalists have values different from their own.

A more scientific approach to the question of media bias was conducted by Tim Groseclose, a professor of political science and economics at the University of California, Los Angeles. He constructs precise quantitative measures of the slant of television, radio, and print media. He estimates something he calls the SQ (slant quotient) of various news outlets.

In his book, *Left Turn: How Liberal Media Bias Distorts the American Mind*, Groseclose reports the results of his research, including: **(1) that nearly all mainstream media outlets have a liberal bias; (2) that many so-called conservative outlets are in fact less tilted toward the right than the typical mainstream outlet is tilted toward the left; and (3) the bias has shifted the average American's PQ (political quotient) significantly to the left.**

He cautions that it is important to remember the journalists who will help establish the campaign agendas are not an all-American mix of Democrats, Republicans, and independents, but an elite group whose views veer sharply to the left. We all saw this play out in the choice of Left-leaning questions and topics poised in Presidential debates. Hopefully, that last circus will lead to disbanding the sham left-leaning "Commission on Presidential Debates."

In fact, surveys over the past 25 years have consistently found that journalists are more liberal than the rest of America.

Left-leaning media watchdogs like FAIR (not to be confused with the immigration policy group) claim that they are being objective when they are really wolves hidden in academic sheepskins, bent on attacking the few conservative news programs found in the mainstream media. Organizations like this and of course Google claim that there is not a liberal bias in the media. In all fairness to FAIR, much public confusion exists regarding what is liberal and what is conservative.

A UCLA political scientist, for example, found that the *Wall Street Journal* has a conservative editorial page but liberal news pages. They are, in fact, even more liberal than those of the *New York Times*. While public television and radio were found to be conservative compared to the mainstream media, public and media professionals themselves strongly disagree, saying that almost all "major media outlets tilt to the Left."

Even self-described liberals agree that there is a liberal bias: 41% see the media as liberal, compared to only 22% that find the news conservative.

There is an interesting perception that the higher your level of education and the more you participate in politics, the more biased you are. This might help explain why left-wing faculty members and students tend to be such biased liberals.

U.S. Media Polarization and the 2020 Election: A Nation Divided

Deep partisan divisions exist in the news sources Americans trust, distrust, and rely on. In the heated 2020 presidential election year, a new Pew Research Center report finds that Republicans and Democrats place their trust in two nearly inverse news media environments.

Overall, Republicans and Republican-leaning independents view many heavily relied on sources across a range of platforms as untrustworthy. At the same time, Democrats and independents who lean Democratic see most of those sources as credible and rely on them to a far greater degree, according to the survey of 12,043 U.S. adults conducted Oct. 29–Nov. 11, 2019, on Pew Research Center's American Trends Panel.

These divides are even more pronounced between conservative Republicans and liberal Democrats.

Moreover, evidence suggests that partisan polarization in the use and trust of media sources has widened in the past five years. A comparison to a similar study by the Center of web-using U.S. adults in 2014 finds that Republicans have grown increasingly alienated from most of the more established sources, while Democrats' confidence in them remains stable, and in some cases, has strengthened.

The study asked about use of, trust in, and distrust of 30 different news sources for political and election news. While it is impossible to represent the entire crowded media space, the outlets, which range from network television news to Rush Limbaugh to the *New York Times* to the *Washington Examiner* to *HuffPost,* were selected to represent popular media brands across a range of platforms.

Greater portions of Republicans express distrust than express trust in 20 of the 30 sources asked about. Only seven outlets generate more trust than distrust among Republicans—including Fox News and the talk radio programs of hosts Sean Hannity and Rush Limbaugh.

For Democrats, the numbers are almost reversed. Greater portions of Democrats express trust than express distrust in 22 of the 30 sources asked about. Only eight generate more distrust than trust—including Fox News, Sean Hannity, and Rush Limbaugh.

Another way to look at the diverging partisan views of media credibility: Almost half of the sources included in this report (13) are trusted by at least 33% of Democrats, but only two are trusted by at least 33% of Republicans.

Republicans' lower trust in a variety of measured news sources coincides with their infrequent use. Overall, only one source, Fox News, was used by at least one-third of Republicans for political and election news in the past week. There are five different sources from which at least one-third of Democrats received political or election news in the last week (CNN, NBC News, ABC News, CBS News, and MSNBC). *All these sources, as I have said earlier, spew the same mantra about left-wing myths exposed in earlier chapters, thus serve as propaganda arms for the on-going brainwashing. This doctor's advice is take these outlets only in small doses and avoid them like the China plague if you scored high on the brainwashing test in Chapter One.*

And in what epitomizes this era of polarized news, none of the 30 sources is trusted by more than 50% of all U.S. adults.

The Fox News phenomenon - The Public Is More Conservative Than the Media

There is also a clearly conservative bias on certain networks like FOX. Why do more people watch FOX? The media tends to forget that members of the public were more likely than journalists to consider themselves conservative.

A Princeton Survey Research Associates report for the Kaiser Family Foundation compared views of media professionals and the public. Here are some key findings: *Members of the public were six times more likely than journalists to consider themselves "conservative," and seven times more likely to identify themselves as "Republican" than were members of the media.*

In the more compact Republican media ecosystem, one outlet towers above all others: Fox News. It would be hard to overstate its connection as a trusted go-to source of political news for Republicans. About two-thirds (65%) of Republicans and Republican leaners say they trust Fox News as a source. Additionally, 60% say they got political or election news there in the past week.

Among Democrats and Democratic leaners, CNN (67%) is about as trusted a source of information as Fox News is among Republicans. The cable network is also Democrats' most commonly turned to source for political and election news, with about half (53%) saying they got news there in the past week. The big difference is that while no other source comes close to rivaling Fox News' appeal to Republicans, a number of sources other than CNN are also highly trusted and frequently used by Democrats.

The impact of political ideology on Americans' trust in news outlets

The partisan gaps become even more dramatic when looking at the parties' ideological poles—conservative Republicans and liberal Democrats. About two-thirds of liberal Democrats (66%) trust *The New York Times*, for example. In comparison, just 10% of conservative Republicans trust the *Times*, while 50% outright distrust it. Rush Limbaugh, meanwhile, is the third-most trusted source among conservative Republicans (38%) but tied for the second-most distrusted source among liberal Democrats (55%).

At the same time, the gap is less pronounced among the more moderate segments in each party. For example, three-quarters of conservative Republicans trust Fox News, while just about half (51%) of moderate or liberal Republicans do. Conversely, moderate and conservative Democrats are more than twice as likely as liberal Democrats to trust Fox News (32% vs. 12%).

The divide widens over time

There is also evidence that suggests that these partisan divides have grown over the past five years, particularly with more Republicans voicing distrust in a number of sources. A comparison to a similar study of web-using U.S. adults conducted by the Center in 2014 finds that Republicans' distrust increased for 15 of the 20 sources asked about in both years—with notable growth in Republicans' distrust of CNN, *The Washington Post*, and *The New York Times*.

Democrats' levels of trust and distrust in media sources have changed considerably less than Republicans' during this time span. Even accounting for the modest methodological differences between the two studies, these differences hold. All in all, it's not that partisans live in entirely separate media bubbles when it comes to political news. There is some overlap in news sources, but determining the full extent of that overlap can be difficult to gauge. One factor is that getting news from a source does not always mean trusting that source. Indeed, the data reveals that while 24% of Republicans got news from CNN in the past week, roughly four-in-ten who did (39%) say they distrust the outlet. And of the 23% of Democrats who got political news from Fox News in the past week, nearly three-in-ten (27%) distrust it.

The Importance of Social Media

The importance of social media played in this year's Presidential race cannot be overstated. Currently 72% of U.S. citizens of voting age actively use some form of social media, while 69% of Americans in the same group use Facebook alone, according to data from Socialbakers. The social media marketing platform found that while President Donald Trump's use of Twitter has been widely acknowledged, and certainly had a tremendous impact on the outcome of the 2016 elections, former Vice President Joe Biden has actually surpassed the President in many key engagement metrics.

Moreover, while President Trump has some 87 million followers on Twitter to Vice President Biden's 11 million followers, both candidates have seen a massive and continuous increase in engagement during this election cycle. Additionally, the Socialbakers data found that Biden's three highest performing tweets have nearly double the amount of interactions compared to Trump's respective tweets, despite Biden's drastically lower follower count—another testament to the irrelevance of follower count on a stage this large.

In the lead up to and just following the debates between the two candidates, social media users spent a lot of time discussing the candidates. Data from Hootsuite showed that from Oct. 21 to Oct. 23 there were 6.6 million total mentions of Trump and Biden, with Biden owning 72% of those mentions.

During the actual debate, mentions for Biden spiked up to 511,000 with a sentiment breakdown of 14% positive, 38% neutral, 48% negative—while mentions for Trump spiked up during the debate to 244,000 with a sentiment breakdown of 10% positive, 41% neutral, and 49% negative.

The Public Recognizes the Media's Liberal Bias

Americans' perception of the national media as too biased and too liberal has grown significantly over the past two decades. In less than twenty years, since the 1985 Times Mirror polls began routinely assessing the public's perceptions of the national media, the percentage of Americans who perceive a liberal bias has doubled from 22 percent to 45 percent, nearly half the adult population. Even Democrats now generally regard the press as a liberal entity.

Three in Four See Bias: Pew's pessimistic findings were matched by a Harris poll of more than 3,000 adults conducted for the Center for Media and Public Affairs (CMPA). According to CMPA's analysis, "nearly two-thirds (63 percent) believe one side is favored in presentation of the news; an even larger majority of 77 percent thinks that there is at least a fair amount of political bias in the news they see."

"This bias is described as liberal by a plurality (43 percent) of all adults," the report continued, while 19 percent described a conservative bias. CMPA discovered that "nearly three-quarters (73 percent) of all Republicans believe that the news media favor one side in their reporting ... compared with only two of five (40 percent) Democrats."

Interestingly, CMPA's analysis concluded that while "complaints about bias used to come mainly from political conservatives, our survey indicates that this limitation no longer exists... Even self-described liberals agree: 41 percent see the media as liberal, compared to only 22 percent who find the news to be conservative. Among self-designated conservatives, of course, the spread is even greater: 57 percent say the media are liberal and 19 percent see them as conservative."

"These findings challenge the argument of some journalists that bias is purely in the eye of the beholder. Although conservatives are three times more likely to see liberal rather than conservative bias, moderates and liberals alike see liberal bias in the media twice as often as they see conservative bias," CMPA concluded.

Plurality of Democrats See Liberal Bias:

In a survey, Pew found that twice as many Americans (51 percent) believed news organizations have a liberal bias than a conservative bias (26 percent). Not only did a majority of Republicans and independents hold this view, but *a plurality of Democrats (41 percent) thought the media had a liberal bias, compared with 33 percent of Democrats who saw a conservative bias.*

The public is not wrong: news organizations are, in fact, disproportionately liberal, and far too many reporters approach their stories with a liberal mindset. Every study of the past 25 years has proved this point. The only question is when will the media elite recognize that a liberal bias erodes their credibility with mainstream and conservative audiences, and make ideological diversity in their newsrooms a goal?

This MRC Special Report summarizes the relevant data on journalist attitudes, as well as polling showing how the American public's recognition of the media's liberal bias has grown over the years:

- **Journalists Say They Are Liberal:** Numerous surveys from 1978 to 2004 show that journalists are far more likely to say they are liberal than conservative, and are far more liberal than the public at large.

- **Journalists Reject Conservative Positions:** None of the surveys have found that news organizations are populated by independent thinkers who mix liberal and conservative positions. Most journalists offer reflexively liberal answers to practically every question a pollster can imagine.

- **Women are more liberal.** In a sign that the media's desire for demographic diversity might result in even more solidly liberal newsrooms, ASNE also found that "women are more likely than men to fall into one of the liberal/Democrat categories," as just 11 percent said they were conservative or leaned that way. Minorities also "tend to be more liberal/Democrat," with a piddling 3 percent of Blacks and 8 percent of Asians and Hispanics putting themselves on the Right.

- Pew also asked journalists to name a news organization that seemed to cover the news from an especially liberal or especially conservative angle. When it came to a liberal news outlet, most of the national journalists were stumped. A fifth suggested the *New York Times* was liberal; ABC, CBS, CNN, and NPR were each named by two percent. One percent of reporters said NBC was liberal. So compared to the public, including a plurality of Democrats; reporters, Google, and their fake news accomplices are either playing dumb or refuse to accept the obvious fact of left-wing media bias. But journalists did see ideology at one outlet: "The single news outlet that strikes most journalists as taking a particular ideological stance—either liberal or conservative—is Fox News Channel," Pew reported. More than two-thirds of national journalists (69 percent) tagged FNC as a conservative news organization, followed by the *Washington Times* (9 percent) and the *Wall Street Journal* (8 percent).

Hopefully, I objectively proved that the media has a strong left-wing bias and that contributed massively to the effective brainwashing of many Americans. With all the other sectors of society parroting the same propaganda for so long, can you now at least open the possibility that so much of what you believe is myth? How sad it is when you can't use Google to check facts because they are also swimming in the left-wing swamp. The facts will eventually seep out; hopefully before you bought the Brooklyn Bridge and the greatest country in history loses America's Cultural Revolution.

WEAPONS OF MASS MEDIA SMEAR AND BIAS (WMB'S)

What if the proverbial man from Mars came to Earth disguised as an Earthling child? His assignment was to spend 25 years evaluating America's culture and then report back what he found. In our schools at the elementary level he learned being White was bad and being Black you are a victim of systemic racism. Those views were reinforced even through his graduate level studies. He would eventually report that America was a racist country from its founding and has no redeeming values worth preserving. That view would be validated during his interaction with friends on social networks. He would later watch riots and looting on the streets of major cities and learn this was part of an on-going revolution against racism and for social justice. He would cheer with his friends as newly elected President Joe Biden said eliminating "systemic racism" was at the top of their agenda.

These riots are happening lately, he is told, because of a pandemic of police targeting and killing Blacks. He watched on TV as left-wing activists and sports celebrities condemned this racism by defaming the symbols of their country. At his workplace he observed as civil right advocates, with support from the government's own EEOC, sued his company because it did not have a representative proportion of minorities in all sectors of the company. He eagerly participated in company-wide diversity training programs.

The Martian however, was confused. His research and education clearly showed that hiring and admission to education institutions based on race and sex, rather than merit, went against the very core of America's stated values expressed clearly in the constitution and in Section 703j of the Civil Rights Act. Moreover, when he investigated facts about cases of police killing Blacks, he found the police are almost always later found innocent in a court of law.

To clear up his confusion about these and other issues the activists on the street are concerned about, he decided to use Google search. The result from scouring the front pages of his searches consistently supported what he was told by the left-wing and diversity groups rioting in the street. It confirmed all he learned in years of schooling, from politicians, church, professional organizations, charitable foundations, celebrities, and those in civil rights movement about the need to dramatically reform this racist capitalist society, into one more socialist oriented.

Before meeting his saucer to return to Mars and make his report, he decided he needed to research if the media would also validate what all the other segments of society thought about American culture. Not surprising, they were almost unanimous in confirming the victimization and all the other concerns raised by the social justice warriors on the Left.

His report concluded that if all segments of American society say something is true then it must be. *Certainly isn't that what the brainwashed masses in Nazi Germany or during Mao's Cultural Revolution believed?*

But as the song line goes "it ain't necessarily so!"

How does bias in the news manifest itself? Unfortunately, it's not always easy to recognize. No self-respecting reporter is going to come right out and say "And this next sentence is biased, so watch out!" Rather, we must try to find bias ourselves, and in order to do so we must know where to look. We have found that the most common ways that bias manifests itself in the news are through word choice, omissions, the limiting of debate, framing of the story, and a biased selection and use of sources.

Let's look at specific examples of the unethical methods used daily by the media to successfully brainwash the public into accepting their dangerous agenda. Don't take it anymore! Be aware at all times that you cannot trust most of the media. Only after learning to distinguish truth from propaganda can we right our moral compasses and identify good from evil.

Fake news—the Left's propaganda arm

Those of you who depended on CNN, Comcast's MSNBC, ABC, NBC, CBS, *NPR*, Bezo's *Washington Post, New York Times,* or Ms. Job's *The Atlantic* for your news are fed similar lies independent of which of these sources you're using. Also BBC sadly relies heavily on these same sources for news about America. These outlets, some owned by Big Tech oligarchs, act like a propaganda arm for the Democratic Party, left-wing radicals, and professional race hustlers. They act like a news monolith and will often use the same terms like a "bombshell disclosure" before presenting some statement from an "anonymous source" regarding something negative about Trump or his family or administration on all these cable outlets. These attacks are so often misleading, lies or much ado about nothing; that this group deservedly earned the moniker of "fake news."

1- Trump Russia Collusion Hoax nightly coverage—"Obamagate" rarely covered

As Victor Davis Hanson, a great clear minded truth-teller commented: "Shortly before Trump's inauguration, President Barack Obama called Vice President Joe Biden, national security adviser Susan Rice, Deputy Attorney General Sally Yates and FBI Director James Comey into the Oval Office. The purpose of the meeting was reportedly to correlate progress reports about how best to continue government surveillance of Trump's designated national security adviser, Michael Flynn, and thereby disrupt the transition.

"Flynn's name was soon unmasked, apparently by Obama administration officials, and then illegally leaked to the press. The harassment during the transition became thematic for Trump's next four years, which saw false evidence submitted to federal courts and other classified documents illegally leaked. "

"No prior president has faced such hysterical opposition bent on removing him from office by a special prosecutor, concocted charges that he should be deposed under the 25th Amendment, and, finally, a failed attempt at removal via impeachment. The president's private phone calls to foreign leaders were leaked. Media darlings and anonymous opponents within the government boasted of sabotaging Trump's initiatives. Washington analysts and retired military officers hyped coup scenarios about how best to use force to remove him from office."

"So it is a bit rich for the media to now warn of Trump's dangers to the spirit of smooth presidential transitions. Such protocols were deliberately rendered null and void in 2016."

After numerous and costly investigations, we learned that Trump's team never did collude with Russia, but instead was the victim of one of the most egregious frame-ups and misuse of our intelligence agencies in our history. The coup attempt based on an infamous fake dossier, paid for by Clinton and pushed by the Obama team will hopefully finally come out in the Durham report. Like the famous Dreyfus case in France where the media tarnished an innocent man's reputation with a false charge of treason, MSNBC and CNN spent years spinning what turned out to be a complete hoax during prime time nightly, unfairly targeting Trump and his administration.

Media and academia will continue to intimidate, in their gestapo-style, fair and balanced conservative voices from being heard in our schools and communication outlets. This will ensure the brainwashing continues, the uncovering of the origins of the many myths against Trump never heard, and propaganda accepted as truth.

As Nazi propaganda minister Goebbels said; a lie told often enough becomes the truth. Repeating lies brainwashed Germans during the war then, as today's media lies are brainwashing generations of Americans to destroy their own great country from within.

A few other specific media lies you were fed about Trump

- On June 22, 2017, CNN reported that Trump aide Anthony Scaramucci was involved with the Russian Direct Investment Fund, under Senate investigation. He was not, and CNN retracted the story. Three reporters who published it resigned, according to CNN.
- In May 2018, some progressive activists, journalists, and former Obama speechwriter Jon Favreau criticized the Trump administration's treatment of unaccompanied children at the U.S. border, citing a picture of children sleeping in an enclosure surrounded by a chain link fence, along with an AZCentral.com article titled, "First glimpse of immigrant children at holding facility." The article and photo were from 2014, during Obama's presidency.
- In February 2019, a blog published on AllSides reported how the media reports hate crimes are either rare or common, depending on their bias. Law enforcement reported hate crimes to the FBI in 2017, up from 2016. Although the numbers increased over the year, so did the number of agencies reporting hate crime data—with 1,000 additional agencies contributing information. Both Left media outlets (CNN, Vox) omitted the fact that more agencies were reporting, in order to present a view that hate crimes were on the rise to make Trump look bad.

2- China virus selective media bias

I will make no apology for calling the current plague the "China virus." I detest media collusion to protect China from any consequences for releasing this destructive historic global pandemic and for once again sticking Trump and any one not using the corona virus moniker with their flaccid racist label. One such woke journalist, Niha Masih, working as the Indian correspondent for the left-wing international media outlet, *The Washington Post*, went as far to take to Twitter to denounce India for tweeting on "#corona virus as #ChineseVirus19". Niha called it a nasty and racist attempt to defame China.

What is sickening and more dangerous is how Google and other media (as I have shown throughout this book, Google now operates more as a content provider than an objective search engine) are colluding to provide cover for China, our most significant adversary role in this disaster.

Searching Google about media bias regarding the China virus, I found most media sites attacking America for China bias and racism. I finally came upon an article online from *The Epoch Times*; a news source I found trustworthy in the past. The article is titled, "China silenced doctors who warned of the new virus."

To my shock, I was immediately hit with warnings about the source—including an unwelcomed video popping up with some high-tech sellout to China, warning that the claims and site are not valid, and banners directing me to other sites. As you have learned throughout the book, I've been outraged and surprised by the search engine becoming a propaganda tool for brainwashed social justice warriors. But with the multimedia barrage when I opened the *Epoch Times* site, I felt I had inadvertently opened a door into some Orwellian society; with a brutal policy of draconian control by propaganda, disinformation denial of the truth, doublethink, and manipulation of the past.

It became very clear that I must add foreign adversaries like China, Russia, and Iran to the cabal of domestic institutions and groups committed to brainwashing the masses and overturning our democracy. Moreover, like the corrupt World Health Organization, Google is deep in bed with China and has become a leader in purveying its Communist Party propaganda.

Media Spinning China Virus Statistics

Media fear and smear campaign destroyed our economy, education and got Biden elected.

As we have been isolated in our homes, we are subjected by media headlines nightly about record breaking numbers of those infected by the China virus in various locales in the U.S. and around the world. Such news provided the Biden campaign an opportunity to blame Trump for his handling of the pandemic and was the major reason for a Biden win. Indeed, before the pandemic Trump's historic accomplishments assured him of an easy victory.

Trump was bashed by the monolithic fake news despite the fact that he effectively led the largest medical mobilization in world history—bringing supplies and even vaccines at warp speed. Even his nemeses Gov. Newsom and Cuomo publicly praised his achievement. There was little media coverage of the Governors' comments and complete shade was provided about the most deadly wrong decision of the pandemic. That, of course, was Cuomo ordering nursing home patients with the virus back into nursing homes to free up hospital space. With Trump supplying hospital space in the Javits Center, Central Park, and by sending a hospital ship, it turned out that there was a massive amount of unused beds and Trump equipment and supplies. Trump also banned travel from China and Europe while the Democrats were holding a sham impeachment and Pelosi was standing with a crowd in Chinatown, telling the public there is nothing to worry about and to come visit.

Examples of media's and Googles effective fear and smear campaign that got Biden elected:

Did your media source tell you that COVID was less harsh on kids than the flu? This year's stats show for younger people, seasonal flu is "in many cases" a deadlier virus than COVID-19. Even Left leaning *PolitiFact's* rules that the statement by Senator Ron Johnson: Mostly True.

Here's why: As schools across the country open for the uncertain, unprecedented school year to come, opinions are split on how to do so safely. Some districts have opted for completely virtual learning. Others will try a mix of both online and in-person classes, or will send younger children to school while older kids stay home, or will phase students back to the classroom gradually. Others still are calling for schools to reopen completely for those who feel well enough to teach and attend, and who aren't especially vulnerable to COVID-19.

Is Johnson correct that COVID-19 is less deadly for children than the flu?

To back up his claim, Johnson's office sent statistics from the Centers for Disease Control and Prevention on flu and COVID-19 deaths among Americans under age 18. During the 2018-19 flu season, the CDC reported approximately 480 flu deaths among children ages 0-17, about 30% of whom had a lab-confirmed case of influenza. Comparably, 90 American youth have died from coronavirus complications from the beginning of the pandemic through mid-August, according to the American Academy of Pediatrics.

More than 46,000 children were hospitalized for the flu in that 2018-19 period. The hospitalization rate among children 5 to 17 was 39.2 children per 100,000 children. For COVID-19, that hospitalization rate is 6 per 100,000 children ages 5 to 17, the CDC says.

In a report detailing the differences between COVID-19 and the flu, the CDC states that "the risk of complications for healthy children is higher for flu compared to COVID-19."

And data from Wisconsin echoes that sentiment. Since the pandemic began, no children have died from COVID-19 complications, according to that state Department of Health Services death data, and 147 people ages 0-19 have been hospitalized. In contrast, three pediatric flu deaths occurred during this year's flu season, DHS data show, and 605 kids ages 17 and under have been hospitalized.

Overall fatality rate

In March, we heard much about the case fatality rate of the China virus. In the U.S. it was roughly three percent—nearly three out of every hundred people who were identified as cases of the China virus died from it. Compare that to today when the fatality rate is less than one-half of one percent. In other words, when the World Health Organization (WHO) said three percent of those who get the virus die from it, they were wrong by at least one order of magnitude. The rate is closer to 0.2 percent. The reason for the highly inaccurate early estimates is simple; we were not identifying most of the people infected by the virus.

When the Trump team dramatically increased testing, CNN sneered at the president for misleading people by claiming the U.S. did more COVID-19 tests than any other country. They, correctly, pointed out that per capita, "South Korea and Italy tested many times more." CNN was right to adjust for population. But then, to make Trump look worse, CNN suddenly stopped adjusting for population. They scolded the president, saying, "The U.S. had more corona virus cases than any country in the world!" But that's just wrong! Adjusted for population, 28 countries, including France, England, Ireland, and Norway had more cases.

More nasty from MSNBC host and former John McCain 2008 campaign aide Nicolle Wallace: "This moment is like every other in Donald Trump's presidency, where it's about his fragile, teeny-tiny ego, and the vast nation that he leads, and he's making all his decisions based on press coverage. ... The difference here ... is that people are dying; more than 30,000 people have died. The virus is still spreading across the country and Donald Trump today, like a punk, seemed to tweet about protesters."

Wallace ignores the administration's mitigation efforts many believe have sharply reduced the number of projected deaths from 2.2 million to fewer than 50,000 to date. As Trump said at Monday's briefing, if he discovered a pill that cured the virus, the media and Democrats would still criticize him.

This is from *New York Times* columnist David Brooks on the PBS News Hour: "If you said anything nasty about Donald Trump, you don't qualify for the [reopening] committee. And that basically guarantees a very low level of competence from that committee. The North Korean-style, you know, loyalty tests are going to be crushing to the competence of any effort going forward."

New York Times' Thomas Friedman echoed his colleagues who seem to daily ratchet up new labels to apply to the president. Friedman recently called the president "unhinged" and "reckless."

MSNBC host Joe Scarborough, a former Republican congressman from Florida, got Newsbuster's No. 1 award for saying the following: "The Republican Party claims to be the party of life, if you're talking about the unborn. But if you're the born, my God, watch out. If you're especially in the Greatest Generation, if you're a World War II veteran in your 90s, if you're a Vietnam veteran in your 60s, if you're a Korean War veteran in your 70s or 80s, well, the hell with you. ... They're saying, 'Well, yeah, they're gonna die.' Yeah, we know older people are gonna die. The Greatest Generation, a lot of people are going to die there. A lot of people are going to die that are Korean War vets and Vietnam vets. But you know what? We have gotta get Wall Street purring again."

3. George Floyd Death

Rioting, looting, burning, assaults, and deaths resulted due to the cause of his death being suppressed by Google and the media. The media stirred up public outrage after the video of a cop putting his knee on Floyd's neck seemingly killing him. But have you heard anything on the media about what the medical examiner found as the actual cause? Probably not!

Did you know that Floyd had a "fatal level of Fentanyl" in his system?

New documents filed give information about the Hennepin County Medical Examiner's findings in Floyd's autopsy. Notes of a law enforcement interview with Dr. Andrew Baker, the Hennepin County Medical Examiner, say Floyd had 11ng/mL of Fentanyl in his system. "If he were found dead at home alone and no other apparent causes, this could be acceptable to call an OD. Deaths have been certified with levels of 3," Baker told investigators. Moreover, new documents say Floyd had a "heavy heart and at least one artery was approximately 75% blocked." How much death and destruction could have been avoided if the facts came out immediately and we had an honest press?

4. Joe Biden Scandal

We have a corrupt media that serves as a propaganda arm. Our media works for the Democrat party. Indeed, less than a week before our most important election we hit the lowest points in history of the press in America. In an unprecedented attempt at election interference, the mainstream media and the oligarchs in Big Tech decided to put a "protective wall" around Joe Biden's candidacy. The *Wall*

Street Journal's editor at large called out the "lapdog press" for blacking out explosive Tony Bobulinski claims during a Tucker Carlson interview. Bobulinski, a former decorated Navy officer and former business associate of Hunter Biden, met with Joe Biden twice; he said Biden's brother shrugged off concerns that Joe Biden's ties to his son's business deals could put a future presidential campaign at risk. They said they would use "plausible deniability" if they were caught (which they have been). This is further proof that Google and the "lapdog press" are not worthy of public trust. This historical censorship of the massive corruption charges against Biden probably cost Trump the election.

Moreover, the fact that the FBI is also looking into pedophilia charges against Hunter after viewing his laptop, or Tara Reade's sexual assault by Joe Biden hasn't even elicited a whisper from the "me too" women's movement and the media, screams of their hypocrisy.

5. President Trump calls neo-Nazis "very fine people"

Like the "Hands up don't shoot" and "No justice, no peace" harmful but baseless slogans; the Left uses "There are good people on both sides" as a statement they attributed to Trump after Charlottesville. Did he say that during a famous press conference following the Charlottesville riots of August 2017? The major media reported that he did.

But what if their reporting is wrong? Worse, what if their reporting is wrong and they know it's wrong? A straight exploration of the facts should reveal the truth. This is what the liberal media did to President Trump following the melee in Charlottesville. They convicted him as a supporter of white supremacy simply for having the wisdom to wait until facts emerged. They declared his statement too little too late.

Proof Trump is not a racist, but rather a victim of an ongoing media smear campaign, was presented in an earlier chapter but is worth mentioning again. Even the transcript of his remarks on left-leaning FactCheck.org, proves Trump condemned white supremacy several times. Indeed, he was referring to the pulling down of a statue of Robert E. Lee when he spoke of "very fine people." People do disagree with the destruction of statues, and that is their right to do so. Moreover, on the day of Heather Heyer's savage killing, he unequivocally issued a statement condemning hatred and violence by anyone. You can fault President Trump for many things, but distorting what he said at Charlottesville and thereafter is not good journalism; it's grasping at some political advantage.

Another ongoing hoax easily disproved by serious journalism is that proud Americans, who support Trump and counter the BLM Antifa's rioting and destruction of our cites, are White Supremacists. The "Proud Boy" hoax is a good example of the on-going smear tactics used to reinforce left-wing brainwashing.

Enrique Tarrio insists that the Proud Boys aren't White Supremacists, and he would be in a position to know. For one, he's the international chairman. For another, **he's Black.**

"I denounce white supremacy," Mr. Tarrio said in a Thursday interview with WSVN-TV in Miami. "I denounce anti-Semitism. I denounce racism. I denounce fascism. I denounce communism and any other -ism that is prejudiced toward people because of their race, religion, culture, and tone of skin."

6. What Riots?

As reported by Steve Krakauer in the Hill, *The New York Times* has introduced a new term into our political lexicon—"rage moms." Its Aug. 17 story described "fired up" mothers supporting protesters in Portland, Ore., and the caption on the story's photo declared: "The Wall of Moms that emerged from the Portland protests is one of the latest examples of parents engaging in activism to strengthen the social safety net." Democrats, the Times said, are "counting on" these "rage moms" to help them win in November. They did but also reinforced the negative stereotype of women acting out of emotion and not logic. Their families will pay the price for not considering the negative impacts of their decisions, some of which I predicted in the beginning of this book, if Biden won and the Senate went Blue.

Meanwhile, *The Washington Post* wrote a glowing profile of Portland's protesters, complete with a photo shoot in protest garb and the headline that "protest is what Portland does best." I'm waiting to see that slogan in the Chamber of Commerce pitch for visitors. They can offer a free circus as well, with the Governor and Mayor performing a dog and pony show while the city burns in the background.

These are just two examples of the absurd lengths to which the "Acela Corridor media" (the biased left-wing media named for the Amtrak service that runs between, and is largely based in, New York City and Washington, D.C.) has gone to glamorize the violent riots that have emerged from what began as peaceful protests around the country. Portland is not a model of peaceful protests, no matter how the media tries to spin it through a bias of omission of the reality on the ground.

Here's the truth: Over a recent weekend, a man was violently assaulted to the point of being rendered unconscious by a mob that said he tried to run over people. Without social media, no one would likely have any idea that this happened. This is not new; violent rioters are regularly clashing with police officers in Portland. Portland Mayor Ted Wheeler (D) has largely stood on the sidelines during this mayhem, but even his call to the crowd that they are "attempting to commit murder" has gotten barely any coverage from the legacy media outlets, except for Fox News.

When the media does cover Portland rioting, it often misses the story. There are the subtle ways, like how CBS News picks up a story about rioting by describing it passively as "riot declared" by police, rather than stating that a literal riot happened. Or you have something more egregious, like the *Times* story about "Bible burning" and flag burning in Portland. The Times described it as "the first viral hit in Russia's 2020 disinformation campaign" and claimed the story spread by conservatives was "too good to check."

In reality, even somewhat Left-biased Snopes described the story as "true"—not "Russia disinformation," as the *Times* alleged. Several Bibles were, in fact, burned. An American flag was, too, as a crowd cheered. Stating these facts is not "disinformation," nor does it mean all protesters burn Bibles and American flags. But reporting the truth was mischaracterized by the *Times* as disinformation.

And this is the crux of the issue: The *Times* and others in the media are so resistant to describe the violent looting and rioting happening in America as what it is, because they believe it will take away from the legitimate social-justice protests which spurred these latest actions. In fact, by spinning the violence as part of the protests, the media take away from the cause they are trying to protect. Peaceful protesters don't assault police officers; they don't burn or loot buildings. That sort of criminal behavior should be covered, and not ignored—so it can be contrasted with the coverage the media gave to the legitimate protests in June and early July.

It's no longer relegated to protests. Portland saw more homicides in July than during any month over the past 30 years. And it's not just Portland, either. In Chicago earlier this month, massive looting was condemned by the mayor but not by media forces covering for Black Lives Matter. On CNN, the incident was barely covered. In New York City, gun violence has skyrocketed—and it's fallen to sites like the Gothamist and other local outlets to cover it, since the national media has largely ignored it.

The media refusing to do their job as a fair, neutral purveyor of information has real-world consequences. Following the media's rosy portrayal of the illegal occupation of Seattle by the CHAZ/CHOP group (which led to violence and other criminal behavior), Seattle's city government eventually caved to many of their demands. In response, Seattle's black female police chief resigned this month. "It really is about the overarching lack of respect for the officers, the men and women who work so hard, day in and day out," said Chief Carmen Best.

What we used to call "mainstream media" is now "woke" media. Many don't even try to be objective. Watching CNN during this summer's protests, I noticed that reporters kept calling protests "mostly peaceful," even when reporting violence. CNN posted the words, "Mostly peaceful protests" on the screen when flaming cars were on the street behind their reporter.

CNN defended itself, citing a study that said "93% of protests were peaceful." But that's silly. When planes crash, we don't put "99% landed safely" on the screen. As Joe Concha put it, "When people start dying and losing their businesses, that's your story!" And then there is the media's most potent power: the power to ignore certain stories.

For those who are passive in the way they receive information—that is accepting what the major media "report" and say—these and worse comments are accepted as truth. That is a major reason the brainwashing happened. It is why socialism and the Democratic Party, which offer free stuff in exchange for votes, are so appealing to especially the young.

The media's liberal slant is likely a major factor contributing to the decline of newspaper circulation and broadcast news ratings. It is all so predictable that people don't need to waste their time (or money) reading and watching. American taxpayers have long subsidized the indoctrination efforts of the Public Broadcasting Service (PBS). PBS has now become a major component of leftist broadcasting. In fact, millions of people wonder what public PBS thinks it is broadcasting to? Is it useful to include every point of view simply to cover every base? Even PBS Senior Producer Linda Harrar said that PBS' programming is virtually impossible for their audience to sort out. We agree, but PBS' listeners are more conservative and do not appreciate the historical revisionism and moral relativism found throughout PBS programming, right down to kids programming.

EPILOGUE

L'Chaim (to life)

- Jewish toast

Tikkun Olem (repair the world)

- Jewish motto

I wrote this book because as I've expressed in earlier books, I am deeply concerned that the futures of our children and grandchildren are in serious jeopardy. I've been obsessed in my efforts to warn voters before the election that America as we know it would change dramatically for the worse if Biden won. Moreover, his win and, if the Democrats take control of the Senate, our constitution with its protections and brilliant system of checks and balances could be destroyed.

In the beginning of this book, I stated my outlandish thesis: that a large percentage of Americans have been as brainwashed as the Red Guards during China's Cultural Revolution. I further attributed this brainwashing as a key factor in the Biden win.

I too would have labeled someone with such a thesis as a kook of the flying saucer variety. But with five decades of successful written predictions, even during confusing times with weak signals, I asked you to give me the benefit of the doubt and keep an open mind while I presented my case. I've had a lifelong obsession to myth-busting, using objectivity, observation, logic, and facts as my weapons. I have great confidence in my brainwashing and an American Cultural Revolution thesis, because it is based on my personal time and chance encounters, and my years of synthesizing seemingly random data into comprehensive frameworks. In this case, a random series of events and actions beginning in the 1960s unleashed a cascade of negative, unintended consequences that few people understand or can explain. The impact of these events, reinforced by many segments of society, became a commonly accepted progressive belief system worshipped unquestionably like some religious myths.

Like one would explain how life evolved, step by step in warm water from blue-green algae slime, I explained the determinants of the brainwashing and how they progressed over time. The elements necessary included:

A history of actual minority injustice, ending in most part by the 1980s and a majority of fair-minded people who detest injustice particularly of minorities.

Hijacking of the civil rights movement by black radicals wanting more than equal justice—an American Revolution. Fair-minded people not understanding the radical, sharp, dangerous turn in the civil rights movement's direction and goals.

Left-wing students being infatuated by the Black Power movement's radical anti-America agenda, subversive ranting, and dress.

Universities giving black radicals teaching positions. Radicals bullying establishment professors and degrading Western Civilization courses and replacing them with hyphenated Black and Feminist studies.

Government, worried about riots, uses a boatload of lawyers to search for discrimination in Employment headed by the EEOC.

Racial hustlers like Jessie Jackson find it very lucrative to target deep pocket business to exploit.

They employ "The Great Con"—since the business does not have as many Blacks as would be represented in the population, they must be discriminating against Blacks. They ignore the myriad of other reasons, including the most obvious, a lack of qualified Blacks.

With EEOC threats that could do serious damage to the business hanging over them, organizations always settle out of court. The race hustlers win, and victimization and diversity grows into a multibillion-dollar business.

These actions completely contradict section 703j of the Civil Rights Act that says there shall be no preference due to race, sex, etc. But few in business have the backbone to stand up to these radicals.

In academia, the radicals are bringing in more of their friends into administration and other positions. They overturn the Sproul Clause that prohibits faculty from presenting their own one-sided propaganda to students. The brainwashing on campus takes off big time.

The flames of rage after some high profile killing of Blacks by police are fanned across the media, which is being populated by brainwashed graduates, radical faculty experts, and left-wing sycophants for the Democratic Party. Rather than just presenting the facts, they consistently side with the black victim and the rioters over the police.

They amplify slogans created by the race baiters and their supporters that, like in Mao's Revolution, incite riots but are not true; "Hands up don't shoot," "Police target Blacks," and "systemic racism," the worst of them all.

Radical groups like Marxist BLM and Anarchist Antifa, initially supported by George Soros and his Tides organization, begin to grow with the big dollar support of major foundations and companies. These groups, like the Black Power movement of old, have an agenda to destroy America through a Socialist style revolution.

Media and academia are joined by: Google and other social media oligarchs, businesses, civil rights leaders, professional organizations, professional teams, leagues, universities, churches, charities, foreign countries, clubs, communication providers, utilities, star athletes, sports leagues, search engines, unions, major consumer brands, the entertainment industry, judges, and government. These brainwashed puppets uniformly repeat Left and Black slogans and aggressively defend and support the groups using these slogans. **With everyone singing from the same hymn book, it made societal brainwashing not only plausible, but very probable.**

Hundreds of facts over myths are spread over the pages of this book. Can you give some examples of systemic racism in the past ten years? Did you look at the facts over the myth of police targeting Blacks? Did George Floyd die of a Fentanyl overdose? Etc!

I rest my case! You are the jury. *Did I make my case about Brainwashed America's coming Cultural Revolution?*

I pray together we can alleviate some of the turbulence and have a controlled soft landing. But we need the backbone to stand up and to shine the light of truth to dissolve the myths created by those hiding behind the curtain and pulling the strings.

As Joseph Conrad noted and I wrote at the beginning of this book, "the messenger can't rest until the message is delivered." This messenger delivered his message and can now relax peacefully until he rests in peace.

www.ingramcontent.com/pod-product-compliance
Lightning Source LLC
Chambersburg PA
CBHW050110280326
41933CB00010B/1043